Incorporate
Your Business

Incorporate
Your Business
When To Do It and How

ROBERT A. COOKE

WILEY

John Wiley & Sons, Inc.

Published by John Wiley & Sons, Inc., Hoboken, New Jersey.
Published simultaneously in Canada.

For general information on our other products and services please contact our Customer Care Department within the United States at (800) 762-2974, outside the United States at (317) 572-3993, or fax (317) 572-4002.

Wiley also publishes its books in a variety of electronic formats. Some content that appears in print may not be available in electronic books. For more information about Wiley products, visit our web site at www.Wiley.com.

Library of Congress Cataloging-in-Publication Data:
Cooke, Robert A., 1931–
   Incorporate your business : when to do it and how / Robert A. Cooke.
     p. cm.
   Includes index.
   ISBN 0-471-66952-0 (pbk.)
    1. Incorporation—United States—Popular works. 2. Corporation law—United States—Popular works. I. Title.
KF1420.Z9C65 2004
346.73′06622—dc22   2004042247

Printed in the United States of America.

10 9 8 7 6 5 4 3 2 1

CONTENTS

CONTENTS

Contents

CONTENTS

Incorporate
Your Business

CHAPTER 1

Why Should I Incorporate My Business?

The short answer is: It depends on circumstances. Here's one in which the corporation form of doing business helped cut the tax bite.

Many entrepreneurs start their businesses by sliding into them. Paul did that. Three years ago, he started keeping a few plumbing tools and fittings in the back of his minivan, from which he did plumbing repairs for friends and neighbors on weekends. His reputation for quality work spread, so he was soon able to chuck his day job. (It helped that his wife, Yvonne, pulled down $100,000 per year as an advertising rep.) Life was simple then, for he just drove to customers' homes, made plumbing repairs, wrote up bills, and collected his money. Because he took care of his customers (and even responded to emergencies at 3 A.M.), his business grew so that he had to hire two more plumbers, two helpers, and buy three trucks for the crews. Along with the increasing business and higher profits came various hassles, such as license requirements in surrounding towns, satisfying tax collectors and other negative manifestations of our complex society, and hiring an accountant to keep track of his expanding empire.

"You probably could save some taxes by incorporating," said Amos, his accountant, as he handed Paul his tax return on April 15.

"Later," said Paul. "It sounds like more hassle, and more hassle is what I don't need."

Then in the fall of that year, Paul ran into an unfortunate situation with a customer. One of his recently hired plumbers did not stick around and check his work as he should have. The consequence was that the leak in the bathroom, which was to be repaired, apparently was not. The resulting trickle of water soaked the carpet in the hallway, requiring that it be replaced at a cost of $500. Paul paid that out of his pocket, as it was below the deductible amount on his liability insurance policy.

Then, a few months later, Paul received a letter from an attorney representing this customer. She was claiming that she had slipped on the wet carpet before it was replaced and suffered extensive injuries. She was seeking $10 million from Paul.

Fortunately, the company that insured Paul was able to settle the case for $1,000, but in the process, Paul spent many sleepless nights. Again, he heard the same thing from Larry, his lawyer, that he had heard from his accountant: "You should consider incorporating."

"What if that customer had prevailed and you had found yourself facing a judgment for $10 million?" Larry asked. "Your liability insurance policy covers only $1 million. You could lose not only your trucks and other business property, but much of your personal assets, such as investment accounts, your boat, and other items. I can't guarantee it, but if your plumbing business did operate as a corporation, it's very likely that you would be able to keep your personal assets, although the business assets would be gone." Paul listened to that advice with increasing interest but still took no action.

We will come back to Paul and his plumbing business later, after we have discussed the points that his story illustrates thus far.

What a Corporation Is and What It Is Not

Essentially, a corporation is created as a separate entity by a government, such as state, federal, and most foreign governments. Corporations can be formed for a variety of purposes, the most common of which is conducting a profit-making business. They can also be formed as vehicles for conducting nonprofit activities such as charitable organizations, social clubs, political activities, and so on. For the most part, this book is devoted to a discussion of corporations that are in business to earn a profit for their owners, but nonprofit charitable corporations are covered briefly in Chapter 6. Almost all of these corporations are created by one of the 50 states, the District of Columbia, Puerto Rico, the Virgin Islands, or Guam. Most foreign governments also provide for the formation of corporations. If you would like a more formal definition of a corporation, here is one:

> CORPORATION   A fictitious legal entity/person which has rights and duties independent of the rights and duties of real persons and which is legally authorized to act in its own name through duly appointed

agents. It is owned by shareholders. Usually created under the authority of state law (*Bouvier's Law Dictionary 1865*).

For many of us, the term *corporation* conjures up images of behemoths such as Microsoft, Wal-Mart, and General Motors. But those corporations have not always been the organizations they are today with thousands of shareholders. The first two started as enterprises owned by one or two people and the third one is a combination of several small companies started in garages by one or two successful dreamers.

Notice that a corporation does *not* exist just because one or a few entrepreneurs hang out a shingle with "Inc." after the name of the business. A corporation exists only by action of the state or other governments just mentioned, as well as the federal government for certain quasi-government purposes.

Who Starts and Who Owns a Corporation?

Corporations come into being because one or more individuals, called *incorporators*, request a state to form a corporation. (The detailed procedure is described in Chapter 6.) The for-profit corporations are owned by stockholders, who may or may not be the same individuals as the incorporators. (The term *stockholders* includes not only individuals but also entities such as other corporations, partnerships, and limited liability companies.) While stockholders share in the hoped-for profits generated by the corporation, nonprofit corporations are not owned by stockholders. The most common use of the latter corporations is for charitable purposes, in which case the theory is that they are owned by the public for the public good.

Reasons to Incorporate Your Business

There are several reasons to incorporate your business. Some entrepreneurs are primarily concerned with limiting their liability for business debts, while others find tax reasons to be the primary motive for incorporating.

Limiting Your Liability for Business Debts

Perhaps the biggest fear of entrepreneurs is that, despite their best efforts, the business will not succeed. If the venture results in failure, that is generally accompanied by excessive debts. The result, for a sole proprietor, is often bankruptcy. That means the entrepreneur faces losing not only business assets, such as equipment and inventory, but personal assets such as savings accounts, securities, vehicles, rental real estate, and possibly his or her residence. (The answer to the question of whether bankruptcy involves loss of residence and certain other assets varies with the laws of each state.)

If, however, you operate your business as a corporation, that may protect you against having to part with personal assets to meet business debts. Remember, a corporation is an entity separate from its owners (stockholders). If I become a spendthrift and run up large bills I cannot pay, you are not responsible for paying my bills (unless you have guaranteed them). Generally, you are not responsible for paying the debts of a corporation, even if you are the sole stockholder, as a corporation is treated as another person. So, if the corporation fails in its business, the creditors of that incorporated business could cause the assets of the corporation to be sold so its debts could be paid, but, with some exceptions, it could not cause your personal assets to be sold to pay corporate debts. (This protection provided by a corporation is often called the *corporate veil*.)

If you buy stock in Ford Motor Company and, due to poor design, someone is injured in one of their products, that injured someone may well collect damages from Ford, but his or her chances of collecting from you as a stockholder are nil, even if the judgment were so large that Ford went bankrupt.

Why do states confer this limited liability on corporations? We have to go back to the 1600s to answer that question. It was the desire of monarchs to increase the economic activity in their kingdoms that prompted the concept of limited liability for business ventures. Monarchs had other uses for the tax revenues, such as fighting wars with neighboring kingdoms. They needed investment money from the rising merchant class to finance such operations as the Hudson's Bay Company, the East India Company, and similar entities. But merchants would not invest because

The IRS and the Corporate Veil

While the IRS normally can look only to the assets of the corporation to collect corporation income taxes, withheld payroll taxes are a different story. Any individual who is responsible for paying over those withheld taxes to the IRS and fails to do so can be held responsible for those taxes, and the IRS can collect by levying on that individual's personal assets. While the responsible individual of a closely held corporation is usually a stockholder, a nonstockholder individual, such as a bookkeeper, could be the responsible person and end up in serious financial straits.

of the high risk of losing their capital and becoming destitute. So the kings and queens promised that the investors could not lose any more money than what they had invested in the exploration and trading venture. Beyond that, the creditors of the venture were out of luck. That is, the investors were promised *limited liability*.

Indeed, without the limited liability of corporations, we could not have the amassing of funds that enables capital-hungry industries, such as railroads, airlines, and many industries, to operate.

Liability of Stockholders Who Are Also Employees of Small Corporations. As we read news accounts of both civil and criminal actions against owners of businesses that operate as corporations, we may arrive at the conclusion that a corporation does not provide a bulletproof corporate veil. Indeed, lawyers for creditors of a corporation will attempt, in any way they can, to pierce the corporate veil. On what basis do they attempt this?

First, they will attempt to prove that the business was not operating as a corporation because the correct procedures to set up a corporation were not followed. For instance, if you fail to register your corporation with the state, you do not have a corporation, and the attorney for your creditors has an easy task in grabbing your personal boat, airplane, and Lamborghini with which to pay the debts of your business. Also, most states require that a corporation hold at least an annual meeting of stockholders and that the minutes of that meeting be recorded. (As a minimum, the minutes should include the annual election of officers, authorization of officer salaries, authorization of distributions to stockholders, and whatever else may be required by the rules of the particular state.)

Second, even though the corporation is properly registered and performing as required, the creditors can claim that you operated outside the corporation. That is, if you write business letters on your personal stationery and sign the letters as an individual, that would be operating outside the corporation. This is particularly important when you sign order blanks that are made out to you personally, rather than to the corporation.

The third way the corporate veil may be pierced is if actions you took personally were illegal, fraudulent, or even with intent to commit fraud. While the most notable of this type of situation involves major corporations, such as Enron, it also applies to small one-owner corporations. While a corporation, as an abstract entity, cannot be put into jail, the corporate officer who directed the illegal act well could spend hard time in some prison.

So, while the corporate veil is not pierced frequently, if you are a *stockholder/employee* of a corporation, your stock holdings are significant, and you are a decision maker. Take pains to dot the *i*'s in corporate documents.

A *stockholder/employee* is a stockholder of the corporation who also is an employee of the corporation. The conventional use of the term appears to assume that the stockholder/employee is in a management position and owns a significant amount of stock. In sections of the Internal Revenue Code, the law regards ownership of more than 2 percent of the outstanding stock as significant.

Two other instances of piercing the corporate veil should be mentioned. One is the situation in which a stockholder voluntarily subjects himself or herself to be exposed to personal liability. The best example of that is a bank loan to the corporation wherein the bank requires that the major stockholder(s) sign a personal guarantee of the loan. The other situation is one in which professionals, such as architects, engineers, accountants, and so on, conduct their professional practice within a corporation. While the corporate form should shield the professional from normal business liabilities, it will not protect against liability for professional malpractice. The professionals must find other ways to protect their assets, such as professional liability insurance or holding assets jointly with spouses or other family members. (The details of the latter are beyond the scope of this book and definitely demand competent legal advice.)

Save Payroll Cash by Incorporating

If you are not yet at the point of having to hire experienced executives and managers to help you run your business, you may arrive at that point soon, we hope. It is difficult to hire these people when you are competing with large corporations and the high salaries they pay for effective managers. But you can compete, if you hire people with some entrepreneurial leanings and reward them with an interest in a piece of your business. That is not to say you should give away your business, but stock and stock options used properly can reduce a need for large cash bundles with which to pay executives. Admittedly, you may not be at this point yet, but when the time comes that you must hire that first executive, you will probably be way too busy and submerged in management tasks to take the time to set up a corporation.

Tax Savings

With proper planning, a corporation can generate a lower tax bill for your enterprise. As is true of any question that deals with the intricacies of the Internal Revenue Code, explanation of an answer will take many words—enough words to be a separate chapter (Chapter 2).

Prestige of a Corporation

Although most of us now realize that the process of incorporation costs very little, and in many cases can be a do-it-yourself project, there is still an air of stability and continuity that is attached to a corporation. If you have paid a sole proprietor for an annual furnace maintenance contract, and he suddenly dies, will someone else perform the maintenance? Maybe the answer is no. If the same business were incorporated, the answer could still be no. However, the fact that it is incorporated makes it more likely that your furnace man paid some attention to planning. That means he probably has provided the means by which his corporation will continue to provide services and collect income for the sake of his heirs.

Ease of Transferring Ownership

Transferring a sole proprietorship from one individual to another is an impossibility, inasmuch as a sole proprietorship is the individual himself or herself. The only way a sole proprietorship business can be bought and sold is by the buyer purchasing the assets of the sole proprietorship. This creates a bookkeeping nightmare for the selling sole proprietor when he or she computes the income tax bill from the sale, and it leaves open the question of the value of goodwill, patents, and trade names that the buyer would want to purchase along with the tangible assets. On the other hand, if the business operates as a corporation, transfer is a simple sale and purchase of the common stock. Also, the gain to the seller should be all long-term capital gain (taxed at a lower rate). It is also much easier to sell or give (as to an adult child) a fraction of the business if it operates as a corporation.

Transferring a partnership interest can be even more complicated. Depending on state law, attempting to transfer more than one-half of a partnership interest actually may cause a partnership to cease existence, and that requires the formation of a new partnership. Obviously, wading through this is going to cost some expensive professional accounting and legal help.

Reasons *Not* to Incorporate Your Business

Many small businesses are sole proprietorships by default. That is, because they have never taken the necessary steps to become a corporation, nor have they taken in a partner, they have always remained a sole proprietor. They are sole proprietors by default. Besides this inertia, there are several reasons offered by people in business for not changing to this other form of conducting business.

Corporations and Other Business Forms Are Too Complicated

Yes, corporations can be complex, but a simple corporation owned by one individual stockholder requires little formality. If there are two or more

Sole proprietorships are also informally known by the initials DBA, which stand for "doing business as," followed by the business name. Because *sole proprietorship* is the term used in legal and tax documents, it is the term used throughout this book. Also, the use of DBA can lead to confusion, as partnerships, corporations, and limited liability companies can also "do business as" some name other than the name of the entity. Example: "The Bicycle Shop, Inc., doing business as Two-wheeled Speed Demons."

owners (stockholders) of the corporation, the formalities are greater, but if the owners did not create a corporation, they would have a partnership, and those animals can be even more complicated than a corporation.

However, keeping it simple can be a valid reason to do business as a sole proprietorship in certain limited and specific circumstances. If the business is tiny, the profits are small, and the proprietor has no other assets than the business assets, going the sole proprietor route may make sense. (In essence, having no assets but those used in the business makes one *judgment proof*. That is, it would not be worthwhile for a creditor to go through the expense of hiring a lawyer and paying court fees when the business owner has nothing that can be turned into money.)

Corporations Cost Too Much to Set Up and Operate

Yes, there is a cost, in both time and money, in operating as a corporation. Operating a corporation entails more income tax forms, more records to keep, and more planning of financial transactions to keep taxes at a minimum. However, if you do have personal assets that are not used for business purposes, such as stocks, bonds, mutual funds, residence, vacation cottage, boat, airplane, jewelry, art works, and so on, then you need to do a little arithmetic. Make a list of all of your nonbusiness assets and for each assign a replacement value. (That is what it would cost you to buy those items at current prices.) Add those values. Then list all mortgages and loans that are secured by those assets, total them, and subtract that total from the total of the asset replacement values. The result is the net replacement value of your assets. Let us say that number is $300,000. Then, ask your lawyer and your accountant how much their fees will increase if you change to the corporate form. Assume their answers total an increase of $3,000. That means that you would be paying $3,000 a year to protect assets with the net value of $300,000. That's only 1 percent of the asset value. Isn't that a nominal fee to protect those assets?

My Business Is Too Small to Incorporate

It's difficult to find any validity in this argument against incorporating. In the first place, the state laws and the bureaucracy that creates corporations do not specify any minimum size of the enterprise. If you wanted to incorporate your 10-year-old daughter's lemonade stand, that could be done. Remember, it's the value of your nonbusiness assets, rather than the size of your business that makes incorporation and the limited liability attractive.

A Corporate Form Does Not Entirely Protect Professionals

This is true. The corporate veil generally will not be effective protection against liability for leaving the sponge in the incision, designing a bridge that falls down, giving grossly incorrect advice, or other acts of malpractice. However, the client who slips on a banana peel or is folded in two by the collapsing waiting room chair is not harmed by professional malpractice, but by corporate negligence. That is, it is the corporation, not the individual owners, who is liable. In other words, the corporate form generally should protect your personal assets in the banana peel situations. (Do not assume, however, that the lawyer for the folded-up former client will not try to collect from you. His or her position could be that you, as an individual, knew or should have known that the chair was in poor condition and should have rectified the situation.) Will the court rule in favor of the client? We do not know until a court decision is handed down, but the fact that you have set up a corporate veil ups your odds for a ruling favorable to you.

CHAPTER 2

How Incorporating Can Result in Tax Savings

Tax Savings in a Corporation? Maybe

If a corporation is operated properly, and if the right elections are filed with the IRS, the corporate form of doing business may well reduce total tax expense. If a corporation is managed haphazardly and tax planning is a low priority item, a corporation could well cost far more in taxes than would a sole proprietorship, so this chapter will help you stay the course that results in tax savings.

As I write this, our tax life is operating under the Jobs and Growth Tax Act of 2003. The results of the elections in 2004 and 2006 could mean that the present tax cuts, particularly the tax rate on dividends, could continue to be in effect, or could result in a return to higher tax rates. Also, present law schedules a return to higher rates in 2009 and 2010. For that reason, this chapter covers both the lower and higher rates, particularly the rates on corporate dividends.

The Organization of this Chapter

Although this is not a tax book, corporation and individual income tax rules do affect your decision to incorporate as well as your decision as to which of two methods will be used to compute and pay your corporation's income tax. We start the chapter by considering the basic method by which corporations have computed their taxes for decades. (This is covered under Chapter C of the Internal Revenue Code and these corporations are therefore known as *C corporations*.) Then we move on to consider corporations that have elected to be taxed under Chapter S of the Internal Revenue Code and are known as *S corporations*. A somewhat incorrect but popular definition of taxation under Chapter S is that the corporation is taxed as if it were a partnership.

The examples in this chapter consider not only income taxes levied on individuals and corporations, but, in addition, the Social Security taxes levied on the first $87,900 (in 2004) of earnings plus the Medicare tax levied on all earnings without limit. (Note that Social Security and Medicare taxes are levied on earnings from employment or self-employment. They are not levied on investment income such as capital gains, dividends, interest, and, in most cases, rent.)

An Example of Tax Saving from a Corporation

Take Paul's plumbing business (see Chapter 1) as an example. In 2004, the plumbing business earned a net income of $100,000, before any reduction for payments to Paul for his salary, income tax, and Social Security and Medicare taxes. Yvonne, his wife, earned $100,000 in salary from her advertising job. Paul withdrew $50,000 from the business during the year, leaving the other $50,000 for the purchase of equipment and working capital in 2005.

If Paul operated as a sole proprietor, the total tax (income, Social Security, and Medicare) for him and Yvonne (filing a joint return) would be $60,507. If he operated as a corporation (a regular C corporation, not an S corporation), the total tax (income, Social Security, and Medicare) for him and Yvonne (filing a joint return) would be $45,173. In this case, the saving would be $15,334.

It is important to note that this significant saving applies in the circumstances described for this example. For other circumstances, the results would be different. For instance, if Paul wanted to withdraw all the earnings from the plumbing business, the tax bite difference between a sole proprietorship and a corporation would be small and might be zero.

Some Background, Concepts, and Explanations

In order to explain how corporate income taxes and a business owner's personal taxes interrelate, we have to use some financial terms, such as *balance sheet, income statement, assets, liabilities, equity, depreciation*, and so on. It is always difficult for an author to write at the level of expertise of the readers, when he or she cannot foretell just who will buy the book. For that reason, I have not included an interminable list of technical terms here, but they can be found in Appendix D. Appendix C is a short course in how these terms interrelate.

How Your Business Tax Picture Changes When You Incorporate

Yes, your tax picture will change if you form a corporation or a limited liability company (LLC). As you might expect, there is no magic rule that says you will be better off taxwise if you incorporate, nor is there a rule that says that an LLC or a sole proprietorship would be preferable. So, we start with the basic rules and build on them throughout this chapter.

How a Sole Proprietorship Is Taxed

A sole proprietor computes his taxable income from his business as in Table 2.1, which is fairly straightforward. You might ask why there are two sections listing deductions from total sales, specifically cost of sales and expenses. Without getting into a lot of accounting theory, let us just accept the fact that this is the way the IRS lays out the tax return form (Schedule C) for sole proprietors. And yes, I know, there are omissions in Table 2.1, such as depreciation. However, they are intentionally omitted so we can keep the examples simple and to the point of the concept under discussion.

While this format for computing taxable income from a business is relatively simple, the IRS directs that what we do with the results of this computation is not so simple. The taxable income is then added in with all the other items of income and deductions on the owner's personal income tax return.

Note that it is the taxable income that is carried to the proprietor's personal income tax return. The amount of the cash that the proprietor takes

PAUL'S PLUMBING

Computation of Taxable Income for the Year

Income:		
Sales		$500,000
Subtract cost of sales:		
Labor (not including Paul)	$180,000	
Material & supplies (pipe, bathtubs, etc.)	100,000	
Total cost of sales		280,000
Gross profit (sales minus cost)		220,000
Expenses:		
Warehouse & office rent	40,000	
Truck operations	30,000	
Office staff (bookkeeper/receptionist)	25,000	
Insurance	14,000	
Licenses, fees, taxes other than income	5,000	
Miscellaneous	6,000	
Total expenses		120,000
Taxable income		$100,000

TABLE 2.1   Computation of Taxable Income for a Sole Proprietorship

out of the business or contributes to the business has no effect on how much income tax the proprietor pays.

The result is that the income tax *rate* on the profits of the business is not dependent on how much the business made, but on the total income picture of the owner. If the owner has other income that elevates his tax rate to 35 percent, that is the rate he or she will pay on the business profits. At the other extreme, if the owner of the business had ordinary losses from other sources, he or she would end up paying at a substantially lower rate, or possibly at a zero rate, on the business profits. (Notice the word *ordinary* as related to how other losses can affect the tax rate on business profits. *Capital* losses are of almost no help in lowering the rate of tax on *ordinary* income, which includes business income.) Of course, if the business owner is married and files a joint return, the income of the spouse enters the picture and affects the income tax rate on the business profits.

So because the total financial picture of a sole proprietor affects the tax picture of the business, it is impossible to state a general rule as to whether there would be a tax advantage for a particular business if it incorporated. All we can do is work out the numbers for a specific situation and make a decision. As we go through the process of generating numbers to help you make a decision, you will be further confounded by the history of Congress playing whimsical games with the tax code, but we will try to keep it as simple as possible.

There are more taxes for the sole proprietor to send off to the IRS. Social Security and Medicare taxes are computed on the taxable income of the sole proprietorship. These taxes are at the same rate regardless of the level of the sole proprietor's other income or losses. Specifically, sole proprietors pay the Medicare tax at the rate of 12.4 percent on the first $87,900 of income from his or her business. In addition, the Medicare tax is levied at the rate of 2.9 percent on all the taxable income from the business of the sole proprietor, with no limit. (These rates are double the rates for Social Security and Medicare taxes that are withheld from one's salary as an employee. The theory, which is valid, is that in the case of an employee the employer matches what is withheld from the employee's paycheck. Therefore, the government collects the same amount from self-employed people as it does from employees.)

How a Corporation Is Taxed

By definition, corporations are separate entities existing almost as if they were a person. As such, they pay their own taxes, but have no responsibility to pay the income taxes of the stockholders. Similarly, stockholders pay their income taxes and have no responsibility to pay the income tax of the corporation. (The S corporation is an exception to this rule and is discussed later in this chapter.) The income tax is computed by first computing taxable income in the same way that the taxable income for a sole proprietor is computed. In other words, the computation starts with the total income or revenue of the corporation and from that are deducted the costs of sales and deductible expenses. The resulting taxable income is multiplied by the appropriate rates to arrive at an income tax figure. The tax rate schedule for corporations consists of brackets and percentages that are different from any of the personal tax rate schedules, and they are displayed in Table 2.2.

CORPORATION TAX RATE SCHEDULE 2004 (Unless changed by Congress)

		If taxable income is:				Of the amount over:
Over:	But not Over:	The tax is:				
$0	$ 50,000		+	15%	$	0
50,000	75,000	$ 7,500	+	25%		50,000
75,000	100,000	13,750	+	34%		75,000
100,000	335,000	22,250	+	39%		100,000
335,000	10,000,000	113,900	+	34%		335,000
10,000,000	15,000,000	3,400,000	+	35%		10,000,000
15,000,000	18,333,333	5,150,000	+	38%		15,000,000
18,333,333	—		+	35%		0

TABLE 2.2   Corporation Tax Rate Schedule for 2004

You are undoubtedly familiar with the taxes and the tax rates that we, as individuals, pay. Whether or not you agree with it, we have a *progressive* tax system by which the rate of the tax increases as income increases. For instance, married individuals filing jointly for a 2004 return with the taxable income under $14,000 are taxed at 10 percent. The same class of taxpayers with taxable income over $311,950 pay at a rate of 35 percent on the income that is more than that $311,950 figure, added to the tax from lower rates applied to income below the $311,950. In other words, the severity of the income tax *progresses* to higher levels as incomes increase.

Corporate income tax rates used to be a simple progression as are the individual rates. However, Congress in its wisdom has seen fit to set up a table that is both progressive and regressive. Note how the rates progress up to 39 percent, and regress to 34 percent, then progress up to 38 percent, and regress to 35 percent. What this does is structure the tax so that corporations with high incomes lose the benefit of the lower rate brackets enjoyed by small corporations. In other words, for very large corporations, the rate is 35 percent from the first to the last dollar of profits. (The Internal Revenue Code actually accomplishes this with a surtax routine. However, the result is a convoluted rate schedule in Table 2.2.)

A complication exists for corporations as it does for individual taxpayers, namely the Alternative Minimum Tax (AMT). It affects those corporations with substantial incomes—generally those with gross receipts of more than $5 million. Although computing it is mostly a mechanical exercise based on figures that should already be in corporate books, it seriously can skew tax planning. Although professional-grade tax software can make the computations, if your business has gross receipts of more than $5 million, or you expect it will soon reach that level, you also need to seek a professional tax person who can help you with your tax planning around the AMT.

Double Taxation of Corporate Profits

As covered earlier, all a sole proprietor has to do to take profits out of his or her business is to write a check to himself or herself, or just take the money out of the cash box. The money flows from the sole proprietorship to the proprietor without tax implications, as the taxes are computed on the *taxable income* of the business rather than what is *withdrawn* by the owner.

In the case of a corporation, life is not so simple. The stockholders receive their share of the profits as dividends, and these differ from the withdrawal of cash (or other assets) by a sole proprietor in two ways. First, the withdrawal of funds is more formal, as the dividends should be formally authorized by the board of directors. Secondly, dividends are paid out of what taxable income is left after the resulting income tax has been computed and subtracted. Then, in the hands of the stockholders, the dividends are taxed again as income of each stockholder. This is true even if there is only one stockholder who owns the entire corporation.

Let us look at an example of a profitable corporation's income tax picture in 2002. (We look at the rules in 2002, as the 2002 rates will return to us in 2009—perhaps sooner, depending on political winds.) The Soleful Shoe Corporation earned $20 million on which it paid federal income tax of $7 million, leaving $13 million that could be paid to the stockholders as dividends. The corporation paid those dividends to the stockholders and all the stockholders were high-income individuals in the 35 percent bracket, so the total income tax the stockholders paid on those dividends was $4,550,000 (35 percent times $13 million). This left only $8,450,000 in the stockholders' pockets out of that original $20 million of taxable income. That amounts to a federal tax bite of 57.7 percent, and in addition there was state income tax to pay! Certainly, you want to avoid having your corporation grow into this situation.

How to Cope with Double Taxation of Your Corporation

In the minds of many people, the only solution to the double taxation of dividend dilemma is the S corporation. However, S corporations have their own disadvantages, so I cover the other methods of avoiding this duplicate tax first.

Pay Dividends Between May 6, 2003 and December 31, 2008. At this writing, those are the dates between which the maximum individual tax on most dividend income is 15 percent. If the Soleful Shoe Corporation had the same taxable income of $20 million in 2004, the tax picture would not be quite as disastrous. Specifically, the total corporate and individual tax would be 44.7 percent versus the 57.7 percent it was in 2002— still too high.

Keep Earnings in the Corporation. In the preceding example, the Soleful Shoe Corporation paid all of its earnings out as dividends. Theoretically, that can be done, but it is highly impractical. Most businesses keep at least part of their earnings within the business in order to purchase new equipment, do additional advertising, and make other expenditures designed to grow the business. As you are probably aware, many high-tech companies follow this policy in order to fund their fast growth. Not paying dividends, at least in theory, does not shortchange the stockholders because the reinvested dividends will generate higher profits and that will increase the market value of the stock. The stockholders can then sell the stock at the higher price and receive their investment return that way. (In many circumstances, that has the additional advantage of converting earnings into long-term capital gain for the stockholders, and that gain may be taxed at a lower rate.) Of course, this has not worked in the case of many high-tech companies that bit the dust after the high-tech bubble-burst of the late 1990s.

Pay Salaries to Stockholders/Employees. In many small corporations the stockholders are also employees of the corporation. In that case, paying salaries to those people generates a tax deductible transfer of money to the stockholders, while paying a dividend is not a deductible item. Unfortunately, there is a downside to paying salaries in that they are subject to Social Security tax (12.4 percent) on wages and salaries up to the current per employee limit ($87,900 in 2004), and Medicare insurance at 2.9 percent on all wages with no upper limit.[1] This has a different impact depending on the size of the profits of the corporation.

For small corporations—those in which the funds transferred to stockholder/employees are less than the Social Security limit—it might appear that it makes little difference whether that transfer of funds to the employees takes the form of salaries incurring a 15.3 percent Social Security and Medicare tax bite or a dividend incurring a 15 percent income tax on the dividend. This is true if both the corporation and the stockholders/employees are in the 15 percent (on dividends) income tax bracket. It is also true in certain other instances, but rather than delve into sophisticated mathematics, I suggest you work out the actual tax picture for your situation and determine whether dividends or salaries a preferable to take money out of your corporation.

For large corporations where stockholder/employee compensation may be in the six or seven figures, taking funds out of the corporation by salaries is almost always preferable. That is because the portion of the salaries above the Social Security maximum limit (as $87,900 in 2004) escapes Social Security tax (12.4 percent) while providing a tax deduction for the corporation. However, in some family-owned corporations, some dividends may be preferable to salaries. For instance, some family members may be active as employees of the corporation while other family members are passive investors, so some dividends to the investors may be necessary. (At this writing, while we have a maximum income tax rate of 15 percent on dividends, it makes this the time to declare and pay them before there is an upward change in the law that sets the rates.)

The IRS Position on Salary Levels for Stockholder/Employees. When the tax rate on dividends is whatever bracket the stockholder is in for regular income (up to 35 percent) instead of the current 15 percent, it is far preferable for all but the smallest corporations to pay deductible salaries rather than nondeductible dividends. For example, let us look at Ralph's Rotund Restaurant, Inc. In December, Ralph finds that he has an extra $100,000 of earnings in his corporation. Ralph's corporation is in the 39 percent bracket and his personal tax picture puts him in the 33 percent bracket. If Ralph causes the corporation to pay him a $100,000 dividend, the corporation would pay $39,000 tax on that $100,000 (because the corporation cannot deduct it), and Ralph would pay $33,000 income tax on the dividend, making a total tax of $72,000 on the $100,000 bundle paid to Ralph. On the other hand, if Ralph causes the corporation to pay him a bonus via a payroll check, he would pay income tax of $33,000 plus Medicare insurance of $1,450. His corporation would pay only the Medicare insurance share of $1,450, making a total income tax and

Medicare insurance tax of $35,900. If you were Ralph, would you pay $72,000 or $35,900?

It seems obvious that you should never declare dividends but should always take an additional salary or bonus out of your corporation, but that is not the case. If your total compensation is a couple of hundred thousand dollars, that should be no problem. But if you are successful and find the need to take a couple of million out of your corporation, and you do that all as salary, the IRS probably will disagree with your position that the lump sum payment was not a deductible salary, but really a disguised dividend, which is not deductible by the corporation. If that happens, that agency has the power to reclassify your salary as a dividend and subject you to the extra corporate tax involved, along with charges for penalties and interest. In other words, the IRS could wipe out that $2 million bonus.

It would seem that a possible solution to this bonus-versus-dividend dilemma is not to pay either but to leave most of the cash the corporation has earned in the corporate bank account. Of course, you would invest that cash so it would grow just as if it were in your hands. (This assumes you have already taken maximum advantage of tax-deferred accounts for your personal future.) Down the road, when you are ready to sell your corporation and retire, you hope you will be able to extract the cash from the sales transaction as capital gain, which is usually taxed at lower rates than ordinary income. Unfortunately, the IRS has a weapon with which it can force you to pay dividends. It is called the accumulated earnings tax and it works this way: If you leave more earnings in your corporation than you reasonably need for the future of the business, the IRS can levy and collect a tax on those excess earnings. The rate of that tax is the same as the rate of tax on dividend income to individuals.

How do you justify to the IRS that you do need to keep your accumulated earnings in the corporation rather than pay dividends? The IRS will accept the need for adequate working capital (what you have tied up in inventory and accounts receivable minus accounts payable); what you need for expansion of your business by internal growth or the acquisition of other companies, provided your business has a history of expansion; formal projections of future cash needs; and expansion plans that have been reduced to writing, such as in the corporate minutes (see Chapter 6). Before the IRS assesses a retained earnings tax on your corporation, you should engage a competent accountant to help you calculate working capital and expansion needs.

You can also use your corporate minutes to help justify paying salaries instead of dividends to stockholders/employees in more profitable years. In the corporate minutes, record the fact that the top executives (maybe it is only you) could command much higher salaries than they are currently receiving from your corporation, and that the shortfall is being recorded with the intention that it will be paid later in more profitable years. For instance, if you are taking a salary of $50,000 per year from your corporation, but as a CEO of a business like yours would command a salary of $400,000, there is a shortfall of $350,000 in your salary. Keep a permanent record of those annual shortfalls and pay them when your business is more profitable. The fact that you have maintained that record may justify unusually high salaries in later profitable years.

Pay Interest to Stockholders. You may have thought of this tax dodge already: Instead of issuing a lot of stock to yourself and other stockholders, simply issue one share of stock, for one dollar, to each stockholder and then supply your corporation with the operating cash it will need by loaning the money to the corporation. Then you can pay yourself interest monthly and, as it is interest and not dividends, it will be a deductible expense for the corporation. *Voila!* You have avoided the double tax and have income from the corporation that is not subject to Social Security and Medicare taxes. Does it sound too good to be true? Of course it does. If you handle your corporation that way, the IRS will reclassify the loan as common stock and the interest as a disguised dividend. In other words, you will have accomplished nothing except to pay additional penalties to the IRS when they catch this gimmick two years after you have filed the corporation's income tax return. Could you possibly do something less drastic, such as fund the operating cash needs of the corporation one-half by sale of common stock to the stockholder(s) and the other half as a loan from the stockholder(s)? Something like that might be possible if you follow the IRS guidelines for the capital structure of a corporation. They are reprinted in Appendix A.

Alternative Minimum Tax on Corporations

Yes, just as for individuals, there is an alternative minimum tax (AMT) for corporations. The one bit of good news about corporate AMT is that there is an exemption for small corporations. A corporation having annual gross receipts of $5 million or less is exempt. Even better, a corporation that has been in existence for at least three years with less than $7.5 million of gross receipts in each year is exempt.

The computation of the corporate AMT is even more complex than that for individuals. Included in Appendix A is Form 4626, Alternative Minimum Tax—Corporations, along with the IRS form Adjusted Current Earnings Worksheet, the completion of which is necessary to fill in the

AMT form. It is included in Appendix A for two reasons: The first is to provide a list of factors that affect the computation of the AMT. The second reason is to support my suggestion that if you do not qualify for the small-corporation exemption from the AMT, you will need professional help in completing the income tax forms for your corporation.

What If the Corporation Has a Net Loss Instead of Net Taxable Income?

If your corporation has a major sales slump and lots of expenses, its books will probably show a loss, and losses can be carried back and/or forward to profitable years and applied to reduce the taxable income in the other year(s). That loss belongs to the corporation, not to the stockholders. In other words, the only one who can use that loss is a corporation, and it can use it only if it has positive taxable income in any of the following 20 years or past two years.

Can you have what amounts to a reverse dividend? In other words if you have to pay tax on dividends the corporation pays to you, can you pay a corporation a reverse dividend and deduct the amount of the dividend on your personal tax return? The answer, unfortunately, is no, even though you might have to invest more money in the corporation to keep it afloat and out of the bankruptcy court. Those additional funds you invest are just that—investments. That cash increases what you paid for the stock (the *basis*), but that increase in basis will benefit you only if and when you sell the stock in your corporation years later. (It will reduce your capital gain.) Just as we say about the proverbial dollar: It is worth more today than a dollar you will receive in the future; a tax deduction is worth more today than it will be years hence.

There is one exception to this locked-in loss. If you own other C corporations, you can apply the loss from one owned corporation against the taxable income of another owned corporation. This generally will work if you own at least 80 percent of the stock in each corporation. If you own less, seek professional help to determine if this application of loss would still be possible in your group of corporations.

If you are just starting your business and incorporating it at the same time, initial losses as the business gets started are a real possibility. That situation should prompt you to consider other alternatives than a C corporation for your startup period. Possibilities are a limited liability company or an S corporation, the discussion of which follows.

S CORPORATIONS

Up to this point, we have been considering the generic C corporation that, at least in the eyes of the IRS, is separate and apart from its stockholders. Years ago, Congress took note of the fact that double taxation and other corporate tax rules were a burden on small businesses, so the federal legislators set up a tax system for closely held corporations, which avoided the double taxation and other complexities of tax law to which large corporations are subject. The basic element of the tax rules for S corporations is that, generally, the S corporation pays no tax. Instead, the income of the corporation is divided among the stockholders of the corporation, and the stockholders add that income to their other income (or losses) when they compute their individual income tax. In other words, there is only one level of taxation of S corporation income, and that is at the stockholder level.[2] As this concept is also basic in the taxation of partnerships, the S corporation concept is often referred to as a system that taxes the business as a partnership even though it is a corporation. (Do not take this partnership analogy as entirely correct. There are significant differences between partnership and S corporation tax rules.)

How Stockholders Take Profits out of an S Corporation

The first method of extracting funds from the corporation is that of paying *distributions* to the stockholders. As for dividends from C corporations, distributions should be authorized by the board of directors and each share of stock should receive the same amount in distributions. Also, like dividends from C corporations, the distributions to S corporation stockholders are not deductible in computing taxable income. However, there is one big difference between dividends and distributions. While dividends from C corporations are taxable to the stockholder, distributions from S corporations are not. In other words, there is no double taxation of distributions from S corporations. Neither are the distributions subject to payroll taxes.

The second method the stockholders of an S corporation should use to extract the funds from the corporation is that of stockholder/employee salaries. As with C corporations, salaries and wages do not come out whole. That is, they are subject to Social Security and Medicare insurance taxes, payable one-half by the employee and one-half by the corporation.

Every reader, at least those paying attention, will now ask, "Why would anybody take money out of the corporation in a way that subjects the payment to payroll taxes when there is another alternative?" The answer is that the IRS will do very unpleasant things if stockholders/employees do not receive a reasonable amount as compensation for services (translation: salaries) rather than as distributions. In other words, the IRS wants to collect Social Security and Medicare taxes insofar as it can. (You can somewhat soften this situation by remembering that Social Security *might* increase your retirement income someday.)

So just how much does your corporation have to pay out in salaries and how much in tax-free distributions? Some years ago, the IRS published guidelines to determine that, but it has since withdrawn them. They took the position that what is a fair return on your investment in the business should come out as distributions and the rest should be salary. The opposition to this position argued that salaries should be in line with the market value of any services performed and the rest of the profits should come out as distributions. In other words, you are left without firm guidelines. The only other comment I can make on this is that the IRS has taken some tax professionals to court when the tax professionals set up an S corporation for their practice and took zero salaries. (They should have known better!) In each case, the IRS won, so take out at least a significant sum as salary.

The Disadvantages of an S Corporation

There is really only one significant advantage of the S corporation over a C corporation, and that is the single tax on corporate profits that are distributed to stockholders. However, there are some disadvantages and a discussion of them follows.

Type of Stockholders. Basically, only individuals can own stock in an S corporation, so that eliminates corporations that are owned by other corporations or limited liability companies as stockholders in an S corporation.

There are certain trusts and estates that may own an S corporation's stock, but they generally are trusts that benefit only individuals and usually come about in estate planning and administration.

Number of Stockholders. The tax code limits the number of stockholders to 75 individuals. The exception is that a married couple who own stock are counted as one stockholder.

Use of the Corporation's Loss, If It Has a Bad Year. As is the case with a sole proprietor, a loss in the business of an S corporation can usually be applied to offset other income in the stockholders' personal tax returns. Yet the income tax code does not allow that in all circumstances. Specifically, they must have a basis in their stock that is greater than the loss to be applied to other income. What is the stockholders' basis? Essentially it is what they paid for the stock when they acquired it. (In the case of a new corporation that would be on the date the corporation was formed.) A basis is increased in the amount the corporation earns each year as taxable income, and is reduced by any losses (loss years) and distributions to the stockholders. At the end of any given year, if the loss is greater than the basis, the part that is greater cannot be deducted from other income of the stockholders.

While we are on the subject of basis, beware of the guaranteed loan trap. If you own stock, with a basis of $1,500, in an S corporation, and close to the end of the year you realize that the S corporation will have a loss of $2,500, it would behoove you to increase your basis to $2,500 by investing another $1,000 in your corporation so that your basis would now be $2,500. You could invest that either by increasing your permanent investment (technically *additional paid-in capital*) or loaning $1,000 to your corporation. What will not work, but many people innocently try, is to guarantee a loan that a bank makes to your corporation. The IRS does not consider that to be an increase in basis of the stock, so if you took that course, you would still have a $1,000 loss that you could not use. (Even though that loss cannot be used in the current year, it can be carried over to future years, so in the meantime you should make arrangements to fund additional basis in your stock.)

This quirk in basis computation is peculiar to S corporations. The amount of a guaranteed loan generally does increase basis in the business in the case of C corporations, limited liability companies, partnerships, and sole proprietorships. The denial of this to S corporation shareholders has been tested in court several times, so remember it is fruitless to attempt using a guarantee in this computation. The better procedure is for the stockholder to borrow the funds from the bank, then turn around and loan the funds to the S corporation.

Flow-through of Certain Tax Attributes to the Stockholder. The computation of taxable income from an S corporation consists of adding the income of the corporation that is generated by the basic business of the corporation and then deducting business-related expenses. However corporations may have other revenue and disbursements that are not strictly business related. While in a C corporation these items are reported on the corporation's income tax return and have no effect on the stockholders, the picture for an S corporation is more involved. Certain items flow through the S corporation to the stockholders, who then may have complications in integrating those items into their own tax picture.

For instance, charitable contributions are such an item. If the S corporation makes a donation to The Salvation Army of $1,000, it does not deduct that contribution on its tax return. Instead, it reports the contribution as a separate item to the stockholders. The stockholders then deduct that contribution as an itemized deduction on their individual income tax returns. The rub comes when a stockholder does not itemize his or her deductions but instead takes a standard deduction. For that stockholder, the deduction of his or her share of the $1,000 donation is lost forever.

For a complete list of what items flow this way from an S corporation to the stockholder, look at Schedule K of Form 1120S, which is in Appendix A.

For more in-depth coverage of S corporations, see my book, *How to Start Your Own S Corporation*.[3] Although it was last revised in 2001, most of the information is still current.

S Corporations Are Limited to One Class of Stock. The Internal Revenue Code limits an S corporation to one class of stock. If the corporation violates that law, it loses its S corporation status. This could be a disadvantage if, for instance, your rich uncle invested heavily in your business, so he wants to receive dividends on his stock before you receive any dividends on yours. He gets paid first; you get paid second. As that would amount to two classes of stock, you could not utilize the S corporation form of doing business.

You might try to keep your uncle happy by structuring his investment as a loan, rather than as a stock purchase. However, the IRS could reclassify the loan as stock if any of these rules are violated.

- The terms of the loan must include a written, unconditional promise to pay on demand or on a specified date a specific sum of money.

- The interest rate and payment dates must not be contingent on profits or other factors.

- The loan must not be convertible into stock.

- The lender must be an individual, estate, or trust that is qualified to be an S corporation stockholder, or an entity that is engaged in the business of lending money, such as a financial institution.

Different stockholders could have different voting rights when it comes time to elect a board of directors and appoint officers, but the IRS does not consider that to be a second class of stock.

When to Use an S Corporation

An S corporation may be your best business form if you expect to have people such as key executives as part-owners of your business. As key executives may come and go, you will need to change who those part-owners are, and with a corporation changes in ownership consist only of transferring stock or issuing additional stock. Also, you may want to transfer part-ownership to children or other relatives, and transferring corporate stock is an easy way to accomplish that.

If your corporation is small and pays you and other stockholders less than the Social Security maximum ($87,900 in 2004), the idea of paying stockholders/employees partly as salaries, subject to Social Security tax, and partly as a distribution of profits, not subject to Social Security tax, can be appealing. Just be sure you have allocated enough to salaries to, it is hoped, keep the IRS happy and justify your allocation in your corporate minutes. (See Chapter 6 regarding corporate minutes.)

The IRS Wants It Two Ways

Yes, our favorite government agency wants it both ways. If you have a regular C corporation, the IRS wants all the money you take out of the corporation to be classified as a dividend, which, of course, means you get to pay double taxation! On the other hand if you have an S corporation, the IRS wants you to take all the money out as salaries so they get to collect Social Security and Medicare taxes. Does the IRS often win both ways? Of course—the game is called Gouge the Taxpayer!

But for awhile—as long as we have the maximum of 15 percent tax on dividends—the taxpayer can win. If you have an existing corporation with excess cash in the till, now is the time to extract it at a minimal tax rate. (That 15 percent rate is reduced to 5 percent if you are in an income tax bracket lower than 25 percent.)

NOTES

1. As stated here, the Social Security and Medicare taxes totaled 15.3 percent, while most people think in terms of 7.65 percent being withheld from their payroll checks. We use the 15.3 percent, as that includes not only the employee contribution but also the employer contribution of 7.65 percent. In the case of stockholders/employees, you can envision the corporations' cash and the stockholders' cash as being held in one big bucket. Any disbursement for taxes by the corporation and/or the stockholders/employees comes out of that bucket.

2. If you own an S corporation that was a C corporation at one time, the S corporation may have to pay its own taxes on certain income, such as some capital gains.

3. Robert A. Cooke. *How To Start Your Own S Corporation.* 2001, New York: Wiley, 2d edition.

CHAPTER 3

The Alternatives to Forming a Corporation

The corporate form of doing business can answer the needs of many businesses, and within the corporate form there is more flexibility in that either a C corporation or an S corporation can be elected. Also, a change from a C corporation to an S corporation and vice versa can be made, albeit that change can be made only once every five years. Even then, it may be that another form of business structure would better fit your situation. In case that is true, this discussion of those other forms should provide some help in making a decision.

Sole Proprietorship

We have already discussed this at some length. Beyond simplicity, it is difficult to find a reason to do business in this form, given its exposure to unlimited liability. For small businesses with a taxable income of less than $90,000, there is an additional disadvantage in that all taxable income is subject to Social Security and Medicare tax, even the income that is reinvested in the business rather than providing a spendable income to the owner.

General Partnership

Like the sole proprietorship, a general partnership is the default organization if two or more people start a business together. Although it does, like a corporation, allow for additional owners, there is strenuous bookkeeping involved in keeping track of who owns how much of the business and who takes home how much of the profits. In this basic form, it provides no limited liability. There is a further disadvantage in our general partnership in that the bookkeeping when partners enter or withdraw from the partnership is complex and definitely requires guidance from a knowledgeable tax professional to get it right. Failure to handle the bookkeeping correctly can lead to a tax disaster.

If there are no changes in ownership during a year, the bookkeeping for a partnership is little different from that for a sole proprietor. Indeed, he could visualize the partnership as two or more sole proprietors working together in a business venture. The taxable income is computed as in the example in Chapter 2 and then allocated to each partner. This allocation is computed in accordance with the partnership agreement (every partnership should have one), or if that is not addressed in the agreement, the taxable income is allocated in the same percentage as each partner's ownership in the partnership (commonly called the *partnership interest*) is to the total ownership. The result is that the taxable income allocated to each partner is taxed at the partner's individual tax rate, and net income includes earnings that are retained in the partnership and not distributed to the partner. We have already heard about that situation, as it arises in an S corporation as discussed in Chapter 2. Also, if the partnership business is small and there are many partners, so each share of the taxable income is less than $90,000, each partner ends up paying Social Security tax on money he or she may never receive. And all partners pay Medicare tax on all of their share of taxable income.

If you get an uncontrollable urge to form a partnership, first look at forming a *limited liability company (LLC)*, which is discussed later.

Despite this preference for LLCs, there are still many general partnerships in existence.

Limited Partnership

This is a special form of partnership in which the inactive, or passive, partners do not participate in management and are therefore granted limited liability by state law. There has to be one general partner who does have unlimited liability for the debts of the partnership, although this disadvantage can sometimes be overcome by forming a corporation (with limited liability) to be the general partner. This business form is little used today as, again, a limited liability company is usually easier to manage.

Limited Liability Company (LLC)

Essentially, this is a partnership in which all the partners (called *members* in an LLC) have limited liability. Like a corporation, the limited liability of an LLC is conferred on the entity by state law. Like the corporation, it is necessary to follow a strict procedure to cause the state to create your LLC. If an LLC makes no election to the contrary, it is taxed in the same manner as a general partnership.

The major advantage of an LLC is that it provides limited liability to all owners of the entity while avoiding the double taxation to which C corporations are subject. A specific instance would be a business, such as a real estate investment operation, that had many passive owners. That is, those owners took no active part in the management of the business. As they were not involved in day-to-day operations, there would be no justification for distributing earnings as salaries to them, and the IRS would strongly object if that were tried. If the real estate operation were incorporated as a C corporation, it would be able to distribute earnings to these owners only as dividends subject to double taxation, so an LLC form of business probably would result in a lower tax bite on those earnings that are distributed.

A situation in which an LLC would be preferable to an S corporation is if the enterprise is to be owned by other LLCs, corporations, or partnerships, as well as individuals. Any of these entities could be members in an

Unlike the corporation, an LLC can elect to be taxed as another type of entity. Practically, that means that an LLC could be taxed as a corporation if it so chose. It would make no sense for an LLC to elect taxation as an S corporation, and if taxation as a C corporation would benefit the LLC, it might be better off to simply incorporate.

LLC, while the rules about S corporations prevent all but individuals and certain trusts to own S corporations.

Unlike partnerships, an LLC may be owned by only one individual, or other entity, such as a corporation, trust, or another LLC. (Such an LLC becomes known as a *single-member LLC*.) Also, because there is only one owner, the IRS says the single-member LLC is generally taxed in the same manner as a sole proprietorship. Or if the LLC is owned by a corporation, its income would flow to and be taxed as is the income of the corporate owner.

Why would anyone form a partnership instead of a limited liability company? The answer is historical: Until the early 1980s the LLC form was unknown in the United States, although many foreign countries were creating these types of entities. Beginning in the 1980s, various states enacted laws granting limited liability to the members of LLCs until today all 50 states have procedures for setting up LLCs. So, due to inertia or not getting the word, we still have general partnerships in our midst. Also there are certain special situations in which a general partnership does have a tax advantage. For example, a working interest in an oil or gas well is not considered a passive activity if that interest is owned by an individual or by a partnership that does not provide limited liability for its partners.

Other Entities with Limited Liability of the Owners

You may see initials other than LLC after the name of some entities, such as LLP, which stands for *limited liability partnership*. This is an entity that grew out of the LLC concept that is applicable to professional practices. It allows limited liability to the professional for the acts of his or her partners, without infringing on the long-standing concept that professionals cannot have limited liability protection for their own acts of malpractice. LLLP stands for *limited liability limited partnership*. This entity is for limited partnerships where the limited partners wish to participate in management without losing their limited partner status. Most people will not run into the need to form one of these esoteric entities, so there is no need to memorize their specific application. Just be aware that they are special instances of the LLC concept.

Passive Losses

This is a subject that can affect your choice of entity. If your enterprise will have passive investors—individuals who are not active in your business but are strictly investors—any income they receive from your LLC or S corporation will be labeled as passive income. Your investors get to pay income tax on that just as they would any other income. However, if your enterprise suffers a loss, that loss is passed through to the individual investors as a passive loss. If the investors have other passive income, that loss can be applied to reduce the income from passive activities and thereby reduce income tax. If those investors do not have passive income to which to apply passive losses, they cannot use the passive losses to offset income such as wages, salaries, dividends, interest, or capital gains.

This passive loss rule applies to all taxpayers except C corporations that are not closely held. For this purpose, the IRS defines *closely held* as having less than five stockholders. If you are operating an entity from which you expect a stream of passive losses for several years, you may want to structure your affairs such that this entity is owned by a C corporation with more than five stockholders. That corporation could apply the passive losses to ordinary income, thereby reducing the corporate tax.

Which Business Form Best Attracts Investors to Your Enterprise?

Basically, investors look for the highest rate of return on their investment coupled with the least risk. While a return on an investment vehicle such as a bond or a savings account can be measured in terms of percentage rate of return, risk is much harder to quantify. Also, it is difficult to quantify the potential long-term return from the hoped-for gain in value of an investment in the ownership of a business, such as an investment in common stock. One thing is pretty much certain about how much risk an investor will assume, and that is that while he or she may understand that they are risking the dollar amount invested, they certainly do not want to risk other personal assets. That leaves only a corporation or an LLC as a business form with which you can entice others to invest.

The LLC form may be preferable for the sophisticated investor who understands partnership taxation and the many ways in which LLCs can allocate profits and losses to the partners. However, for those who like to keep things simple, the concept of corporate stock may be more appealing. This is particularly true where the investor may hold only a small percentage of total ownership of the enterprise, which can result in having to pay tax on part of an LLC's income without receiving any distribution of funds with which to pay the tax.

For example, Lenora has $5,000 to invest. If she invests that in an LLC that is seeking investments totaling $100,000, her $5,000 share makes her a minority member with little influence as to management of the LLC. The promoters who manage the LLC could arbitrarily decide to make no cash distributions to the members, even though the LLC earned $200,000 during the tax year. Lenora's share of those earnings is $10,000, so she would receive a statement (on IRS form K–1) that tells the IRS that she should pay income tax on the $10,000 of income that is her share. She can cry that she has no funds with which to pay the tax, but the IRS will say "Tough, pay the tax."

On the other hand, if the entity were a C corporation, Lenora would pay no tax on the earnings of the corporation unless it declared and paid a dividend, and then she would pay tax only on that dividend. So Lenora would probably prefer to invest in the enterprise if it were a C corporation. Note that an S corporation has the same downside as an LLC in this respect. That is, a stockholder could be liable for income tax on the S corporation's earnings even though the corporation distributed no cash to the stockholder.

In essence then, if you are attempting to finance your enterprise with several small investments by individuals, a corporate form may be more attractive to them. If you are attempting to finance it all with funds from Uncle Harry, he may prefer the LLC form, which avoids the corporate double taxation.

Another consideration in the Lenora story is this: If she had withheld her investment until the partnership agreement specified that there would be distributions of cash adequate to pay the LLC members tax on the LLC profits, she might also have preferred the LLC route. In other words, there is no definitive answer as to which entity form best attracts investors, but this short discussion can kick off your thought process in making that determination.

As you go about seeking investors, remember to check out your state's laws regarding the sale of securities. If your search takes you to other states, check with the federal Securities and Exchange Commission as to registration requirements.

CHAPTER 4

How to Structure
a Corporation

In a free enterprise system, all businesses consist of the business owner, those who are employed by the business, and the equipment and other assets with which the business carries out its function. In the case of a really small business, the distinction between the employer and the employee may be blurred because both functions are carried out by the same person. Similarly, the distinction between equipment that is owned personally by the owner and that which is owned by the business is also blurred. If you operate a part-time woodworking business in your garage, it is hard to say whether your power saws are owned by you or the business. If you are not incorporated, deciding which entity owns the equipment would be only a theoretical academic pursuit were it not for the fact that if you consider your equipment to be owned by the business, you may be able to generate some depreciation deduction on your tax return.

One of the advantages of a corporation is that it formalizes this distinction between owners and employees, and it defines the ownership of equipment.

In its simplest form, the structure of a corporation is easy to set up and maintain. However, there are some options of which you should be aware; they may be applicable to your circumstances, and in some instances they could generate tax savings or, at least, keep you out of trouble with the IRS. So, with some trepidation about using a scary phrase, I say that what follows is a short, but simple, discourse about *corporate structure and finance*.

The Basic Corporation

In its simplest form, we can envision a corporation, called Arbar, Inc., which is owned 50 percent each by Arnold and Barbara. The only asset of the corporation is $100,000 in the corporate bank account. The source of the $100,000 was the $50,000 that Barbara and Arnold each paid for 5,000 shares of common stock at $10 per share.

At this point, I have to use some basic accounting and finance terms. If you find this an unfathomable area, read through the next paragraphs to get the gist of it and do not worry about signing up for an MBA program. If you are already familiar with the terms *balance sheet, assets, liabilities*, and *equity*, read on. If you are somewhere in between, here is a brief explanation of the basics.

Assets, Liabilities, and Equity

This initial picture of Arbar, Inc. can be laid out in a format called a *balance sheet* as in Table 4.1. Notice that the total of liabilities and equity on the right-hand side equal the total assets on the left-hand side. That is, the two sides of this report equal, or *balance*, each other. That is why it is

ARBAR, INC.
Initial Balance Sheet

Assets		Liabilities	
Cash	$100,000		
		Total liabilities	0
		Equity	
		Common stock	100,000
		Total equity	100,000
Total assets	$100,000	Total liabilities & equity	$100,000

TABLE 4.1   Initial Balance Sheet of Arbar, Inc.

called a balance sheet. There are three main parts to a balance sheet, and they can be defined as follows:

- An asset is something you own, such as your house and car. In the case of this corporation, it owns the $100,000 in the bank.

- A liability is the amount that the corporation would owe some third party. At this point, Arbar, Inc. owes no one. One of the first tasks by Barbara and Arnold is to buy two desks and two chairs in the name of the corporation. If they agreed the corporation would pay $1,000 for those items within 10 days, the balance sheet would change this way: Assets would be increased to $101,000 (cash and desks), and the $1,000 owed to the office supply company would appear as a liability on the right-hand side of the balance sheet. (It would still balance, as the total assets would be $101,000 and liabilities and equity on the right-hand side would be liabilities of $1,000 and equity of $100,000.

- Equity is the third part. You are probably familiar with the term *equity* in relation to owning your house. If the value of the house (an asset) is $150,000 and your mortgage balance is $100,000, your equity is the difference, or $50,000. Essentially, this same concept of equity applies to a corporation balance sheet, with some modification. (Accountants, for technical reasons we do not get into here, generally value assets as the price paid for them rather than the current market value—although there are some exceptions to that rule.) In the case of this corporation, the asset of $100,000 was created because that is what the stockholders (Arnold and Barbara) paid for their stock in the corporation. So the balance sheet, under the heading of equity, displays the stockholders' ownership interests by listing that as the value of common stock. That equity interest is documented by stock certificates that are issued to Arnold and Barbara.

How to Invest in Your Corporation

We continue the example of Arbar, Inc. The corporation needed an additional $199,000 of equipment making a total investment in equipment of $200,000. While it could have bought half of this equipment with the $100,000 in the bank, it would have left the corporation with no *operating capital*. That is, it would have no funds with which to pay employees, buy advertising, and pay other expenses that are involved in day-to-day operations of the business. So Barbara and Arnold had to look elsewhere for funds with which to buy the equipment.

Each provided another $25,000 by purchasing additional stock, totaling $50,000. Their local friendly neighborhood banker agreed to loan the corporation $80,000, secured by the equipment that would be purchased. They now had $130,000 additional funds and needed $70,000 more.

Operating capital can be defined as the capital, or funds, that is necessary for the corporation to operate. Almost every business will find times when it has more cash outgo than intake. For instance, it is usually necessary for a business to pay employees, buy materials, and cover other expenses before it will collect from customers for the service provided or the goods manufactured. Whatever the amount of money needed to pay for those initial expenditures is the minimum operating capital that a business needs, and when the business collects for its sales, the cash from those collections becomes the operating capital for the next cycle of paying employees and other expenditures before it can collect from customers.

As a next-to-last resort, Barbara and Arnold borrowed all the balances ($40,000) in their retirement plans at prior employers and loaned that amount to the corporation. They made that a loan, rather than a purchase of stock, as they expected that the corporation would earn enough to pay the loan back during its first two years, but right now they still needed another $30,000.

Their last resort was to ask Barbara's Uncle Harry to loan the corporation the $30,000. However, Uncle Harry was an astute investor and was not much interested in loaning money to a speculative enterprise at a nominal interest rate. Instead, he agreed to invest $30,000, by purchasing stock in the corporation, with this provision: He would receive dividends of $6,000 per year (20 percent return on his investment) before either Barbara or Arnold received any dividends.

The result of all of this high finance is displayed in Table 4.2. Comparing it to Table 4.1 indicates the equipment has been purchased and shows up as an additional asset that costs $200,000. The loan from the bank in the

ARBAR, INC.

Balance Sheet after Funding the Corporation

Assets		Liabilities	
Cash	$100,000	Loan from bank	$ 80,000
Equipment	200,000	Loan from stockholders	40,000
		Total liabilities	120,000
		Equity	
		Preferred stock	30,000
		Common stock	150,000
		Total equity	180,000
Total assets	$300,000	Total liabilities & equity	$300,000

TABLE 4.2   Balance Sheet of Arbar after Funding of the Corporation

amount of $80,000 plus the $40,000 loan from Arnold and Barbara are liabilities totaling $120,000. Common stock, under equity, displays the additional $50,000 of stock that Arbar purchased. Also under equity is the $30,000 that Uncle Harry invested, but it is not the same class of stock as issued to Arnold and Barbara for it has some preferences over their stock, and that is why it is called *preferred* stock.

This preferred stock is something of a hybrid. It is stock in that it represents ownership in the corporation, but it resembles a loan because Uncle Harry is guaranteed a payment of $6,000 per year. There are almost limitless modifications that can be added to preferred stock. For instance, the stock certificate could contain a provision that the preferred dividends will be paid regardless of the earnings of the corporation, or it could specify that the preferred dividends would not be paid unless there were adequate earnings to cover that payment. Another clause should specify whether or not the preferred dividends were cumulative. That is, if the corporation had a loss in one year and therefore did not pay preferred dividends, those dividends would accumulate for each year they were missed, and the accumulated total would have to be paid to the preferred stockholders before the common stockholders received any dividends. Note that the bank loan and a loan from stockholders are liabilities, and unless there is some agreement to the contrary, the interest on those loans must be paid before dividends are paid to stockholders, both common and preferred.

If you are operating as a small corporation, this coverage of preferred stock is probably academic and of little interest. However, the message here is that different stockholders can be treated differently when it comes to paying dividends. While it is unusual for a small corporation to issue preferred stock, it is not impossible and sometimes can be a means of attracting capital without incurring the need to pay interest in the first year or so of the business.

To summarize, when there are insufficient earnings or assets to pay lenders (the corporation is insolvent), preferred stockholders and common stockholders, the preference as to who gets paid first is this:

1. Secured lenders (creditors) who have a lien or mortgage on the assets of the corporation. As a practical matter, they get paid first because if

Additional paid-in capital is another item you may see in the equity section of the balance sheet. When Arnold and Barbara invested another $50,000 in the corporation, they chose to do so by purchasing additional shares of stock. They also could have simply poured another $50,000 into the corporation without issuing any additional shares to themselves. In that event, that extra $50,000 would be called *additional paid-in capital* and would appear as another line item in the equity section of the balance sheet.

they do not, they could repossess the equipment and virtually close the business. In our example, the bank is a secured lender.

2. Unsecured lenders, such as the desk supplier in our example. If they are not paid their due, they could petition the court to sell the assets that were not pledged to the secured creditors, probably through the bankruptcy process, and could collect the money through that sale.

3. Preferred stockholders, as discussed previously (Uncle Harry in our example), get any cash and other assets after all creditors have been paid.

4. Common stockholders get anything that is left, and it is improbable that there will be anything left.

Debt versus Equity

This boils down to the fact that how the corporation is capitalized has a great deal of flexibility. Perhaps you already discerned a major tax issue that arises in this process and is reflected in our example. That is, stockholders can invest money in the corporation not only by purchasing stock, but also by loaning money to the corporation. There is some tax advantage in this, in that dividends paid to stockholders are subject to double taxation, as dis-

Funding, as used in this context, refers to the source of cash that will be used for working capital, equipment purchases, initial set-up costs, and other business-related expenditures.

To capitalize, as used here, refers to the process of investing in the corporation by sale of common stock (investment in equity) or borrowing (incurring debt). The investments generally fall into three basic categories: common stock, preferred stock, and debt (loans).

To fund is often used as a synonym, although it also carries the connotation of determining the source of funds to start a business.

ARBAR, INC.

Balance Sheet as a Thin Corporation

Assets		Liabilities	
Cash	$100,000	Loan from bank	$ 80,000
Equipment	200,000	Loan from Uncle Harry	30,000
		Loan from stockholders	189,000
		Total liabilities	299,000
		Equity	
		Common stock	1,000
		Total equity	1,000
Total assets	$300,000	Total liabilities & equity	$300,000

TABLE 4.3   Balance Sheet of Arbar, Inc. as a Thin Corporation

cussed in Chapter 2. However, interest on loans made to the corporation by stockholders can be as deductible as is interest paid to any other person or institution. Obviously, then, the best way to capitalize the corporation is with one-dollar's worth of common stock and the balance as a loan to the corporation by the stockholder(s). This is demonstrated in Table 4.3 where, instead of showing common stock of $150,000 and a stockholder loan of $40,000, it reflects the fact that the corporation issued only $1,000 of common stock to Arnold and Barbara and received the other $189,000 as a loan from the stockholders. That lets the corporation pay substantial interest to the stockholders (which would be deductible by the corporation) and pay only token dividends, making the double taxation an insignificant consideration.

The same concept can apply to the preferred stock issued to Uncle Harry. Instead of classifying it as stock, the corporation could have issued him a promissory note that specified the 20 percent *interest* rate. Otherwise, the note could specify the same terms as does the preferred stock–that interest must be paid before any dividends can be paid to the common stockholders.

The IRS Position on Debt versus Equity

If you envisioned this before reading the previous discussion, I give you a gold star with a commendation for your tax-planning acumen. However, the IRS is more likely to award you significant penalties. The reason: The IRS views a situation as portrayed in Table 4.3 as a *thin corporation*. That is, if the value of the common stock is very small as a percentage of total liabilities and equity, the IRS says the corporation is thinly capitalized. In other words, most of the stockholders' investment in the corporation really represents stockholders' equity, and therefore should be treated as common stock. The result of the IRS reclassifying the interest (and it does have the power to do that) is that the interest changes to a dividend that the corporation cannot deduct, and therefore corporation taxes will be much higher. As the IRS generally does not get around to auditing a corporate tax return until at least a year after it is filed, there are not only additional taxes assessed on the corporation, but also penalties for disregard of tax rules plus penalties for late payment of the additional tax.

The moral is that you should finance an adequate percentage of your corporation through the issuance of stock, as opposed to long-term loans from stockholders. What is an adequate percentage of stock to total investment? The IRS will not say, and neither will it look at your proposed method of capitalizing your corporation and tell you whether or not it will fly. Years ago, the IRS guidelines did indicate that if the debt was no more than three times the investment in stock, the arrangement would be accepted. That is no longer the case, so if you propose to fund your corporation by buying a little stock and loaning far more to the corporation, you should engage an experienced tax professional to help you plan your capitalization. The best that exists in the way of guidelines on how much cap-italization can be in the form of loans from stockholders is from a con-gressional committee report in 1989 that summarizes the results of the very many court cases in this area. The guidelines are in Appendix A.

As you know by now, the significance of this question is currently not as great as it once was, as the maximum income tax rate on dividends is only 15 percent. However, that rate is subject to change in the political winds and is currently scheduled to expire at the end of 2008. As the impact of substantial double taxation may reappear, it may be a good idea to plan some of your corporation's capitalization to include loans from the stock-holder or stockholders. Read the guidelines in Appendix A and seek pro-fessional help before you proceed.

As a practical matter, if you loan your corporation some money to get it through a tight spot in its cash flow and that loan is repaid within a year, the IRS is unlikely to try to reclassify, so do not treat a short-term emer-gency loan as purchase of the corporation's stock. If it turns out that the loan probably will never be repaid, and it appears prudent to reclassify as an investment in corporate stock, that can be accomplished by a book-keeping entry that reduces the loan to zero and increases the investment in common stock by the same amount. Such an entry should be supported by a resolution in the corporate minutes.

How to Invest in Your S Corporation

Because there is no double taxation of dividends or distributions from an S corporation to the shareholders, there is little or no benefit in structuring some of your investment as a loan to the corporation if you expect that money to stay forever invested in the corporation. However, if you expect to pull out some of your investment as soon as the corporation has cash with which to repay you, then structure it as a loan. To be correct, the loan should carry a reasonable interest rate and should be paid at least annually. Note that this interest payment has little effect on the income tax bill, inasmuch as the interest is deductible by the corporation and as income to the stockholder. As that deduction of interest by the corporation actually flows to the stockholder within the flow of taxable income to the stockholder, both the deduction and the income are contained and offset each other in the stockholder's individual income tax return.

Remember, as covered in Chapter 2, that you should not fund an S corporation by having the stockholder(s) guarantee a bank loan. It would not increase the basis in the loan, and therefore if operating losses ensue, the stockholder(s) may not be able to deduct those losses.

Keep Control of Your Corporation If Possible

This is another situation that may appear as only academic if you own all the stock of your corporation. However, it is almost never too soon to contemplate who will control your corporation when you provide others the opportunity to purchase stock in your enterprise. You might do this to attract people with executive skills, marketing know-how, and other valuable attributes. Indeed, control becomes a major consideration at such time as you might enter into agreements with venture capitalists and when you might sell shares in your corporation to the general public and become a publicly held company. This last entails compliance with federal securities laws, state laws, and regulatory agencies such as the federal Securities and Exchange Commission (SEC); those details are beyond the scope of this book.

When an employee receives a very small percentage of the outstanding stock of your corporation, he or she probably is not concerned with the element of ownership control represented by that stock. More likely, the individual is motivated by the expectation that the value of stock will rise, and the enterprise may someday become a publicly held corporation, perhaps making his or her stock worth millions! Where control of management of the corporation is presumably not a concern to the recipient, it makes sense to issue it as *nonvoting stock*. If you become involved with a venture-capital firm as an investor, or even with your Uncle Harry as an investor, you may find that these people want a voice in the management of the corporation and in some circumstances may even wish to have majority control. If you need the venture capitalists more than they need you (you are desperate for cash), you may have to allow them control. Try first, though, to make their stock nonvoting until such time as the corporation fails to meet certain goals, such as earning a respectable net income. In other words, investors generally are not interested in micromanaging an enterprise unless they deem their investment to be at substantial risk.

The point of this last discussion is that nonvoting stock can be a useful tool. Be sure to note that merely having some stock classified as nonvoting and some as voting stock does not create two classes of stock for purposes of an S corporation. However, if you go further in creating rights for one class of stock and not another, such as a difference in dividend payout rate, you will have caused your corporation to lose its S status (see Chapter 2).

CHAPTER 5

Planning Your Corporation

The process of setting up a corporation used to be shrouded in mystery with many formalities that could be completed only by an expensive lawyer. Those arcane formalities have now given way to routines that can be followed by anyone who can read and follow directions. This is not to say that you should undertake all the following steps without advice from a professional, particularly if there will be more than one stockholder of the corporation. However, much of the process can be a do-it-yourself procedure.

Do-It-Yourself Incorporation

Essentially, the process involves dealing with the bureaucracy of an individual state, and normally that state agency is called the *Secretary of State* or something similar such as the *State Corporation Commission*. Naturally, there will be forms to fill out and fees to pay, but the process is simpler than dealing with many government forms, such as those for computing your income tax. The agency with whom you file various forms for each state is listed in Appendix B, along with address and phone number. For most states, we also list the web site where information can be obtained and forms downloaded, but web site addresses frequently change, in which case you would need to use a search engine to locate the web site. This chapter discusses the forms that need to be filed and applies to almost all states. (That is partly because the American Bar Association has developed a Model Corporation Act in the hope that all states would adopt the same rules. As you might expect, state legislatures are too independent to do that, but generally most procedures contained in the model act are followed by most states.)

Using Professionals

Although you may want to do the paperwork yourself, it may be a good idea to have professionals review your work. If that is the case, search for professionals who will provide a review as opposed to those who insist on doing *all* the work in their office. (This is often the case in large firms, where the lawyers or accountants will delegate the incorporation job to the clerk who follows a certain routine.)

Incorporating your business entirely as a do-it-yourself project is appropriate only if you will be the sole stockholder of your corporation. See the discussion under stockholder agreements later in this chapter.

Choosing an Attorney

Even if you file the forms with your state yourself, it would be a good idea to retain an attorney for advice when you are unsure of your best course. If there are other stockholders involved, you will need a stockholders' agreement (discussed later), and you definitely need a lawyer's input in developing that.

The best way to select an attorney is to ask for recommendations from other small-business people. (A membership in the local Chamber of Commerce can provide you with contacts who can offer suggestions.) You want an attorney who practices business law, as opposed to domestic relations, criminal law, and so on. At this stage of your corporate life, you do not need the lawyer who represents large corporations and charges accordingly. This individual also probably practices tax law. Although that is a plus, if you choose your accountant carefully, you should get adequate tax advice from him or her.

Choosing an Accountant

Although not all accountants are certified public accountants (CPAs), all CPAs are accountants, by definition. In other words, for corporate tax work choosing a CPA, rather than someone who just hangs out a shingle as a tax accountant and has few credentials, is generally the preferable selection. Many non-CPA tax preparers who do outstanding work in preparing individual tax returns have little or no training in business law, corporation finance, and taxes. However, you can be reasonably assured that any individual who is licensed as a CPA has taken courses in business law and corporation finance, as well as in-depth tax courses—but that does not mean that you would want just any CPA to advise you on your corporation. Some CPAs tend to concentrate on creating and auditing financial statements and do not stay current on income tax rules, while other CPAs do concentrate on corporate taxation, including S corporations. Again, obtaining referrals from local businesspeople is the best way to choose an accountant.

Planning the Specifics of Your Corporation

Your planning should start from one of two situations. You are either starting a business from scratch and are planning to incorporate prior to opening the doors of your business, or you are already running an established business and, after reading this book, have decided you would be better off operating as a corporation. Where this difference is relevant, we cover each of the two possibilities.

Decide on the Size of the Initial Investment in the Corporation

If you are setting up your corporation for a new business, you should have already developed a business plan that includes a cash flow budget. If you have not made such a plan that projects your cash needs, you should do so prior to deciding on your initial investment. There is no more sure way to fail than to start with inadequate working capital or equipment. If you are not familiar with cash flow budgeting, you should be before starting a business. There are several good writings on cash flow budgets, two of which I have authored.

If you are already operating a business, the fact that you change to the corporate form of doing business does not change your need for working capital and equipment. In other words, you know how much you have invested in the business in terms of cash and equipment, so the simplest procedure is to transfer not only your business' cash, but also all of your business equipment to the corporation in exchange for common stock.

However, the simplest is not always best. As we plan, we want to expect great success, where funds will be more than adequate to provide the standard of living to which we would like to become accustomed. While that is a healthy attitude to have, in-depth planning requires planning for the best scenarios, worst scenarios, and several levels in between. In Chapter 4 we have already looked at the best scenarios, where the corporation grows quickly, profits are high, and initial public offering of stock is imminent, as is instant billionaire status!

Unfortunately, as things do not always work as planned, we have to look at the worst-case scenario. What if the economy turns sour or your market disappears and your business falls on hard times? Part of that scene generally involves owing other businesses, government agencies, and individual's money. The business cannot pay its bills, so bankruptcy sales ensue. As your business operates as a corporation, the bankruptcy will affect only your corporate assets, but they will disappear as the bankruptcy trustee sells them off. So although you will still have your home, your BMW, and your boat, you will no longer have your own warehouse building, machinery, display cases, computers, or other business assets. You may be reduced to the untenable situation of having to work a nine-to-five (that's 9 A.M. to 5 A.M.—a 20-hour day!) job.

You may have been able to prevent this loss of business assets by retaining ownership of the assets when you incorporated and leasing them to your corporation. Then, if the business went bankrupt, while you would lose some business assets such as accounts receivable and inventory of goods, you would still have your commercial building, computers, and so on (assuming that your creditors cannot reach through the corporate veil as covered in Chapter 1). If you set up a corporation in this manner, the only assets that you would initially transfer to the corporation in exchange for common stock would be the cash for operating capital. You might also transfer inventory and accounts receivable in order to keep your bookkeeping simple, but keeping title to fixed assets and leasing them to your corporation often makes good sense and does not unduly burden your bookkeeping procedures.

Obviously, if you keep many of the assets in your name, your initial investment will be less than what it would be if you transferred all the assets to the corporation. (Not only cash but all assets transferred to the business are considered to be the investment in the corporation.)

Size Your Investment to Qualify for Treatment as a Small-business Corporation

A small business corporation is a corporation that has not received more than $1 million in exchange for stock, both common and preferred. Section 1244 of the Internal Revenue Code provides special treatment for the stockholders of this corporation if the corporation goes defunct or the stockholder sells his or her stock at a loss. That special treatment is that the stockholders can treat the loss as ordinary and is not limited, as would otherwise be the case, to treating it as a capital loss. (A capital loss is deductible only to offset capital gains and can offset other income to a maximum of $3,000 per year. An ordinary loss can be applied to other income in full in the year of the loss.) In order to qualify for

Section 1244 treatment, the stock must have been issued in exchange for money or other property, not other stock, securities, or services. And the corporation must show that more than 50 percent of its receipts were from business operations.

Try to arrange your corporate affairs to qualify for this treatment. If you suffer a disaster in your business and have to close it, you will be glad you took pains to so qualify, as it will result in the IRS partially reimbursing you for the loss, via a tax deduction.

Who Will Be the Owners (Stockholders) of Your New Corporation?

If you are incorporating an existing business, this question is probably already decided. In other words, if you are operating as a sole proprietorship and are changing to the corporate form, you probably will be the sole stockholder of your corporation. However, that is not necessarily true in all cases, because incorporating your business makes transfer of ownership easier, and that may open some estate planning opportunities for you. For instance, you may want to issue the stock in a corporation to yourself and your spouse jointly (assuming you have a stable marriage), as that would enable him or her to easily continue the operation of your business if you should die or become disabled. Estate planning is beyond the scope of this book, but it would be well to check with your attorney, accountant, or financial planner, as to what family members should be the owners of the corporation, or who will inherit how much of the corporation sometime (in the distant future, we hope).

If you are already operating as a partnership and you and your partner have decided to incorporate, the stock normally would be issued in the same proportions as are the present percentages of ownership of the partnership. For instance, if yours is a two-person partnership and you and your partner are equal partners, the corporation's stock would be issued one-half to each partner. That is not to say that the allocation of stock has to be that way. It can be any way that you and your partner wish. For instance, it may be that one of the partners wants to retire and part of the retirement process could be to incorporate and issue a smaller percentage of the stock to the retiring partner.

If you are starting a business as a corporation from day one, your choices as to who will own stock in your corporation are unlimited. Bear in mind, though, that if you intend to elect S corporation status, you are limited to eligible stockholders (individuals and certain specific trusts and estates), as explained in Chapter 2.

Whether you are incorporating a new or old business, remember that it is much easier to issue stock or to transfer stock to a new stockholder than it is to retrieve the stock if that becomes necessary. In other words, do not be in a rush to issue any stock in your corporation to other individuals until you are confident they are the individuals with whom you want a long-term business relationship and that they will be motivated by an opportunity to share in the growth of your business.

Determine How Many Shares of Stock Will Be Authorized and Issued

When a state authorizes the existence of your corporation, it will issue a corporate charter which, among other things, will specify how many shares of stock are authorized and how many are issued to stockholders.

This is a scenario where many incorporators take the easy route and come to regret it later. In other words, if Aunt Bessie sets up a small corporation to sell her needlework, she may decide that she needs only one share of stock to be authorized by the state and that one share is to be issued to her. Business is good, and Bessie gets behind in filling her orders. She invites Lorna to help her in exchange for a one-third share of the business. Now Bessie has a problem of how to divide one share of stock. While some states permit fractional shares to be issued, it certainly is not the easiest way to keep track of who owns how much of the corporation. So Bessie may decide that she needs to have more shares authorized by the state, which, although generally possible, entails more forms to be completed and submitted to the state along with a fee! While using fractional shares would be relatively simple for Bessie and Lorna (two-thirds for Bessie and one-third for Lorna) it can get messy when more investors want on board. Such is the following example:

Jim started a corporation with one share authorized. When three others joined him, he issued fractional shares out of his one share. For various reasons, each had a different fraction of the share, and it ended up this way: Jim owned six-seventeenths of a share, Mary owned three-elevenths, Phyllis owned four-thirteenths. Bert owned how much? It takes a math major to figure it out, but you get the idea: Fractions of shares can be a pain. It is much easier to request the state to authorize many shares at the inception of the corporation, even though only a few shares may be issued to the original stockholder(s). If Bessie had originally requested that the state authorize 1,000 shares and then issued 100 of them to herself at the inception of the corporation, she would be in a position to issue, in exchange for some investment, 50 shares to Lorna at some future date. That is much easier to comprehend and record than dealing with parts of one share.

When it comes to deciding on how many shares of stock will be authorized and how many issued, there are other factors to consider. Check with your state's corporation authority as to fees involved, both at the inception of the corporation and annually. Some states base fees on the number of shares authorized and/or issued, regardless of the value of each share. If that is the case in your state, do not overdo the number of shares authorized and issued if that is going to create a significantly larger annual fee that has to be paid to the state.

Determine What the Price per Share of Stock Will Be

If you have followed the preceding steps, you know how much you will invest (cash and other assets) in your corporation, and you know how many shares of stock will be issued to each stockholder. To determine the price, you obviously divide the total investment by the total number of shares to be issued to arrive at a price per share. This is what the corporation's stockholders will pay for their stock; how it appears on the corporation's books and balance sheet will be in one of two ways. This example will illustrate.

Oliver and Olivia started an olive pitting company, which they decided would operate as a corporation. From the cash flow projections they prepared, they decided that each of them should invest $1,000 in the corporation. When they applied to the state for their corporate charter, they specified that the corporation should be authorized to issue 10,000 shares of stock. Then they actually issued 100 shares each to themselves. The result is that their corporate records and the equity section of the corporation's balance sheet indicated "10,000 shares of common stock authorized, 200 shares issued and outstanding: $2,000."

Through hard work developing a more efficient way of extracting the pits from the olives, and expert marketing, their sales grew rapidly to the point that they needed more working capital. They solved that problem by agreeing to let Preston invest in their profitable enterprise. However, as Preston was not there to take the original risks of starting a business, Oliver and Olivia required that he pay $75 for each share of stock. Preston elected to buy 25 shares at the $75 price for a total investment of $1,875. Now the common stock records indicated outstanding stock as follows:

Oliver	100 shares @ $10	$1,000
Olivia	100 shares @ $10	1,000
Preston	25 shares @ $75	1,875
Totals	225 shares	$3,875

Obviously, dividing the total dollars received for the shares by the number of shares outstanding yields an average price of $31 per share. This is something of a meaningless figure, inasmuch as nobody paid that specific price. There is nothing wrong with keeping the accounting records and the balance sheet in this manner. The stock transfer records provide any

You need not be too concerned about the details of accounting for common stock. Failure to take the time to digest this is not a reason not to incorporate, but remember that this discussion is here in case you are bewildered by what your accountant includes in your financial statements.

needed information relative to shares issued and outstanding—and who owns them.

However, if this bothers you and you would like to see a direct relationship between a price per share and the number of shares outstanding, you can elect to be authorized to issue common stock with a *par value* or *stated value*. That would result in the stock records showing the stock issued to Preston as having a par value of $10, like the earlier stock issued, and the 25 shares at $10 would be shown as $250 of common stock issued to Preston. As Preston still paid the sum of $1,875 for the stock, that leaves $1,625 unaccounted for in this stock record. As good accountants never leave anything unaccounted for, this last sum is called *additional paid-in capital* or the older term of *capital surplus*, and appears as a separate item in the equity section of the balance sheet.

Which is the better way to keep the accounting for common stock? It makes very little difference in most cases. The only technical difference is that in some states dividends can be paid out of capital surplus even if the corporation earned no profits. However, for small corporations with a few stockholders who are also employees of the corporation, planning on more than token dividends are unnecessary, as profits can be extracted as salaries to stockholders/employees. (If your profits are too big to all be extracted as salaries, there would be no reason to pay dividends out of capital surplus.)

There is one last point about par value stock before we move on. If a stockholder purchases stock from the corporation for less than par value, that stockholder would be personally liable to creditors for the shortage between the par value and what he or she paid. In the preceding example, if another individual, Quincy, became another stockholder by paying only $600 for 100 shares of $10 par stock, and the corporation became insolvent, creditors could successfully demand that Quincy fork over another $400 to the corporation's treasury.

Determine Who Will Be the Directors and Officers, and Assign Duties

In most corporations, the structure of the management of the corporation appears this way: The stockholders arrive at their status as stockholders by investing in the corporation and receiving corporate stock, as discussed before. If there is only one stockholder, what follows is just a formality, as that one stockholder will manage the corporation (we are talking about ultimate responsibility for management, not a hired gun to operate the business day-to-day).

The stockholders, at a stockholders' meeting, elect a board of directors. Again, where there is only one stockholder that stockholder generally is the sole director, although sole stockholders could elect others as directors

The examples here all contemplate that the stockholders buy their stock from the corporation. If a stockholder acquires his or her stock from another stockholder, that has no effect on the equity section of the balance sheet. This is not to say that the corporation does not keep track of sales from one stockholder to another, for it must keep a record of stock ownership. Otherwise, it would be difficult to declare a dividend and know to whom the check should be sent.

if they wished to. The directors then, by majority vote, appoint the officers of the corporation, which usually consist of at least a president, secretary, and treasurer. (The president and treasurer are usually the same people as the Chief Executive Officer (CEO) and Chief Financial Officer (CFO), and in some states CEO and CFO can be the legal terms used in corporate documents instead of president and treasurer.)

If there is going to be discussion (or an argument) about who is going to be CEO and who is going to fill the lesser jobs, the time to have that discourse is before you go through the formal steps of creating your corporation. Besides determining who will perform as which corporate officer, this is the best time to agree on several other attributes of the corporation. These would include:

- The assignment of responsibilities, such as who is in charge of sales, production, purchasing, bookkeeping, maintaining the bank account in a positive mode, and other areas of your business.

- The specification of which stockholders/employees will devote how much time to the business (full-time, part-time, or some specific number of hours).

- The setting up of compensation amount for each stockholder/employee as well as formulas for computation of bonuses. Be sure that total compensation does not exceed the figures for salaries in your cash flow projection.

- Agreeing that no stockholder will sell his or her stock to another party until a stockholders' agreement (discussed later) is in effect.

- Deciding anything else you can think of that might become a controversial subject after the business has started.

Prepare a Pre-incorporation Agreement

As the human memory is fallible, reduce all points discussed in the previous section to at least a written memorandum that each prospective stockholder initials. If deals had to be cut to reach agreement on these points, or there is a chance of later misunderstanding, it would be preferable to formalize the results of the discussion in a *pre-incorporation agreement*, drawn up by your lawyer. It should include not only the points already discussed, but all the items covered in a stockholders' agreement (discussed later).

Obviously, as this is an agreement among prospective stockholders, if you are to be the only stockholder there is no need for such an agreement. If you appoint nonstockholders as directors or officers, you can assign their duties and change such assignments as you later decide.

Determine Who Will Be the Incorporator(s)

The incorporator is the individual who files the necessary paperwork with the state to cause a charter that will be issued to the corporation. This is usually a perfunctory job that goes away once the paperwork has been submitted, so the attorney or the incorporating service is often the incorporator. If you are setting up a corporation with only yourself as stockholder, you can easily perform the duties of the incorporator yourself. However, if you are asked to be the incorporator of an enterprise that is already making business contacts and negotiating contracts with others, you could incur personal liability if the corporation somehow fails to be organized or is insufficiently capitalized. The problem is that, inasmuch as the corporation does not yet exist, it cannot be a party to the contract, so the incorporator stands in its shoes.

It is for this reason that lawyers always advise against doing business in a corporate name until a state has issued its charter: A corporation does not protect against personal liability until it is a legal entity chartered by the state.

However, if you are sure that no one has contracted with a third party in the name of the corporation, you are relatively safe in acting as the incorporator.

Select a Resident Agent for Your Corporation

If your corporation gets sued or otherwise served by a legal process, where does the process server serve it? As a corporation is an intangible entity, there has to be an individual to receive a summons or other process. That individual is called a *registered agent*, and has to be a resident of the state in which your corporation is formed or another state (foreign state) where your corporation has registered as doing business in that state. So there has to be a different registered agent in each state in which your corporation operates. For closely held corporations, the easiest designation of registered agent is to name the president of the corporation at the business office of the corporation in its home state. Otherwise, it is not uncommon to designate the corporation's attorney as the resident agent. That should ensure that any summons is answered in a timely manner by a competent individual.

If you register and operate in a foreign state, you are required to have a registered agent who or which is a resident of that state. (Some states permit an entity other than an individual, such as another corporation or limited liability company to act as a resident agent.) You can meet the requirement by retaining a lawyer in that state who can act as your registered agent and also can respond to any legal process that is served on him or her as your registered agent. In many states, firms exists that do nothing but register corporations and act as a registered agent. As many of these firms are not operated by lawyers, their fees may be lower, but check out their references and check them out with the Better Business Bureau. Of course, if you do get sued, you will then have to find an attorney. This does not necessarily mean that you have to engage an attorney or hire a registration service in order to register your corporation in another state. You can handle registration in that state by mail, or perhaps on the Internet, just as easily as you can register your corporation in your own state. The only hiring you *have* to do is to fill the registered agent slot in that state. (Hire expensive professionals for their knowledge, not to do clerical work such as filling in simple forms.)

Have All Prospective Stockholders Sign a Stock Subscription

A stock subscription, at this pre-incorporation stage, is a signed promise by a prospective stockholder to purchase a specific number of shares at a specific price as soon as the corporation is formed. If properly drawn, it commits the prospective stockholder to making this purchase, and any stockholder who fails to complete the purchase can be held personally liable to the corporation and to the corporation's creditors for the amount of the promised purchase.

Again, obviously, there is no need for this document in the case of a single-shareholder corporation, and the need for this document is somewhat diminished if the other stockholders are family members and/or close friends (real friends).

Determine the State in Which You Will Incorporate

You have probably seen ads in business magazines and newspapers extolling the benefits of incorporating in Nevada. (See the box for the principal benefits.) However, incorporating in Nevada may be a good idea for you, or it may be full of traps.

Incorporate in Nevada? If the main business of your corporation is that of painting houses on Long Island, New York, and you incorporated in Nevada, you would be required to register your foreign corporation in New York State before you could engage in house painting there. Then the corporation would be liable for corporate income tax for all the busi-

> The principal advantages of incorporating in Nevada, according to the Secretary of State's web page, are:
>
> - No income tax on corporations
> - No income tax on individuals
> - No tax on corporate stock that you own
> - No sharing of information with the IRS
> - Nominal annual fees
> - A list of your stockholders is not available to the public

ness that it does in New York. If that is 100 percent, then incorporating in Nevada has provided no escape from corporation income tax. As for the salary that your corporation pays you, it would be subject to New York State individual income tax because you physically performed your duties in New York State. (You would have the same situation if you were still a sole proprietor. That is, you would end up owing New York State income tax on the money you earned in New York State, even if you moved to Nevada—or New Hampshire—and commuted.)

If you elect S corporation status, the salary that the corporation pays you would still be subject to New York State income tax, as that is where you performed the services. As for the bottom line income from the S corporation (that flows to the stockholders), that would be taxable in the state in which you reside. In other words, if you actually lived in Nevada and commuted daily to work on Long Island you might escape New York State individual tax on the S corporation income. However, the cost of the daily commute from Nevada to New York and return would, I am sure, far exceed the New York State income tax you would have to pay.

What if you just commuted on weekends and maintained a small residence in New York State and your principal residence was in Nevada? Could you avoid state income tax on dividends and S corporation distributions? This gets into the murky area of determining where your *tax home* is. Deciphering that is not a do-it-yourself project, as the states vary in their interpretation of the rules and their aggressiveness in attempting to collect all taxes possible. This often boils down to a constitutional question regarding which state has the right to extract tax money from you, so obtaining advice from a competent tax attorney is a must if you are going to try to finesse your way around some state income tax by this maneuver.

Therefore, if your business is location sensitive, that is, you provide services such as painting houses in a specific state, or you operate at a physical location as does a manufacturer, wholesaler, or retailer, there is probably no advantage in incorporating in another state. All you will have accomplished is the necessity to pay fees and file corporation reports in two states instead of one. (There is an exception: when you grow sufficiently to sell your stock to the public. Delaware becomes the state of choice for most publicly held companies for various reasons. The justification for incorporating in that state instead of the state in which you maintain most of your facilities and/or offer services is complex. Your underwriters, lawyers, and accountants can explain at that time.)

When should you incorporate in Nevada? Alice develops software for several customers in different states. She travels around the country in her RV, visiting customers holing up in various RV parks for a month at a time while she creates and revises software. She really has no permanent home, but for state tax purposes she claims Nevada (no state tax) as her residence. Incorporating in Nevada could strengthen her position that Nevada is her tax home. (She also retains a mail forwarding service there that gives her the Nevada address for herself and her corporation.)

If you have a segment of your business that could be chopped off from your main enterprise and incorporated in Nevada, you might be able to avoid some tax in other states. (Check out setting up your own advertising agency to handle your main corporation's advertising in Nevada—an idea that might work for you.) As your S corporation's taxable income will appear on your personal tax return regardless of where the corporation lives, you would want to operate as an ordinary C corporation in Nevada. Also, you would want the corporation to retain most of its earnings in its treasury, as any payment to you in the form of salary and/or dividends would be taxable where you live. Remember, also, that if the corporation does business in states other than Nevada, it could be subject to taxes in those states. In other words, do some careful tax planning, with the help of a competent tax advisor, before incorporating in some state other than your state of residence, assuming that your business operates or will operate in the same state where you live.

Choose a Name for Your Corporation

If you are already in business and operating under a business name, such as Bob's Beds, you will probably want to maintain the present goodwill of customers by simply naming your corporation Bob's Beds, Inc. If you're starting your new business as a corporation from day one, your choice of names is almost unlimited, but you cannot use a name that is similar to the name of a corporation already registered and active in your state. The state agency that controls the issuance of corporate charters will not permit names for corporations that duplicate or nearly duplicate names of existing corporations. For that reason, you should determine the name of your corporation early in the planning process. Usually, for a modest fee, the state agency that registers corporations will let you reserve a particular name for a period of time. That enables you to order signage, letterheads, business cards, and advertising while you are going through the process of obtaining your state charter for the corporation and planning your organization.

Will you operate in several states? Do not push this question aside because you will be a small business in a small area. Small service businesses near state lines, such as those operating in the Washington, D.C., area inevitably doing business in Virginia, Maryland, or Pennsylvania, plus the District of Columbia, are examples. If that is your case, you will need to reserve a name (and later register) not only in your home state but also in all the states in which you may do business. What if you do not register your corporation in these other states? You will be violating the law in those other states and your corporation will have no legal standing there. That means that if, for instance, your corporation is a builder head-quartered in Maryland and you build a residence for a customer in Virginia without registering your corporation in Virginia, and your customer refuses to pay you for his home, your corporation would be unable to sue him in Virginia, because it is not registered as a foreign corporation in Virginia. So if you operate in more than one state, register your corporation in those other states as a foreign corporation.

The process of reserving a name also assures you that the name is available and that no other corporation has a similar name in your state or any state in which you are reserving the name of your corporation. Not infrequently, a small business will operate successfully as a sole proprietorship within one city, oblivious to the fact that a small corporation operates in another part of the state under the same name. For instance, when Bob

> **When you reserve a name and/or register your corporation in another state, you will find that you are known as a *foreign corporation*. Even though your corporation operates entirely within the United States, it is considered to be foreign in all states except that in which its corporate office resides. (The corporate office may not be the principal business office of the corporation, as that may be in another state. Indeed, a corporate office may be only the file folder in the lawyer's office.)**

started his bed store as a sole proprietor in one city, he was not aware that there was a corporation named Bob's Beds, Inc. operating in another city within the state. Neither did that corporation realize that Bob was using the same name to operate his sole proprietorship. Therefore, when Bob sets up a corporation, the state will tell him of the conflict of name, and then it would be necessary for him to change his business name.

The name of your corporation is important, for as you operate your business you will, it is hoped, build goodwill that is attached to that name. If you later expand your market area, it will be a severe shock to find that someone else is using your business name. This conflict often results in expensive litigation that, usually, results in the business that was registered first with the state winning out. Notice that I use the word "registered" rather than "incorporated." That is because there are other methods to protect your business name in addition to setting up a corporation with that name. Specifically, a trade name (or trademark) can be registered with a state even though the business is a sole proprietorship or other non-corporate entity. Registration of a trade name is usually a matter of filling out a simple form and submitting it to the proper state agency. Even if you were to set up a corporation with a unique name, also registering the trade name should ensure that you have covered all the bases within your state. If you plan to operate in several states, or if that size of operation could materialize several years downstream, register your trade name with the U.S. Patent and Trademark Office.

What name you choose is a marketing decision, so we leave that discussion to marketing books. However, remember that the name of a corporation must identify the entity as a corporation. Generally, this is done by attaching a suffix to the name that does this task. The usual suffixes are Corporation, Corp., Inc., Limited, and a few others. Not all suffixes are accepted by all states, so be sure to check with your state corporation authority. (Corporation, Corp., Incorporated, and Inc. are always acceptable for general business corporations.)

Determine If You Can Use a Simplified Procedure

Many states offer a simplified version of corporation specifically for small, often family-held, corporations. The most obvious simplification is the elimination of the board of directors, leaving the stockholders to operate as this board, appointing officers, setting compensation, and passing resolutions that may be appropriate or required. The number of stockholders allowed in such a corporation may be limited by the state, as in Nevada it is limited to 30. Also, there may be restrictions on the ability of stockholders to sell their shares except to certain eligible individuals, such as other family members. In my opinion, this provision is not significant enough to be a factor in selecting the state in which you want to incorporate. After you have selected the state, a telephone call or e-mail to the state's corporation authority should provide information as to the availability of the streamlined procedure in your state.

This simplified procedure of corporate governance makes sense for almost all closely held corporations. The exception would be the closely

> Examples of forms for reserving a name and various other forms are included in Appendix A. Also in Appendix B, you will find the address for ordering these forms from your state corporation agency. In many cases, the forms can be downloaded from the Internet.

held corporation that is well capitalized, with the expectation that it will expand rapidly and offer its stock to the public in the near future.

These corporations with the streamlined procedure are known as *close corporations* in many states. In other states, the rule about doing without a board of directors is just buried somewhere in the state code. (You can plod through the state code, which many states publish on the Internet, or you can just call the state corporation authority—Secretary of State, and so on—and ask if the state permits a close corporation or something similar. If you have to be more specific, just ask if you can do without a board of directors.)

Prepare a Pre-incorporation Agreement

For almost every corporation that will have two or more stockholders, this is an important document. It consists of stating all the decisions made previously in this chapter and should be signed by all those who have subscribed to the purchase of stock. Clear statements of what has been agreed upon are more important than couching it all in legalese. However, a review of your agreement by a lawyer would be well advised in order to avoid violating some obscure state law.

The *close* as used in referring to corporations, stands for *closely held*. The term *closely held* refers to the fact that the stock is owned by relatively few people. More often than not, in such situations the stockholders are all related, but that is not a requirement for being a close corporation.

The exception to your needing to create this document would be if you are going to hold a substantial majority of the stock yourself, while others will hold a minimal amount of stock. However, be aware that some states have laws protecting the interests of minority stockholders (those who hold less than 50 percent of the outstanding stock), so check that out with your attorney.

If *you* are to be a minority stockholder, then it is in your interest to have a pre-incorporation agreement. Certainly, you would like to receive a return on your investment, but if you have no agreement as to when dividends will be paid, you may never earn anything on your investment. That is, a pre-incorporation agreement could specify that dividends will be paid when earnings reach a certain level or some such criteria.

Prepare a Stockholders' Agreement

The stockholders' agreement is similar to the pre-incorporation agreement and should cover many of the same points as those covered in that agreement. Because this agreement may endure for decades without modification, it should be more formally and carefully drawn, as by a competent lawyer.

Additional subjects that should be covered in this document should answer the question of what happens to shareholders' stock when they retire or die prior to retirement, along with restrictions on to whom an existing stockholder may sell his or her stock. You certainly do not want your fiercest competitor to be able to buy some of your stock and influence corporate decisions that would benefit him or her more than it would your corporation, nor do you want such a competitor to have inside-route confidential information. Also, more likely, you do not want your obnoxious cousin at your stockholders' meetings.

The best way to limit who may be a stockholder is to restrict the sale of stock, as just mentioned, and also to provide a source of the funds with which to buy the stock when a shareholder wants out or dies. The agreement should specify that the stockholders agree to offer the stock first to the corporation before selling it to any other party. There should also be a formula for determination of the price at which the stock will be sold, which could be a specific price—but a more realistic approach is to provide for the increase in price due to profitable operations of the corporation. Rather than a specific price, the price could be determined by some formula based on the average earnings of the corporation over a period of time or simply the book value of the corporation.

Generally, it is more tax efficient to provide that the corporation, rather than the other stockholders, will buy back the shares of stock from the departing stockholder. That is because it will use corporate cash that is left after paying tax only once rather than from the shareholders' cash that is left after having been subject to double taxation.

Book value can be determined from the balance sheet of the corporation. It is the equity (total assets minus total liabilities) divided by the number of shares outstanding. In other words, if total assets are $1,000 and total liabilities are $400, the equity is $600. If there are 100 shares outstanding, the book value is $6 per share.

There should also be a clause that prevents a stockholder from pledging, assigning, or encumbering his or her stock. Such an activity could result in a sale of stock to the party to whom it was pledged, possibly resulting in the stock's eventually being sold to an undesirable individual or entity. Such a restriction should be printed on the face of the stock certificates, so that any bank or other creditor is aware of the restriction. (Use your attorney to draft the exact wording to be placed on the stock certificates.)

Preparing a stockholders' agreement is one of the most important items, and one of the most overlooked, in setting up a corporation. Where two or more stockholders/employees run a business, differences of opinion will inevitably arise. Having a well-thought-out stockholders' agreement could prevent the corporation's being torn apart by such differences. In Appendix A, you can find a Corporate Shareholders Agreement Form. Please do not use this without legal advice, as it may not be effective in all states as it is written. Also, probably not all clauses in the agreement are applicable to your situation.

CHAPTER 6

Steps to Create and Run Your Corporation

With the decisions you made in Chapter 5 firmly in hand, you are ready to start the process of creating and running your corporation through the following steps.

Steps to Forming Your Corporation

As we did in Chapter 5 for the decision you need to make, we cover all the basic steps to create a corporation based upon those decisions. These are the steps to make if you have several stockholders. If yours is a single stockholder corporation, some of the following steps would be superfluous.

Initial Action the Incorporator(s) Should Take

It is the job of the incorporator to obtain the form (Figure 6.1) known as the *Articles of Incorporation* from your state corporation authority.

DEAN HELLER
Secretary of State
206 North Carson Street
Carson City, Nevada 89701-4299
(775) 684 5708
Website: secretaryofstate.biz

Articles of Incorporation
(PURSUANT TO NRS 78)

Important: Read attached instructions before completing form.　　　ABOVE SPACE IS FOR OFFICE USE ONLY

1. Name of Corporation:	
2. Resident Agent Name and Street Address: *(must be a Nevada address where process may be served)*	Name _____, **NEVADA** _____ Street Address　　City　　　Zip Code Optional Mailing Address　　City　　State　　Zip Code
3. Shares: *(number of shares corporation authorized to issue)*	Number of shares with par value: _____ Par value: $_____　Number of shares without par value: _____
4. Names & Addresses, of Board of Directors/Trustees: *(attach additional page if there is more than 3 directors/trustees)*	1._____ Name Street Address　　City　　State　　Zip Code 2._____ Name Street Address　　City　　State　　Zip Code 3._____ Name Street Address　　City　　State　　Zip Code
5. Purpose: *(optional–see instructions)*	The purpose of this Corporation shall be:
6. Names, Address and Signature of Incorporator: *(attach additional page if there is more than 1 incorporator)*	Name　　　　Signature Address　　City　　State　　Zip Code
7. Certificate of Acceptance of Appointment of Resident Agent:	I hereby accept appointment as Resident Agent for the above named corporation. Authorized Signature of R.A. or On Behalf of R.A. Company　　Date

This form must be accompanied by appropriate fees. See attached fee schedule.　　Nevada Secretary of State Form 78 ARTICLES.2003
　　　　　　　　　　　　　　　　　　　　　　　　　　　　　　　　Revised on: 11/21/03

FIGURE 6.1　Articles of Incorporation

The articles of incorporation for Nevada are reprinted there, so you can follow my comments. (See also Figure 6.2: Instructions for Articles of Incorporation, Nevada.)

Box one is the name of the corporation, which you already should have reserved.

Box two should be the name and street address of your registered agent, and that address must be in the state in which you incorporate. The optional mailing address is for use if you have a post office box or a mail forwarding service.

Box three states the number of shares authorized (not the number you will issue), how many you want, and whether you want shares to have a par value or a no-par value. This was covered in Chapter 5, so you already should have made that decision.

Similarly, the names and addresses of the directors should be inserted in box four. (The term *director* applies to for-profit corporations, while *trustee* applies to nonprofit corporations.)

In box five, your purpose should be as broad as possible. In our rapidly changing economic society, you may well start out painting houses and diversify into running a fleet of tugboats, so word your purpose broadly, such as: "To engage in all lawful business except those professions regulated by other state agencies." (Some states, such as Florida, do not require a purpose to be stated in the Articles of Incorporation.) If you do plan to engage in the practice of a regulated profession such as engineering, architecture, accounting, and so on, the regulatory agency that controls that profession probably has more paperwork for you to complete.

DEAN HELLER
Secretary of State
206 North Carson Street
Carson City, Nevada 89701-4299
(775) 684 5708
Website: secretaryofstate.biz

Instructions for
Articles of Incorporation
(PURSUANT TO NRS 78)

IMPORTANT: RE AD ALL INSTRUCTIONS CAREFULLY BEFORE COMPLETING FORM.

1. *Name of the Corporation:* A name appearing to be that of a natural person and containing a given name or initials must not be used as a corporate name except with the addition of a corporate ending such as Incorporated, Inc., Limited, Ltd., Company, Co., Corporation, Corp. or other words that identifies it as not being a natural person. The name must be distinguishable from the names of corporations, limited-liability companies, limited partnerships, limited-liability limited partnerships, business trusts or limited-liability partnerships on file in the office of the Secretary of State. A name may be reserved, if available, for 90 days by submitting a name reservation form with a $25.00 filing fee. For details you may call (775) 684-5708, visit www.secretaryofstate.biz, or write to the Secretary of State, 206 North Carson Street, Carson City NV. 89701-4201.

2. *Resident Agent:* Persons wishing to incorporate in the State of Nevada must designate a person as a resident agent who resides or is located in this state. E very resident agent must have a street address in this state for the service of process, and may have a separate mailing address such as a post office box, which may be different from the street address.

3. State th e number of shares the corporation shall have the authority to issue with par value and its par value in appropriate space provided. State the number of shares without par value in the space provided for shares without par value.

4. State th e names and addresses of the first governing board. Use a separate 8¹/₂ x 11 sheet as necessary for additional members. Direct ors or trustees must be at least 18 year of age.

5. If it appears from the name and/or purpose of the entity being formed that it is to be regulated by the Financial Institutions Division, Insurance Division, State Board of Professional Engineers and Land Surveyors, State Board of Accountancy or Real Estate Division, the application will need to be approved by the regulating agency before it is filed with the Office of the Secretary of State.

6. Names an d addresses of the incorporators are required. Each incorporator must sign. Additional 8¹/₂ x 11 white sheet will be necessary if more than 1 incorporator.

7. Resid ent agent must complete and sign certificate of acceptance at bottom of form or attach a separate signed certificate of acceptance.

8. On a separate 8¹/₂ x 11, white sheet you may state additional information you wish to be part of the articles. This is an optional provision.

IMPORTANT

INITIAL LIST OF OFFICERS: Pursuant to NRS 78.150, each corporation organized under the laws of this state shall, on or before the last day of the first month after the filing of its articles of incorporation, and annually thereafter, file its list of officers, directors and resident agent. The initial list fee is $125.00. Forms will be mailed to you upon the organization of your corporation and annually thereafter to the corporation's resident agent.

COPIES: You *must* send in the number of copies you would like certified and returned to you in addition to the original article to be filed. A filing fee of $30.00 for each certification is required. Copies received without the required fee shall be returned uncertified. NRS 78.105 r equires that a corporation receive at least one certified copy to be kept in the office of the resident agent. Th e Secretary of State keeps the original filing.

FILING FEE: Filing fee is based on the number of shares authorized. Please see the attached fee schedule. Filing may be expedited for an additional $125.00 expedite fee.

Filing may be submitted at the office of the Secretary of State or by mail at the following addresses:

(Regular and Expedited Filings Accepted)	(Expedited Filings Only)
Secretary of State	Secretary of State-Satellite Office
New Filings Division	Commercial Recordings Division
206 N. Carson Street	Washington Avenue, Suite 4000
Carson City, NV 89701-4299	Las Vegas, NV 89101
775-684-5708 Fax 775-684-7138	702-486-2880 Fax 702-486-2888

Nevada Secretary of State Form CORPINST 2003
Revised on: 12/18/03

FIGURE 6.2   Instructions for Articles of Incorporation, Nevada

Do not ignore that requirement, as without the blessing of that agency you may be operating illegally.

Be sure to insert the name and address of the incorporator and have the incorporator (probably you) sign in box six.

The resident agent must sign as accepting the appointment of resident agent. If it is not convenient to obtain the resident agent signature on the Articles of Incorporation, he or she can sign the Resident Agent Acceptance form (Figure 6.3), that is also reprinted here, but that form is unnecessary if he or she signs the Articles of Incorporation.

That is it! Send the form, with the appropriate fee to the Secretary of State or whatever your state corporation authority is called. As soon as the state accepts your Articles of Incorporation, your corporation exists and can begin doing business.

If you are incorporating in a state that provides for a *close corporation*, it may have a slightly different form for such an entity. Use that form if you want to set up a close corporation.

Obviously, if you are operating in other states, you will need to register in those other states as soon as you receive the accepted Articles from your home state. Do not file Articles of Incorporation in the foreign states, but obtain the form for registering a foreign corporation from each state, fill it in, and submit it to that state with, of course, the required fee.

The various state corporation authorities have done a good job of simplifying the process of submitting Articles of Incorporation and other corporate

DEAN HELLER
Secretary of State
202 North Carson Street
Carson City, Nevada 89701-4201
(775) 684 5708
Website: secretaryofstate.biz

Resident Agent Acceptance

General instructions for this form:

1. Please print legibly or type; Black Ink Only.
2. Complete all fields.
3. Ensure that document is signed in signature field.

In the matter of _____

(Name of business entity)

I, _____ ,

(Name of resident agent)

hereby state that on _____ I accepted the appointment as resident agent

(Date)

for the above named business entity. The street address of the resident agent in this

state is as follows:

_____   _____
Physical Street Address   Suite number

_____, **NEVADA**   _____
City   Zip Code

Optional:

_____   _____
Additional Mailing Address   Suite number

_____,_____   _____
City   State   Zip   Code

Signature:

_____   _____
Authorized Signature of R.A.   or   On Behalf of R.A. Company   Date

Nevada Secretary of State RA Acceptance 2003
Revised on: 11/04/03

FIGURE 6.3   Resident Agent Acceptance

documents, as well as the process of annual reporting and paying fees. Years ago, Articles of Incorporation had to be individually drafted on plain paper as a lengthy legal document which, for most people, meant engaging an attorney to draft it. You may still find lawyers who persist in this practice, but that appears unnecessary except in rare and obscure situations, so it could be a make-work-and-increase-billing gimmick.

Hold Organizational Meetings

To activate a conventional corporation, there should be an organizational meeting, first of the stockholders and then of the board of directors. While there are basic requirements as to what should be accomplished in these meetings, there is no requirement that the minutes be couched in legalese and be written by a lawyer. There need be only a record of what took place, much the same way the secretary of your social club would keep minutes of the business meeting.

State law generally requires that notices of stockholders or directors meetings be delivered to the stockholders or directors, respectively, and be received by those individuals a specific number of days in advance of the meeting. This, of course, can be a hassle involving preparing the notice and delivering it by hand, certified mail, or express service. The usual practice for small closely held corporations is to advise participants of the meetings verbally and then include, in the minutes of the meeting, a waiver of notice of the meeting. (See the examples of meeting minutes in Appendix A, Figures A.4 and A.5.)

Also, if a stockholder and/or a director is not present at a meeting, it is good policy to obtain a proxy, if possible, from that individual or entity or to have him or her confirm agreement in writing, with the actions taken at the meeting.

Organizational Meeting of the Stockholders. This meeting should be held as soon as possible after you are notified of the state's acceptance of your Articles of Incorporation. The required function of this meeting is to elect the board of directors. However, if you have elected the close corporation or other simplified procedure, where the corporation is managed directly by the stockholders without a board of directors, this organizational meeting would also include all the business that is conventionally done in the organizational meeting of the board of directors.

Organizational Meeting of the Board of Directors. This meeting is normally held immediately following the organizational meeting of stockholders. The required function is to elect the chairman of the board of directors and corporate officers, who should at least be the president (or CEO), secretary, and treasurer (or CFO). Generally, these three offices can be held by the same person. Other business that should be conducted in this meeting includes the adoption of the corporate bylaws, the opening of a bank account, the purchase of property, the acceptance of the stockholders' offer to purchase shares of stock, or borrowing money from a bank or other entities, the acceptance of significant contracts, and such other business as should be brought before the board of directors. (There are examples of corporate bylaws and a shareholders' agreement form in Appendix A, Figures A.6 and A.7.)

Register Your Corporation with the Internal Revenue Service (IRS)

As you should expect, the IRS wants to know about your corporation. For that purpose, the IRS expects you to fill in a form SS-4, giving it much information about your corporation. What happens if you do not fill it in and send it off to the IRS? You will not receive an employer identification number (EID) for your corporation, and without the number you cannot file a tax return and pay the corporate taxes that are due. And we all know what happens to people who do not pay their taxes for several years and are caught!

You need this new EID for your corporation, even if you have an EID for your sole proprietorship, partnership, or limited liability company. A sample of this form is in Appendix A (SS-4). A couple of the questions on the form deserve comment.

Question 13, the highest number of employees expected in the next 12 months, should be answered "zero" unless you are sure you will have employees soon. Otherwise, you will be deluged by correspondence from the IRS providing you with payroll tax forms and asking why you have not submitted payroll tax reports.

Question 16a should be answered "no." It is the corporation, not you, that is responding to this question. Obviously, the answer would be "no" for a new corporation.

Register Your Corporation with Your State's (and Any Foreign State's) Tax Authorities

Registering with your Secretary of State or whatever your state corporation authority is called, does not register you with your state's tax department. Your state has its own registration process for letting its tax department know about your corporation. Some states have all-purpose forms, and when you fill them in and submit them, you will be on the list to pay not only income and payroll taxes, but many other fees to which your corporation may be subject. Do not fail to submit these forms and pay the taxes; penalties are too severe to ignore this advice.

Elect S Status for Your Corporation If That Is Your Decision

If you want your new corporation to be an S corporation, you have to make that election by filing Form 2553, Election by a Small Business Corporation, before the fifteenth day of the third month of the corporation's taxable year. (See Appendix A, Figures A.8 and A.9.)

Pay Particular Attention to the Initial Corporate Income Tax Return

There are choices (*elections*, in IRSspeak) to make on this first return that will affect many years of your corporate income tax returns. Some elections are impossible to change once made, and other elections can be changed, but only with some difficulty and correspondence with the IRS that will draw attention to your returns already filed. Some of these are:

- How you will value your inventory of goods for sale or goods in process
- Whether you will report your income on the cash or accrual basis
- Method of depreciating assets initially acquired for the corporation

In addition, it is very important that you avoid this scenario: Suppose you had for several years operated a road grading company as a sole proprietor. The road grader you purchased for $100,000 years ago has, through the bookkeeping process of depreciation, ended up with the value of $1.00 on your sole proprietorship books. (Rather than divert into a long explanation of depreciation, trust me, that is the result of years of depreciation expense.) Now you incorporate, and you pay for your stock by transferring ownership of the road grader to the corporation. Although your book value is only $1.00, the market value of the road grader, due to your excellent maintenance, is $50,000. If the IRS was left unchecked, it would tell you that you received $50,000 of stock in exchange for the grader. As the grader is listed at $1.00 on your sole proprietorship books, you have a gain, classified as ordinary income, of $49,999. If you are in the 25 percent tax bracket, that will cause you to send $12,500 off to the IRS. Scary? Of course. Fortunately, Congress came to the rescue years ago by passing Section 351 of the Internal Revenue Code. It provides that if you attach a statement, listing the property that you are transferring to the corporation and some other information, there will be no tax due on this transfer. (The road grader is still booked at $1.00 on the corporate books, so there would be tax due if the corporation sold the grader.)

The message here is that you should engage a qualified tax professional for preparation of at least the first year's tax return. If you transfer any property to the corporation, please make it your responsibility to ensure that the Section 351 statement is attached to the tax return. If your tax professional fails to include this important document in the corporate tax return, find another professional who understands Section 351 and have him or her prepare the document.

Steps to Keep Your Corporation Alive

At this point you have your corporation set up properly, you held the necessary meetings, and you have written the minutes of those meetings. You have drawn the corporate veil that should protect your personal assets from obligations of the corporation. Now the challenge is to keep that corporate veil in place so it continues to protect you should you need it.

Hold the Annual Stockholders Meeting Every Year

Hold this meeting every year on the date specified in your bylaws. As for the organizational meeting of stockholders, the main order of business is to elect the board of directors. (If you do not have a board of directors, the tasks listed under board of directors annual meeting should also be accomplished in the stockholders annual meeting.) Also, changes in the structure of the corporation, such as amending the Articles of Incorporation should be approved by the stockholders. Also, be sure you include a signed waiver of notice of the meeting in the minutes.

If you are the only stockholder of your corporation, it would be time effective to hold these meetings in your automobile on the way to or from work. That efficiency does not, however, relieve you of recording your decisions, actions, and minutes of both stockholders and board of directors meetings.

Hold an Annual Board of Directors Meeting Every Year

As for the organizational meeting, this meeting should elect officers for the following year. It should also take care of any other business that should be approved by the board of directors, such as purchase or sale of property, change banking relationships, significant borrowing, and so on. Again, do not forget a waiver of notice in the minutes.

Special Meeting of the Board of Directors
(or of Stockholders If There Is No Board of Directors)

It is wise to hold special meetings of the board of directors, and record in the minutes whenever there is a major corporate decision to make, such as those just listed for the annual meeting. Some people take a shortcut by passing a resolution in the annual board of directors meeting that confirms all actions taken by the corporate officers during the year. This may or may not fly in your state, so the recommendation to seek legal counsel applies here. Also, be sure to read documents you are asked to sign in connection with opening an account or borrowing money from a financial institution and other significant transactions. For instance, when you open a corporate bank account, one of the documents the bank will probably ask you to sign is actually a resolution of the board of directors of a corporation authorizing the opening of the bank account. Proper handling of that document is to insert it into the corporate minutes book with a waiver of notice for the meeting in the preamble to the minutes, which specifies the time and place of the meeting.

Live Your Corporate Life as If You Meant It

Keep yourself in the posture of a corporate officer at all times when you are conducting corporate business. That means all correspondence, including e-mails, about corporate business should be on corporate letterhead and signed with the writer's corporate title.

In short, if you treat your corporation as a separate entity, it should provide the corporate veil and/or the taxation status that you desire.

Nonprofit Charitable Organizations

Forming a corporation for charitable purposes is a different ball game, played in a different park. If you form this type of organization, you will still need to file Form SS-4 with the IRS. The IRS will then assign your organization an identification number. However, there is much more to do in terms of IRS filings. If you want to be certain that the IRS will recognize your corporation as a charitable organization, and therefore not subject to income tax, you will have to obtain approval from the IRS. You do that by filing Form 1023, which consists of several pages. Form 1023 and instructions for completing it are available from the IRS at 1-800-829-3676 or at the IRS web site at www.irs.gov. After you complete the form, attach the required documents and probably have one or more telephone conferences with IRS personnel, you should receive a letter stating your corporation is classified as nonprofit, under Section 501(c)(3) of the Internal Revenue Code. Thereafter, depending on the size of your operation, you may be required to file annual reports with the IRS on Form 990.

Does this appear like it is more than you want to undertake? Try this. Find a tax-oriented lawyer or CPA who sympathizes with the purpose of your organization and invite them to sit on your board of trustees. They may not do the leg work, but they can be a source of free advice on how to obtain this approval of nonprofit status and comply with annual reporting requirements.

Useful Forms

List of Forms

DEAN HELLER
Secretary of State
206 North Carson Street
Carson City, Nevada 89701-4299
(775) 684 5708
Website: secretaryofstate.biz

Articles of Incorporation of

_____

(Name of Close Corporation)

A Close Corporation
(PURSUANT TO NRS 78A)

(Name of Corporation _MUST_ appear in the above heading)

Important: Read attached instructions before completing form.   ABOVE SPACE IS FOR OFFICE USE ONLY

1. Name of Close Corporation:	
2. Resident Agent Name and Street Address: _(must be a Nevada address where process may be served)_	Name _____ , **NEVADA** _____ Physical Street Address _____ City _____ Zip Code Additional Mailing Address _____ City ____ State __ Zip Code
3. Shares: _(no. of shares corporation authorized to issue)_	Number of shares with par value: _____ Par value: $_____ Number of shares without par value: _____
4. Governing Board: _(check one; if yes, please complete below)_	This corporation is a close corporation operating with a board of directors _____ **Yes** / or _____ **No**
5. Names, addresses, Number of Board of Directors: _(if more than two directors, please attach additional pages)_	1._____ _____ Name Street Address _____ City _____ State ___ Zip Code 2._____ Name Street Address _____ City _____ State ___ Zip Code
6. Purpose: _(optional-See instructions)_	The purpose of this Corporation shall be:
7. Names, Addresses and Signatures of Incorporators: _(if more than two incorporators, please attach additional pages)_	Name _____ Signature _____ Address ___ City ___ State __ Zip Code Name _____ Signature _____ Address ___ City ___ State __ Zip Code
8. Certificate of Acceptance of Appointment of Resident Agent:	I hereby accept appointment as Resident Agent for the above named corporation. _____ _____ Authorized Signature of R.A. or On Behalf of R.A. Company Date

This form must be accompanied by appropriate fees. See attached fee schedule.   Nevada Secretary of State Form 78A ARTS.2003
Revised on: 12/03/03

FIGURE A.1   Articles of Incorporation, Nevada

State of Nevada
Secretary of State
202 North Carson Street
Carson City, Nevada 89701-4201
Phone: (775) 684 5708
Website: secretaryofstate.biz

PROFIT CORPORATIONS INITIAL FILING FEE : Pursuant to NRS 78, 80, 78A, and 89 Domestic and Foreign Corporations, Close Corporations and Professional Corporations.

Fees are based on the value of the total number of authorized shares stated in the Articles of Incorporation as prescribed by NRS 78.760:

$75,000 or less	$75.00
over $75,000 and not over $200,000	$175.00
over $200,000 and not over $500,000	$275.00
over $500,000 and not over $1,000,000	$375.00
OVER $1,000,000	
For the first $1,000,000	$375.00
For each additional $500,000 - or fraction thereof	$275.00
Maximum fee	$35,000.00

For the purpose of computing the filing fee, the value (capital) represented by the total number of shares authorized in the Articles of Incorporation is determined by computing the:

A. total authorized shares multiplied by their par value or;
B. total authorized shares without par value multiplied by $1.00 or;
C. the sum of (a) and (b) above if both par and no par shares.

Filing fees are calculated on a minimum par value of one-tenth of a cent (.001), regardless if the stated par value is less.

The 24-hour expedite fee for Articles of Incorporation for any of the above entities is $125.00 in addition to the filing fee based upon stock.

The 2-hour expedite fee is $500.00 in addition to the filing fee based upon stock.

PLEASE NOTE: the expedite fee is in addition to the standard filing fee charged on each filing and/or order.

24-HOUR EXPEDITE TIME CONSTRAINTS:

Each filing submitted receives same day filing date and may be picked up within 24-hours. Filings to be mailed the next business day if received by 2:00 pm of receipt date and no later than the 2nd business day if received after 2:00 pm.

Expedite period begins when filing or service request is received in this office in fileable form.

The Secretary of State reserves the right to extend the expedite period in times of extreme volume, staff shortages, or equipment malfunction. These extensions are few and will rarely extend more than a few hours.

Nevada Secretary of State Form Fee Schedule-NF Profit pg 1 2003
Revised on: 10/27/03

FIGURE A.2   Profit Corporation Fee Schedule, Nevada

DEAN HELLER
Secretary of State
202 North Carson Street
Carson City, Nevada 89701-4201
Phone: (775) 684 5708
Website: secretaryofstate.biz

Profit Corporation Fee Schedule
Effective 11-1-03
Page 2

OTHER PROFIT CORPORATION FEES:

Articles of Association pursuant to NRS 89.210 (Professional Association)	$75.00
Reinstatement Fee	$300.00
Certificate of Amendment, minimum fee*	$175.00
Certificate pursuant to NRS 78.209 (stock split), minimum fee*	$175.00
Certificate pursuant to NRS 78.1955 (stock designation)	$175.00
Amendment to Certificate pursuant NRS 78.1955 (stock designation)	$175.00
Amendment of Modified Name	$175.00
Restated Articles, minimum fee*	$175.00
Certificate of Correction, minimum fee*	$175.00
Certificate of Termination (includes filings pursuant to NRS 78.209, 78.380 and 78.390)	$175.00
Termination Pursuant to NRS 92A	$350.00
Articles of Merger* or Exchange	$350.00
Dissolution of Corporation	$75.00
Withdrawal of Foreign Corporation	$75.00
Preclearance of any Document	$125.00
Articles of Conversion – contact office for fee information	
Articles of Domestication – contact office for fee information	
Revival of Corporation – contact office for fee information	
24-Hour Expedite fee for above filings	**$125.00**
Change of Resident Agent/Address	$60.00
Resident Agent Name Change	$100.00
Resignation of Director or Officer	$75.00
Resignation of Resident Agent (plus $1.00 for each additional entity listed)	$100.00
Name Reservation	$25.00
24-Hour Expedite fee for above filings	**$25.00**
Apostille	$20.00
Certificate of Good Standing	$50.00
Initial List of Officers and Directors	$125.00
Annual or Amended List of Officers and Directors	See Annual List Fee Schedule
Annual List of Officers and Directors (Professional Association)	$125.00
24-Hour Expedite fee for above filings	**$75.00**
Certification of Documents – per certification	$30.00
Copies – per page	$2.00
Late Fee for List of Officers	$75.00

*Fee will be higher if stock is increased a significant amount, according to the initial filing fee schedule on page 1 of the profit corporation fee schedule. Maximum fee for an increase in stock is $35,000.00.

2-Hour Expedite is available on all of the above filings at the fee of $500.00 per item.

PLEASE NOTE: *the expedite fee is in addition to the standard filing fee charged on each filing and/or order.*

24-HOUR EXPEDITE TIME CONSTRAINTS: Each filing submitted receives same day filing date and may be picked up within 24-hours. Filings to be mailed the next business day if received by 2:00 pm of receipt date and no later than the 2nd business day if received after 2:00 pm. Expedite period begins when filing or service request is received in this office in fileable form. The Secretary of State reserves the right to extend the expedite period in times of extreme volume, staff shortages, or equipment malfunction. These extensions are few and will rarely extend more than a few hours.

Nevada Secretary of State Form Fee Schedule-Profit Page 2 2003
Revised on: 01/06/04

FIGURE A.2   *(Continued)*

DEAN HELLER
Secretary of State
202 North Carson Street
Carson City, Nevada 89701-4201
Phone: (775) 684 5708
Website: secretaryofstate.biz

The following is a list of copies and certification services and the associated fees. Fees are per document unless otherwise noted.

SERVICE REQUESTED:

Copies	$2.00 per page
Certification of Document	$30.00
Search	$50.00
Certificates:	
Certificate of Existence (evidence of good standing – short form)	$50.00
Certificate of Existence (listing amendments – long form)	$50.00
Certificate Evidencing Name Change	$50.00
Certificate of Fact of Merger	$50.00
Certificate of Default	$50.00
Certificate of Revocation	$50.00
Certificate of Dissolution	$50.00
Certificate of Withdrawal	$50.00
Certificate of Cancellation	$50.00
Certificate of Non-Existence	$50.00
Corporate Charter	$50.00
Miscellaneous Certificates	$50.00
Apostille (Hague Treaty Nations)/Certification (Non-Hague Treaty Nations)	$20.00
Exemplification	$50.00

EXPEDITE SERVICE:

Expedite service is available for copies, certificate and certification services. Fees for expedite service are in addition to the fees as listed above.

24 Hour Expedite Service: Order may be picked up or mailed out within 24-hours.

Copies:	
1 to 10 pages	$75.00
11 or more pages	$125.00
Certificates (per entity name & and certificate type):	
1 to 10 certificates	$75.00
11 or more certificates	$125.00
Search:	
Expedite fee on search only; additional expedite fee required for copies	$25.00

4-Hour Expedite Service: Order may be picked up or mailed within 4-hours.
    CERTIFICATES ONLY (per entity name & certificate type):

1 or more certificates	$125.00

BASIC INSTRUCTIONS:

1. All orders may be received in writing with fees enclosed at the above address. Telephone orders with payment by VISA or Mastercard may be called into our Customer Service Department at (775) 684-5708. Trust account and credit card customers may fax *expedite orders only* to (775) 684-5645. Trust account orders must be received on company letterhead.

2. Other than orders specified as a pick-up, all orders are mailed out via first-class mail, unless a prepaid envelope, express mail number or Federal Express number is provided.

3. We *do not* fax orders back to customers. Each order will be returned to one address only.

Nevada Secretary of State Form Fee Schedule- Copies 2003
Revised on: 10/29/03

FIGURE A.3   Copies and Certification Services Fee Schedule, Nevada

Minutes of Organization Meeting of Incorporators Form

'Lectric Law Library   *'Lectric Law Library*   *'Lectric Law Library*

MINUTES OF ORGANIZATION MEETING OF INCORPORATORS

WAIVER OF NOTICE
ORGANIZATION MEETING OF INCORPORATORS
[NAME OF COMPANY]

WE, THE UNDERSIGNED, being all the incorporators of the corporation above named, organized under the laws of the State of [STATE], DO HEREBY WAIVE NOTICE of the time, place and purpose of the organization meeting of said incorporators, and do fix the __th day of ___, ____ at _____ o'clock __.M. as the time, and [PLACE] as the place of said meeting.

And we do hereby waive all the requirements of the statutes of [STATE] as to the notice of this meeting, and do consent to the transaction of such business as may come before the meeting.

Dated:

_____
[Name 1]

_____
[Name 2]

_____
[Name 3]

=======

MINUTES OF ORGANIZATION MEETING OF INCORPORATORS
[NAME OF COMPANY]

The organization meeting of the incorporators was held on the ____th day of ___, 20___ at [TIME] o'clock __.M., at [PLACE] pursuant to a written waiver of notice, signed by all the incorporators fixing said time and place.

The following incorporators were present in person:
[Name 1]
[Name 2]
[Name 3]

being all of the incorporators of the corporation.

[Name 3] acted as Chairman and [Name 3] was appointed Secretary of the meeting.

FIGURE A.4   Minutes of Organization Meeting of Incorporators Form

Recorder of Deeds and instructed the Secretary to cause a copy of the Certificate of Incorporation to be prefixed to the minutes.

Upon motion, duly made, seconded and carried, it was: RESOLVED, That the certificate of Incorporation of the corporation be and it hereby is accepted and that this corporation proceed to do business thereunder.

The Secretary presented a form of By-Laws for the regulation of the affairs of the corporation, which were read article by article.

Upon motion, duly made, seconded and carried: RESOLVED, That the By-Laws presented at this meeting, as amended and attached to the Minutes, were unanimously adopted and the Secretary was instructed to cause the same to be inserted in the minute book immediately following the copy of the Certificate of Incorporation.

The Chairman stated that the next business before the meeting was the election of a Board of Directors.

After discussion, [Name 1], [Name 2] and [Name 3] were nominated for directors of the corporation, to hold office for the ensuing year and until others are chosen and qualified in their stead. No other nominations having been made, the vote was taken and the aforesaid nominees declared duly elected.

Upon motion, duly made, seconded and carried, it was RESOLVED, That the Board of Directors be and they are hereby authorized to issue the capital stock of this corporation to the full amount or number of shares authorized by the Certificate of Incorporation, in such amounts and proportions as from time to time shall be determined by the Board, and to accept in full or in part payment thereof such property as the Board may determine shall be good and sufficient consideration and necessary for the business of the corporation.

Upon motion, duly made, seconded and carried, the meeting thereupon adjourned.

Secretary

___

Contributed to the Library by Richard Widrig

FIGURE A.4 *(Continued)*

We've lots of related material, so wander around & explore places like our
Business Law Topic Area and the **Business Peoples's Lounge** and **Study of Law Study**

▓ Our Main Forms Room ▓
▓ Our Law Practice Forms ▓
▓ Our Business & General Forms ▓

▓ The Library Rotunda ▓

Our Central Hub, Directory and Index

▓ The Reference Room ▓

Dozens of Topic Areas & Our Law Lexicon

Want Forms Programs, other Legal Software & Etexts, Help with Legal Problems or Questions?

Help with Legal Problems & Questions Legal Software, Etexts & Lots More	Join Our	GoldCard Program	Click Here For Info

[Last Revised 3/02]

FIGURE A.4 *(Continued)*

Minutes of First Meeting of the Board of Directors Form

'Lectric Law Library   'Lectric Law Library   'Lectric Law Library

MINUTES OF FIRST MEETING OF THE BOARD OF DIRECTORS

WAIVER OF NOTICE
FIRST MEETING OF THE BOARD OF DIRECTORS
[COMPANY NAME]

WE, THE UNDERSIGNED, being the directors elected by the incorporators of
the above named corporation, DO HEREBY WAIVE NOTICE of the time, place
and purpose of the first meeting of the Board of Directors of said
corporation.

We designate the ____th day of ____, 20____ at 9:35 o'clock __.M. as
the time and [FULL ADDRESS] as the place of said meeting; the purpose of
said meeting being to elect officers, authorize the issue of the capital
stock, authorize the purchase of property if necessary for the business
of the corporation, and the transaction of such other business as may be
necessary or advisable to facilitate and complete the organization of
said corporation, and to enable it to carry on its contemplated
business.

Dated: ____ ____, 20____

_____
[Name 1]

_____
[Name 2]

_____ ____
[Name 3]

===========

MINUTES OF FIRST MEETING OF THE BOARD OF DIRECTORS OF
[NAME OF COMPANY]

The first meeting of the Board of Directors was held at [PLACE] on the
____th day of ____, 20____ at _____ o'clock __.M.

Present:
[Name 1]
[Name 2]
[Name 3]

constituting a quorum of the Board.

[Name 3] acted as Chairman and [Name 3] was appointed temporary
Secretary of the meeting.

The Secretary presented and read a waiver of notice of the meeting,
signed by all the directors.

Figure A.5   Minutes of First Meeting of the Board of Directors Form

The minutes of the organization meeting of incorporators were read and approved.

The following persons were nominated to the offices set opposite their respective names, to serve for one year and until their successors are chosen and qualify:

[Name 2]- Chairman
[Name 3]- Vice Chairman
[Name 1]- President
[Name 3]- Secretary
[Name 3]- Chief Financial Officer

All the directors present having voted, the Chairman announced that the aforesaid had been unanimously chosen as said officers, respectively.

The Chairman thereupon took the chair and the Secretary thereupon entered upon the discharge of his duties.

Upon motion, duly made, seconded and carried, it was
  RESOLVED, That the stock certificates of this corporation shall be in the form submitted at this meeting.

Upon motion, duly made, seconded and carried, it was
  RESOLVED, That the seal, an impression of which is herewith affixed, be adopted as the corporate seal of this corporation.

The Secretary was authorized and directed to procure the proper corporate books.

Upon motion, duly made, seconded and carried, it was
  RESOLVED, That the officers of this corporation be authorized and directed to open a bank account in the name of the corporation, in accordance with a form of bank resolution attached to the minutes of this meeting.

[Name 3] reported the following balances in the bank accounts of the corporation at [BANK]:

Savings #_____: $
Checking #_____: $

Upon motion, duly made, seconded and carried, the following preambles and resolutions were unanimously adopted:

WHEREAS, The following offer has been made to the corporation in consideration of the issuance of full paid and non-assessable shares of the corporation:

Price= $_____ per share
___ shares issued to [Name 1]
___ shares issued to [Name 2]
___ shares issued to [Name 3]
([Name 1], [Name 2] and [Name 3] hereafter known as "Offerors")

WHEREAS, In the judgment of this Board of Directors of this corporation, said offer is good and sufficient consideration for the shares demanded therefor and necessary for the business of this corporation,

Now, therefore, be it

FIGURE A.5 *(Continued)*

RESOLVED, That the aforesaid offer be and is hereby accepted and that the President and Secretary of this corporation be and they hereby are authorized and directed to execute in the name and on behalf of this corporation, and under its corporate seal, such agreement or agreements as may be necessary in accordance with said offer.

FURTHER RESOLVED, That the President and Secretary be and they hereby are authorized and directed to issue and deliver in accordance with said offer certificates of full paid and non-assessable shares of this corporation to the said Offerors.

Upon motion, duly made, seconded and carried, the following preambles and resolutions were unanimously adopted:

WHEREAS, The following loans have been offered to the corporation in consideration of the issuance of promissory notes from the corporation:

[LIST]

WHEREAS, In the judgment of this Board of Directors of this corporation, said offer is good and sufficient consideration for the loan offered therefor and necessary for the business of this corporation,

Now, therefore, be it
    RESOLVED, That the aforesaid offer be and is hereby accepted and that the proper officers of this corporation be and they hereby are authorized and directed to execute in the name and on behalf of this corporation, and under its corporate seal, such agreements, copies of which are attached hereto, as may be necessary in accordance with said offer.

Upon motion, duly made, seconded and carried, it was
    RESOLVED, That in compliance with the laws of the State of [State], this corporation have and continuously maintain a registered office within the State of [State] and have an agent at all times in charge thereof, upon which agent process against this corporation may be served, and that the books and records of the corporation shall be available for examination by any stockholder for any proper purpose as provided by law.

Upon motion, duly made, seconded and carried, it was
    RESOLVED, That the proper officers of the corporation be and they hereby are authorized and directed on behalf of the corporation, and under its corporate seal, to make and file such certificate, report or other instrument as may be required by law to be filed in any state, territory, or dependency of the United States, or in any foreign country, in which said officers shall find it necessary or expedient to file the same to authorize the corporation to transact business in such state, territory, dependency or foreign country.

Upon motion, duly made, seconded and carried, it was
    RESOLVED, That the Chief Financial Officer be and hereby is authorized to pay all fees and expenses incident to and necessary for the organization of the corporation.

There being no further business, the meeting upon motion adjourned.

Secretary

—--

Contributed to the Library by Richard Widrig

FIGURE A.5   *(Continued)*

* <u>IMPORTANT</u> *

A primary purpose of the Library has always been to provide no-cost legal information to anyone who wants or needs it. However,   It's Vital that You Understand that most of our Forms are ONLY General, Generic Examples of possible formats & contents. Legal Requirements for various Business Entity related documents Can and Do Vary Greatly from State to State and can Change Often.   To be Valid - and Not Create More Problems than it Solves - it MUST be Properly Drafted and Modified to fit Your Specific Location and Circumstances!

For Up-To-Date Forms Covering Just About Every State & Situation plus Summaries of Relevant Laws We STRONGLY SUGGEST You Check Out:

'LLL's Premium Forms   25,000+ WILLS, CONTRACTS, DEEDS, TRUSTS, LEASES
ALL SUBJECTS & STATES   · CLICK HERE ·

(This should open a new window. Close it when you're done and you'll be back here.)

'Lectric Law Library   'Lectric Law Library   'Lectric Law Library

We've lots of related material, so wander around & explore places like our <u>Business Law</u> Topic Area and the <u>Business Peoples's Lounge</u> and <u>Study of Law</u>

<u>Our Main Forms Room</u>
<u>Our Law Practice Forms</u>
<u>Our Business & General Forms</u>

<u>The Library Rotunda</u>
Our Central Hub, Directory and Index
<u>The Reference Room</u>
Dozens of Topic Areas & Our Law Lexicon

'Lectric Law Library   'Lectric Law Library   'Lectric Law Library

Want Forms Programs, other Legal Software & Etexts, Help with Legal Problems or Questions?

| Help with Legal Problems & Questions Legal Software, Etexts & Lots More | Join Our | GoldCard Program | Click Here For Info |

[Last Revised 3/02]

FIGURE A.5   *(Continued)*

Sample Corporate Bylaws

'Lectric Law Library   'Lectric Law Library   'Lectric Law Library

SAMPLE CORPORATE BYLAWS

BY-LAWS

"COMPANY"

ARTICLE I - OFFICES

Section 1. The registered office of the corporation shall be at:

"Address"

The registered agent in charge thereof shall be: "Name".

Section 2. The corporation may also have offices at such other places as the Board of Directors may from time to time appoint or the business of the corporation may require.

ARTICLE II - SEAL

Section 1. The corporate seal shall have inscribed thereon the name of the corporation, the year of its organization and the words "Corporate Seal, "State"".

ARTICLE III - STOCKHOLDERS' MEETINGS

Section 1. Meetings of stockholders shall be held at the registered office of the corporation in this state or at such place, either within or without this state, as may be selected from time to time by the Board of Directors.

Section 2. Annual Meetings: The annual meeting of the stockholders shall be held on the 3rd Wednesday of February in each year if not a legal holiday, and if a legal holiday, then on the next secular day following at 10:00 o'clock A.M., when they shall elect a Board of Directors and transact such other business as may properly be brought before the meeting. If the annual meeting for election of directors is not held on the date designated therefor, the directors shall cause the meeting to be held as soon thereafter as convenient.

Section 3. Election of Directors: Elections of the directors of the corporation shall be by written ballot.

Section 4. Special Meetings: Special meetings of the stockholders may be called at any time by the Chairman, or the Board of Directors, or stockholders entitled to cast at least one-fifth of the votes which all stockholders are entitled to cast at the particular meeting. At any time, upon written request of any person or persons who have duly called a special meeting, it shall be the duty of the Secretary to fix the date of the meeting, to be held not more than sixty days after receipt of the request, and to give due notice thereof. If the Secretary shall neglect or refuse to fix the date of the meeting and give notice thereof, the person or persons calling the meeting may do so.

Figure A.6   Sample Corporate Bylaws

Business transacted at all special meetings shall be confined to the objects stated in the call and matters germane thereto, unless all stockholders entitled to vote are present and consent.

Written notice of a special meeting of stockholders stating the time and place and object thereof, shall be given to each stockholder entitled to vote thereat at least 30 days before such meeting, unless a greater period of notice is required by statute in a particular case.

Section 5. Quorum: A majority of the outstanding shares of the corporation entitled to vote, represented in person or by proxy, shall constitute a quorum at a meeting of stockholders. If less than a majority of the outstanding shares entitled to vote is represented at a meeting, a majority of the shares so represented may adjourn the meeting from time to time without further notice. At such adjourned meeting at which a quorum shall be present or represented, any business may be transacted which might have been transacted at the meeting as originally noticed. The stockholders present at a duly organized meeting may continue to transact business until adjournment, notwithstanding the withdrawal of enough stockholders to leave less than a quorum.

Section 6. Proxies: Each stockholder entitled to vote at a meeting of stockholders or to express consent or dissent to corporate action in writing without a meeting may authorize another person or persons to act for him by proxy, but no such proxy shall be voted or acted upon after three years from its date, unless the proxy provides for a longer period.

A duly executed proxy shall be irrevocable if it states that it is irrevocable and if, and only as long as, it is coupled with an interest sufficient in law to support an irrevocable power. A proxy may be made irrevocable regardless of whether the interest with which it is coupled is an interest in the stock itself or an interest in the corporation generally. All proxies shall be filed with the Secretary of the meeting before being voted upon.

Section 7. Notice of Meetings: Whenever stockholders are required or permitted to take any action at a meeting, a written notice of the meeting shall be given which shall state the place, date and hour of the meeting, and, in the case of a special meeting, the purpose or purposes for which the meeting is called. Unless otherwise provided by law, written notice of any meeting shall be given not less than ten nor more than sixty days before the date of the meeting to each stockholder entitled to vote at such meeting.

Section 8. Consent in Lieu of Meetings: Any action required to be taken at any annual or special meeting of stockholders or a corporation, or any action which may be taken at any annual or special meeting of such stockholders, may be taken without a meeting, without prior notice and without a vote, if a consent in writing, setting forth the action so taken, shall be signed by the holders of outstanding stock having not less than the minimum number of votes that would be necessary to authorize or take such action at a meeting at which all shares entitled to vote thereon were present and voted. Prompt notice of the taking of the corporate action without a meeting by less than unanimous written consent shall be given to those stockholders who have not consented in writing.

Section 9   List of Stockholders: The officer who has charge of the stock ledger of the corporation shall prepare and make, at least ten days before every meeting of stockholders, a complete list of the stockholders entitled to vote at the meeting, arranged in alphabetical order, and showing the address of each stockholder and the number of shares registered in the name of each stockholder. No share of stock upon which any installment is due

FIGURE A.6   *(Continued)*

and unpaid shall be voted at any meeting. The list shall be open to the examination of any stockholder, for any purpose germane to the meeting, during ordinary business hours, for a period of at least ten days prior to the meeting, either at a place within the city where the meeting is to be held, which place shall be specified in the notice of the meeting, or, if not so specified, at the place where the meeting is to be held. The list shall also be produced and kept at the time and place of the meeting during the whole time thereof, and may be inspected by any stockholder who is present.

ARTICLE IV – DIRECTORS

Section 1. The business and affairs of this corporation shall be managed by its Board of Directors, ___ in number. The directors need not be residents of this state or stockholders in the corporation. They shall be elected by the stockholders at the annual meeting of stockholders of the corporation, and each director shall be elected for the term of ore year, and until his successor shall be elected and shall qualify or until his earlier resignation or removal.

Section 2. Regular Meetings: Regular meetings of the Board shall be held without notice, at least quarterly, at the registered office of the corporation, or at such other time and place as shall be determined by the Board.

Section 3. Special Meetings: Special Meetings of the Board may be called by the Chairman on 2 days notice to each director, either personally or by mail, fax or by telegram; special meetings shall be called by the President or Secretary in like manner and on like notice on the written request of a majority of the directors in office.

Section 4. Quorum: A majority of the total number of directors shall constitute a quorum for the transaction of business.

Section 5. Consent in Lieu of Meeting: Any action required or permitted to be taken at any meeting of the Board of Directors, or of any committee thereof, may be taken without a meeting if all members of the Board or committee, as the case may be, consent thereto in writing, and the writing or writings are filed with the minutes of proceedings of the Board or committee. The Board of Directors may hold its meetings, and have an office or offices, outside of this state.

Section 6. Conference Telephone: One or more directors may participate in a meeting of the Board, or a committee of the Board or of the stockholders, by means of conference telephone or similar communications equipment by means of which all persons participating in the meeting can hear each other; participation in this manner shall constitute presence in person at such meeting.

Section 7. Compensation Directors as such, shall not receive any stated salary for their services, but by resolution of the Board, a fixed sum and expenses of attendance at each regular or special meeting of the Board PROVIDED, that nothing herein contained shall be construed to preclude any director from serving the corporation in any other capacity and receiving compensation therefor.

Section 8. Removal: Any director or the entire Board of Directors may be removed, with or without cause, by the holders of a majority of the shares then entitled to vote at an election of directors, except that when cumulative voting is permitted, if less than the entire Board is to be removed, no director may be removed without cause if the votes cast against his removal would be sufficient to elect him if then cumulatively voted at

FIGURE A.6 *(Continued)*

an election of the entire Board of Directors, or, if there be classes of directors, at an election of the class of directors of which he is a part.

ARTICLE V – OFFICERS

Section 1. The executive officers of the corporation shall be chosen by the directors and shall be a Chairman, President, Secretary and Chief Financial Officer. The Board of Directors may also choose a one or more Vice Presidents and such other officers as it shall deem necessary. Any number of offices may be held by the same person.

Section 2. Salaries: Salaries of all officers and agents of the corporation shall be fixed by the Board of Directors.

Section 3. Term of Office: The officers of the corporation shall hold office for one year and until their successors are chosen and have qualified. Any officer or agent elected or appointed by the Board may be removed by the Board of Directors whenever in its judgment the best interest of the corporation will be served thereby.

Section 4. Chairman: The Chairman shall preside at all meetings of the stockholders and directors; he shall see that all orders and resolutions of the Board are carried into effect, subject, however, to the right of the directors to delegate any specific powers, except such as may be by statute exclusively conferred on the Chairman, to any other officer or officers of the corporation. He shall execute bonds, mortgages and other contracts requiring a seal, under the seal of the corporation. He shall be EX-OFFICIO a member of all committees.

Section 5. President: The President shall attend all sessions of the Board. The President shall be the chief executive officer of the corporation; he shall have general and active management of the business of the corporation, subject, however, to the right of the directors to delegate any specific powers, except such as may be by statute exclusively conferred on the President, to any other officer or officers of the corporation. He shall have the general power and duties of supervision and management usually vested in the office of President of a corporation.

Section 6. Secretary: The Secretary shall attend all sessions of the Board and all meetings at the stockholders and act as clerk thereof, and record all the votes of the corporation and the minutes of all its transactions in a book to be kept for that purpose, and shall perform like duties for all committees of the Board of Directors when required. He shall give, or cause to be given, notice of all meetings of the stockholders and of the Board of Directors, and shall perform such other duties as may be prescribed by the Board of Directors or President, and under whose supervision he shall be. He shall keep in safe custody the corporate seal of the corporation, and when authorized by the Board, affixe tsame to any instrument requiring it.

Section 6. Chief Financial Officer: The Chief Financial Officer shall have custody of the corporate funds and securities and shall keep full and accurate accounts of receipts and disbursements in books belonging to the corporation, and shall keep the moneys of the corporation in separate account to the credit of the corporation. He shall disburse the funds of the corporation as may be ordered by the Board, taking proper vouchers for such disbursements, and shall render to the President and directors, at the regular meetings of the Board, or whenever they may require it, an account of all his transactions as Chief Financial Officer and of the financial condition of the corporation.

FIGURE A.6   *(Continued)*

ARTICLE VI – VACANCIES

Section 1. Any vacancy occurring in any office of the corporation by death, resignation, removal or otherwise, shall be filled by the Board of Directors. Vacancies and newly created directorships resulting from any increase in the authorized number of directors may be filled by a majority of the directors then in office, although not less than a quorum, or by a sole remaining director. If at any time, by reason of death or resignation or other cause, the corporation should have no directors in office, then any officer or any stockholder or an executor, administrator, trustee or guardian of a stockholder, or other fiduciary entrusted with like responsibility for the person or estate of stockholder, may call a special meeting of stockholders in accordance with the provisions of these By-Laws.

Section 2. Resignations Effective at Future Date: When one or more directors shall resign from the Board, effective at a future date, a majority of the directors then in office, including those who have so resigned, shall have power to fill such vacancy or vacancies, the vote thereon to take effect when such resignation or resignations shall become effective.

ARTICLE VII – CORPORATE RECORDS

Section 1. Any stockholder of record, in person or by attorney or other agent, shall, upon written demand under oath stating the purpose thereof, have the right during the usual hours for business to inspect for any proper purpose the corporation's stock ledger, a list of its stockholders, and its other books and records, and to make copies or extracts therefrom. A proper purpose shall mean a purpose reasonably related to such person's interest as a stockholder. In every instance where an attorney or other agent shall be the person who seeks the right to inspection, the demand under oath shall be accompanied by a power of attorney or such other writing which authorizes the attorney or other agent to so act on behalf of the stockholder. The demand under oath shall be directed to the corporation at its registered office in this state or at its principal place of business.

ARTICLE VIII – STOCK CERTIFICATES, DIVIDENDS, ETC.

Section 1. The stock certificates of the corporation shall be numbered and registered in the share ledger and transfer books of the corporation as they are issued. They shall bear the corporate seal and shall be signed by the President.

Section 2. Transfers: Transfers of shares shall be made on the books of the corporation upon surrender of the certificates therefor, endorsed by the person named in the certificate or by attorney, lawfully constituted in writing. No transfer shall be made which is inconsistent with law.

Section 3. Lost Certificate: The corporation may issue a new certificate of stock in the place of any certificate theretofore signed by it, alleged to have been lost, stolen or destroyed, and the corporation may require the owner of the lost, stolen or destroyed certificate, or his legal representative to give the corporation a bond sufficient to indemnify it against any claim that may be made against it on account of the alleged loss, 'theft or destruction of any such certificate or the issuance of such new certificate.

Section 4. Record Date: In order that the corporation may determine the stockholders entitled to notice of or to vote at any meeting of stockholders or any adjournment thereof, or the express consent to corporate action in writing without a meeting, or entitled to receive

FIGURE A.6 *(Continued)*

payment of any dividend or other distribution or allotment of any rights, or entitled to exercise any rights in respect of any change, conversion or exchange of stock or for the purpose of any other lawful action, the Board of Directors may fix, in advance, a record date, which shall not be more than sixty nor less than ten days before the date of such meeting, nor more than sixty days prior to any other action.

If no record date is fixed:

(a) The record date for determining stockholders entitled to notice of or to vote at a meeting of stock- holders shall be at the close of business on the day next preceding the day on which notice is given,–or if notice is waived, at the close of business on the day next preceding the day on which the meeting is held.

(b) The record date for determining stockholders entitled to express consent to corporate action in writing without a meeting, when no prior action by the Board of Directors is necessary, shall be the day on which the first written consent is expressed.

(c) The record date for determining stockholders for any other purpose shall be at the close of business on the day on which the Board of Directors adopts the resolution relating thereto.

(d) A determination of stockholders of record entitled to notice of or to vote at a meeting of stockholders shall apply to any adjournment of the meeting; provided, however, that the Board of Directors may fix a new record date for the adjourned meeting.

Section 5. Dividends: The Board of Directors may declare and pay dividends upon the outstanding shares of the corporation from time to time and to such extent as they deem advisable, in the manner and upon the term and conditions provided by the statute and the Certificate of Incorporation.

Section 6. Reserves: Before payment of any dividend there may be set aside out of the net profits of the corporation such sum or sums as the directors, from time to time, in their absolute discretion, think proper as a reserve fund to meet contingencies, or for equalizing dividends, or for repairing or maintaining any property of the corporation, or for such other purpose as the directors shall think conducive to the interests of the corporation, and the directors may abolish any such reserve in the manner in which it was created.

ARTICLE IX – MISCELLANEOUS PROVISIONS

Section 1. Checks: All checks or demands for money and notes of the corporation shall be signed by such officer or officers as the Board of Directors may from time to time designate.

Section 2. Fiscal Year: The fiscal year shall begin on the first day of January.

Section 3. Notice: Whenever written notice is required to be given to any person, it may be given to such person, either personally or by sending a copy thereof through the mail, by fax, or by telegram, charges prepaid, to his address appearing on the books of the corporation, or supplied by him to the corporation for the purpose of notice. If the notice is sent by mail, fax or by telegraph, it shall be deemed to have been given to the person entitled thereto when deposited in the United States mail, faxed or with a telegraph office for transmission to such person. Such notice shall specify the place, day and hour of the meeting and, in the case of a

FIGURE A.6 *(Continued)*

special meeting of stockholders, the general nature of the business to be transacted.

Section 4. Waiver of Notice: Whenever any written notice is required by statute, or by the Certificate or the By-Laws of this corporation a waiver thereof in writing, signed by the person or persons entitled to such notice, whether before or after the time stated therein, shall be deemed equivalent to the giving of such notice. Except in the case of a special meeting of stockholders, neither the business to be transacted at nor the purpose of the meeting need be specified in the waiver of notice of such meeting. Attendance of a person either in person or by proxy, at any meeting shall constitute a waiver of notice of such meeting, except where a person attends a meeting for the express purpose of objecting to the transaction of any business because the meeting was not lawfully called or convened.

Section 5. Disallowed Compensation: Any payments made to an officer or employee of the corporation such as a salary, commission, bonus, interest, rent, travel or entertainment expense incurred by him, which shall be disallowed in whole or in part as a deductible expense by the Internal Revenue Service, shall be reimbursed by such officer or employee to the corporation to the full extent of such disallowance. It shall be the duty of the directors, as a Board, to enforce payment of each such amount disallowed. In lieu of payment by the officer or employee, subject to the determination of the directors, proportionate amounts may be withheld from his future compensation payments until the amount owed to the corporation has been recovered.

Section 6. Resignations: Any director or other officer may resign at anytime, such resignation to be in writing, and to take effect from the time of its receipt by the corporation, unless some time be fixed in the resignation and then from that date. The acceptance of a resignation shall not be required to make it effective.

ARTICLE X – ANNUAL STATEMENT

Section 1. The President and Board of Directors shall present at each annual meeting a full and complete statement of the business and affairs of the corporation for the preceding year. Such statement shall be prepared and presented in whatever manner the Board of Directors shall deem advisable and need not be verified by a certified public accountant.

ARTICLE XI – AMENDMENTS

Section 1. These By-Laws may be amended or repealed by the vote of stockholders entitled to cast at least a majority of the votes which all stockholders are entitled to cast thereon, at any regular or special meeting of the stockholders, duly convened after notice to the stockholders of that purpose.
—
Contributed to the Library by Richard Widrig

Lectric Law Library   Lectric Law Library   Lectric Law Library

* <u>IMPORTANT</u> *

A primary purpose of the Library has always been to provide no-cost legal information to anyone who wants or needs it. However, It's Vital that You Understand that most of our Forms are ONLY General, Generic Examples of possible formats & contents. Legal Requirements for various Business Entity related documents Can and Do Vary Greatly from State to State and can Change Often. To be Valid – and Not Create More Problems than it Solves – it MUST be Properly Drafted and Modified to fit Your Specific Location and Circumstances!

FIGURE A.6 *(Continued)*

For Up-To-Date Forms Covering Just About Every State & Situation plus Summaries of
Relevant Laws We STRONGLY SUGGEST You Check Out:

'LLL's Premium Forms 25,000+ WILLS, CONTRACTS, DEEDS, TRUSTS, LEASES
ALL SUBJECTS & STATES · CLICK HERE ·

(This should open a new window. Close it when you're done and you'll be back here.)

'Lectric Law Library   'Lectric Law Library   'Lectric Law Library

We've lots of related material, so wander around & explore places like our
Business Law Topic Area and the **Business Peoples's Lounge** and **Study of Law
Study**

▓ Our Main Forms Room ▓
▓ Our Law Practice Forms ▓
▓ Our Business & General Forms ▓

▓ The Library Rotunda ▓

Our Central Hub, Directory and Index

▓ The Reference Room ▓

Dozens of Topic Areas & Our Law Lexicon

'Lectric Law Library   'Lectric Law Library   'Lectric Law Library

Want Forms Programs, other Legal Software & Etexts, Help with Legal Problems or Questions?

| Help with Legal Problems & Questions Legal Software, Etexts & Lots More | Join Our | **GoldCard Program** | Click Here For Info |

[Last Revised 3/02]

FIGURE A.6 *(Continued)*

Corporate Shareholders Agreement Form

SHAREHOLDERS AGREEMENT

THIS SHAREHOLDERS AGREEMENT is made by and among Shareholder 1 ("Share1"), Shareholder 2 ("Share2"), and Shareholder 3 ("Share3") (Share1, Share2 and Share3 and any subsequent person or entity holding common stock of the Company hereinafter sometimes referred to individually as a "Shareholder" and collectively as the "Shareholders") and Company Name, a Delaware corporation (the "Company").

WITNESSETH:

WHEREAS, in order to insure the harmonious and successful management and control of the Company, and to provide for an orderly and fair disposition of shares of common stock of the Company now or hereafter owned by any Shareholder;

NOW, THEREFORE, in consideration of the mutual promises of the parties hereto, and intending to be legally bound, the parties hereby agree as follows:

1. Definitions.

(a) "Offering Shareholder" means any Shareholder, or his personal representatives, heirs, administrators, and executors, as the case may be, who pursuant to this Agreement must or does offer all or any of his Shares to the Company or the Continuing Shareholders.

(b) "Continuing Shareholders" means all Shareholders other than an Offering Shareholder.

(c) "Shares" means shares of Common Stock of the Company now or hereafter owned by any Shareholder.

(d) "Buyer" means the Company or those Continuing Shareholders who purchase an Offering Shareholder's Shares pursuant to this Agreement.

(e) "Management Shareholder" means Share3, Share1 and Share2.

(f) "Nonmanagement Shareholder" means any Shareholder other than a Management Shareholder.

2. Purchase for Investment. Each Shareholder represents and warrants that he is acquiring and has acquired his Shares for his own account for investment and not with a view to, or for resale in connection with, any distribution thereof or with any present intent of selling any portion thereof.

3. Transfers of Shares. A Shareholder may not transfer, give, convey, sell, pledge, bequeath, donate, assign, encumber or otherwise dispose of any Shares except pursuant to this Agreement.

(a) Transfers to the Company. Notwithstanding anything to the contrary contained in this Agreement, a Shareholder may give, sell, transfer or otherwise dispose of all or any of his Shares to the Company at such price and on such terms and conditions as such Shareholder and the Board of

Figure A.7   Corporate Shareholders Agreement Form

Directors of the Company may agree.

(b) Transfer to Others. Except as provided for in Paragraph 3(a) above, a Shareholder desiring to dispose of some or all of his Shares may do so only pursuant to a bona fide offer to purchase (the "Offer") and after compliance with the following provisions. Such Shareholder shall first give written notice to the Company and the other Shareholders of his intention to dispose of his Shares, identifying the number of Shares he desires to dispose of, the proposed purchase price per Share and the name of the proposed purchaser and attaching an exact copy of the Offer received by such Shareholder.

(i) The Company's Right to Purchase. The Company shall have the exclusive right to purchase all of the Shares which the Offering Shareholder proposes to sell at the proposed purchase price per Share. The Company shall exercise this right to purchase by giving written notice to the Offering Shareholder (with a copy thereof to each of the Continuing Shareholders) within thirty (30) days after receipt of the notice from the Offering Shareholder (the "30 Day Period") that the Company elects to purchase the Shares subject to the Offer and setting forth a date and time for closing which shall be not later than ninety (45) days after the date of such notice from the Company. At the time of closing, the Offering Shareholder shall deliver to the Company certificates representing the Shares to be sold, together with stock powers duly endorsed in blank. The Shares shall be delivered by the Offering Shareholder free of any and all liens and encumbrances. All transfer taxes and documentary stamps shall be paid by the Offering Shareholder.

(ii) The Continuing Shareholders Right to Purchase. If the Company fails to exercise its right to purchase pursuant to subparagraph (i) above, the Continuing Shareholders shall have the right for an additional period of thirty (30) days (the "Additional 30 Day Period") commencing at the expiration of the 30 Day Period to purchase the Shares which the Offering Shareholder proposes to sell at the proposed purchase price per Share. The Continuing Shareholders shall exercise this right to purchase by giving written notice to the Offering Shareholder prior to the expiration of the Additional 30 Day Period that they elect to purchase his Shares and setting forth a date and time for closing which shall be not later than ninety (90) days after the expiration of the Additional 30 Day Period. Any purchase of Shares by all or some of the Continuing Shareholders shall be made in such proportion as they might agree among themselves or, in the absence of any such agreement, pro rata in proportion to their ownership of Shares of the Company (excluding the Offering Shareholder's Shares) at the time of such offer, but in any event one or more of the Continuing Shareholders must agree to purchase all the Shares which the Offering Shareholder proposes to sell. At the time of closing, the Offering Shareholder shall deliver to Buyer certificates representing the Shares to be sold, together with stock powers duly endorsed in blank. Said Shares shall be delivered by the offering Shareholder free and clear of any and all liens and encumbrances. All transfer taxes and documentary stamps shall be paid by the Offering Shareholder.

(iii) Performance of Acceptance. When exercising the rights granted in Paragraphs 3(b)(i) and (ii) hereof, Buyer must elect to purchase all Shares which the Offering Shareholder proposes to sell for the price and upon the same terms for payment of the price as are set forth in the Offer; provided, however, that if said offer received by the Offering Shareholder shall provide for any act or action to be done or performed by the party making such Offer at any time before or within thirty (30) days after the last day for exercise of Buyer's right to purchase pursuant to Paragraphs 3(b)(i) and (ii) hereof, then the Buyer shall be deemed to have complied with the terms and conditions of such Offer if Buyer does or performs such

FIGURE A.7 *(Continued)*

act or action within thirty (30) days after the last day for exercise of Buyer's right to purchase pursuant to Paragraphs 3(b)(i) and(ii) hereof.

(iv) Sale to Third Party. If either the Company or some or all of the Continuing Shareholders do not elect to purchase all of the Shares which the Offering Shareholder proposes to sell, the Offering Shareholder may accept the Offer which the Offering Shareholder mailed with his notice to the Company pursuant to Paragraph 3(b) hereof and transfer all (but not less than all) of the Shares which he proposes to sell pursuant thereto on the same terms and conditions set forth in such Offer, provided that any transferee of such Shares shall be bound by this Agreement as provided by Paragraph 10 hereof, and further provided that if such sale is not completed within one hundred twenty (120) days after the date notice is received by the Company under Paragraph 3(b) hereof, all such Shares shall again become subject to the restrictions and provisions of this Agreement.

(v) Right of Co-Sale. Notwithstanding any other provision hereof, in the event the Offering Shareholder receives an Offer from an unaffiliated third party (the "Offeror") to purchase from such Shareholder not less than 20% of the Shares owned by such Shareholder and such Shareholder intends to accept such Offer, the Offering Shareholder shall, after complying with the provisions of Paragraph 3(b)(i) and (ii) above and before accepting such Offer, forward a copy of such Offer to the Company and each of the Continuing Shareholders. The Offering Shareholder shall not sell any such Shares to the Offeror unless the terms of the Offer are extended by the Offeror to the Continuing Shareholders pro rata in proportion to their ownership of Shares of the Company (excluding the Offering Shareholder's Shares) at the time of such Offer. The Continuing Shareholders shall have 10 days from the date of the foregoing Offer to accept such Offer.

(c) Share1, Share2 and Share3 may each during their lifetimes transfer all, but not less than all, of their Shares to said Shareholder's spouse or a lineal descendant of such Shareholder, so long as prior to such transfer (i) such person, the Company, and all the Shareholders amend this Agreement to the reasonable satisfaction of such person, the Company and all the Shareholders to provide the parties to this Agreement with the rights, remedies and effect provided in this Agreement as if no such transfer had occurred, and (ii) the proposed transferee agrees in a writing satisfactory to the Company and all Shareholders that such person shall vote for Share1, Share3 and Share2 (or their nominees) as directors of the Company in accordance with Paragraph 14 hereof and shall be bound by all the terms and conditions of this Agreement.

4. Right of First Refusal.

(a) Except in the case of Excluded Securities (as defined below), the Company shall not issue, sell or exchange, agree to issue, sell or exchange, or reserve or set aside for issuance, sale or exchange, any (i) shares of Common Stock or any other equity security of the Company which is convertible into Common Stock or any other equity security of the Company, (ii) any debt security of the Company which is convertible into Common Stock or any other equity security of the Company, or (iii) any option, warrant or other right to subscribe for, purchase or otherwise acquire any equity security or any such debt security of the Company, unless in each case the Company shall have first offered to sell to each Shareholder, pro rata in proportion to such Shareholder's then ownership of Shares of the Company, such securities (the "Offered Securities") (and to sell thereto such Offered Securities not subscribed for by the other Shareholders as hereinafter provided), at a price and on such other terms as shall have been specified by the Company in writing delivered to such Shareholder (the "Stock Offer"), which Stock Offer by its terms shall remain open and irrevocable for a period of 10 days (subject to extension pursuant to the

FIGURE A.7 *(Continued)*

last sentence of subsection (b) below) from the date it is delivered by the Company to the Shareholder.

(b) Notice of each Shareholder's intention to accept, in whole or in part, a Stock Offer shall be evidenced by a writing signed by such Shareholder and delivered to the Company prior to the end of the 10-day period of such Stock Offer, setting forth such portion of the Offered Securities as such Shareholder elects to purchase (the "Notice of Acceptance"). If any Shareholder shall subscribe for less than his pro rata share of the Offered Securities to be sold, the other subscribing Shareholders shall be entitled to purchase the balance of that Shareholder's pro rata share in the same proportion in which they were entitled to purchase the Offered Securities in the first instance (excluding for such purposes such Shareholder), provided any such other Shareholder elected by a Notice of Acceptance to purchase all of his pro rata share of the Offered Securities. The Company shall notify each Shareholder within 5 days following the expiration of the 10-day period described above of the amount of Offered Securities which each Shareholder may purchase pursuant to the foregoing sentence, and each Shareholder shall then have 10 days from the delivery of such notice to indicate such additional amount, if any, that such Shareholder wishes to purchase.

(c) In the event that Notices of Acceptance are not given by the Shareholders in respect of all the Offered Securities, the Company shall have 120 days from the expiration of the foregoing 10-day or 25-day period, whichever is applicable, to sell all or any part of such Offered Securities as to which a Notice of Acceptance has not been given by the Shareholders (the "Refused Securities") to any other person or persons, but only upon terms and conditions in all respects, including, without limitation, unit price and interest rates, which are no more favorable, in the aggregate, to such other person or persons or less favorable to the Company than those set forth in the Stock Offer. Upon the closing, which shall include full payment to the Company, of the sale to such other person or persons of all the Refused Securities, the Shareholders shall purchase from the Company, and the Company shall sell to the Shareholders the Offered Securities in respect of which Notices of Acceptance were delivered to the Company by the Shareholders, at the terms specified in the Stock Offer.

(d) In each case, any Offered Securities not purchased by the Shareholders or other person or persons in accordance with Section 4(c) may not be sold or otherwise disposed of until they are again offered to the Shareholders under the procedures specified in Sections 4(a), (b) and (c).

(e) The rights of the Shareholders under this Section 4 shall not apply to the following securities (the "Excluded Securities"):

(i) Any (A) shares of Common Stock or any other equity security of the Company which is convertible into Common Stock or any other equity security of the Company, (B) debt security of the Company which is convertible into Common Stock or any other equity security of the Company, or (C) option, warrant or other right to subscribe for, purchase or otherwise acquire any equity security or any such debt security of the Company (collectively, an "Equity Security") if the issuance of such Equity Security does not alter the respective proportions of ownership (on a fully diluted basis) by Share1, Share2 and Share3, as among themselves, of Equity Securities immediately prior to the issuance of such Equity Security;

(ii) Common Stock issued as a stock dividend or upon any stock split or other subdivision or combination of the outstanding shares of Common Stock;

(iii) Securities issued pursuant to the acquisition by the Company of

FIGURE A.7 *(Continued)*

another corporation to the stockholders of such other corporation by merger or purchase of substantially all of the assets whereby the Company owns not less than 51% of the voting power of such other corporation; and

(iv) Common Stock issued in connection with a firm underwritten public offering of shares of Common Stock, registered pursuant to the Securities Act.

5. Sale Or Redemption Upon Termination of Employment or Upon Disability Or Upon Death. Upon the termination of a Management Shareholder's employmen or other relationship with the Company (including without limitation, any position as an officer, director, consultant, joint venturer, independent contractor, or promoter to or of the Company) for whatever reason, the Disability (as defined below) of a Management Shareholder, or the death of a Management or Nonmanagement Shareholder (any such event hereinafter a "Triggering Event"), such Shareholder (or his heirs, executors, guardian or personal representative) within sixty (60) days after the Triggering Event shall offer to sell all, but not less than all, of the Shares owned by the Shareholder. Each offer shall be made to the Company in writing and shall exist for a period of ninety (90) days after such offer has been received by the Company. If the Company fails to purchase all of the Shares offered, the offer to sell shall be made in writing to all of the Continuing Shareholders in such proportion as the Continuing Shareholders may agree among themselves, or in the absence of agreement, pro rata in proportion to their then ownership of Shares of the Company (excluding the Offering Shareholder's Shares), and shall exist for a period of ninety (90) days after the offer has been received by all of the Continuing Shareholders. For purposes of this Agreement, "Disability" of a particular person means the inability, due to a physical or mental condition, of such person to maintain his employment or other relationship with the Company (including without limitation, fulfilling hi s duties in any position as an officer, director, consultant, joint venturer, independent contractor, or promoter to or of the Company) or to conduct his normal daily activities on behalf of the Corporation for any six (6) consecutive month period.

6. Purchase Price. The purchase price for all Shares purchased pursuant to Paragraph 5 hereof shall be determined as follows:

(a) The Company or the Continuing Shareholders, as the case may be, within thirty (30) days after receipt of any offer referred to in Paragraph 5 above, shall notify the Offering Shareholder of the price at which the Company or the Continuing Shareholders, as the case may be, are willing to purchase the Shares.

(b) In the event the Offering Shareholder objects to the purchase price established in accordance with Paragraph 6(a) above, the Offering Shareholder shall have the right to solicit offers to buy the Shares in accordance with the provisions of Paragraph 3(b) of this Agreement. The right to solicit offers shall be subject to the terms and conditions of Section 3(b) and (c) hereof, including without limitation, the rights of first refusal and co-sale and the period during which any right of first refusal must be exercised but shall not be subject to the one hundred twenty (120) day period referred to in Paragraph 3(b)(iv) of this Agreement.

7. Payment of Purchase Price. The purchase price for all Shares purchased pursuant to Paragraph 5 hereof shall be paid at the closing of the sale.

8. Put and Call Options

(a) Put and Call Options. Each Shareholder shall have the right and option upon the written declaration (a "Declaration") by such Shareholder to the

FIGURE A.7 *(Continued)*

other Shareholders and the Company of the occurrence of an "impasse" (as defined below) to sell to the Continuing Shareholders all of his Shares, and the Continuing Shareholders shall have the obligation to either (i) purchase all of such Shares owned by the offering Shareholder in such proportion as the Continuing Shareholders may agree upon, and if they cannot so agree, pro rata in proportion to their then ownership of Shares of the Company (excluding the Offering Shareholder's Shares) or (ii) if the Continuing Shareholders are unable or unwilling to purchase all of the Shares owned by the Offering Shareholder, sell all of their Shares to the Offering Shareholder, and the Offering Shareholder shall have the obligation to buy such Shares.

(b) Impasse. An "impasse" shall be conclusively evidenced by (i) either Share1, Share3 or Share2 or their respective representative, voting opposite the others at a vote at a shareholders meeting or at a vote at a meeting of the Board of Directors of the Company (or failing to attend such meetings upon due notice if such failure results in the lack of a quorum making such vote impossible), which vote is on a material issue, not in the ordinary course of business, and affecting the business, assets or operations of the Company, including, but not limited to, a proposal to merge, liquidate, consolidate or dissolve the Company, or to sell, lease or dispose of all or substantially all of the assets of the Company or to amend the substantive provisions of the Company's bylaws or articles of incorporation, or to issue or redeem stock, or to declare dividends of any kind, and (ii) either Share1, Share3 or Share2 notifying the others and the Company and any other Shareholders within thirty (30) days after such meeting, proposed meeting or vote than an "impasse" has occurred. The put and call rights granted to each Shareholder under this Paragraph 8 are independent of the other rights granted to the Shareholders and the Company under the other terms of this Agreement and such rights are not mutually exclusive or inconsistent.

(c) Exercise of Option. The Continuing Shareholders shall exercise any option provided for in this Paragraph 8 within thirty (30) days after receipt of a declaration. Any closing of the sale of Shares pursuant to such exercise shall occur within ninety (90) days after receipt of a Declaration.

(d) Purchase Price. Any purchase or sale of Shares sold pursuant to this Paragraph 8 shall be at the price as set forth in the Declaration delivered by the Shareholder exercising his right to sell his shares and shall be paid at the closing of the sale of the Shares.

9. Rights Upon Registration. In the event that the Company shall register or qualify any or all of the common stock of the Company under the Securities Act of 1933, as amended (or any similar statute then in force), on an appropriate registration statement, the Company shall give the Shareholders written notice thereof, and upon written request of a Shareholder, received by the Company not later than fifteen (15) days after receipt by the Shareholder of such notice, the Company will include in the registration statement filed by the Company with the Securities and Exchange Commission all Shares held by such Shareholder with respect to which the Shareholder shall have so requested registration.

10. Agreement Binding on All Persons Interested in Shares. Each person who now or hereafter acquires any legal or equitable interest in any Shares shall be bound by the terms of this Agreement. No issuance or transfer of Shares shall be effective and the Company shall not enter any issue or transfer upon the stock books of the Company or issue a certificate in the name of any person unless the Company is satisfied that such person is, and in a manner satisfactory to the Company has acknowledged being, bound by this Agreement.

FIGURE A.7 *(Continued)*

11. Closing. Except as otherwise agreed to or expressly provided for herein, closing pursuant to the exercise of a right to purchase or sell Shares pursuant to this Agreement shall be held at the principal executive offices of the Company.

12. Entry of Legend Upon Stock Certificates. The following legend shall he immediately entered on each stock certificate representing Shares owned by the Shareholders:

"The gift, sale, mortgage, pledge, hypothecation or other encumbering or transfer of the shares of the capital stock represented by this certificate is restricted in accordance with the terms and conditions of a Shareholders Agreement dated the day of 1996, a copy of which is on file at the principal executive offices of the Company. Said Shareholders Agreement restricts the ability of the Shareholder to sell, give, pledge, bequeath or otherwise transfer or dispose of this stock certificate and the shares of capital stock represented by it."

13. After Acquired Shares – Subsequent Shareholders. The terms and conditions of this Agreement shall specifically apply not only to Shares owned by Shareholders at the time of execution of this Agreement, but also to any Shares acquired by any Shareholder subsequent to such execution.

14. Board of Directors. At each election of the Board of Directors of the Company, the Shareholders shall vote their Shares to elect three directors of the Company, one director being Share1, or his nominee, one director being Share3, or his nominee, and one director being Share2, or his nominee.

15. Community and Marital Property Laws. Notwithstanding anything to the contrary contained herein, the following terms shall control to the extent community property laws or other marital property laws apply to the Shares of any Shareholder:

(a) Lifetime Transfers. The provisions of this Agreement regarding restrictions against the transfer of Shares shall apply to any interest of the spouse of any Shareholder in such Shares (said spouse is hereinafter referred to as a "Spouse").

(b) Transfers Upon Death of Spouse. If the Spouse of a Shareholder predeceases such Shareholder and has failed to bequeath to such Shareholder the deceased Spouse's entire marital property interest, if any, in the Shares held by the Shareholder, or if the Spouse of a Shareholder is adjudicated to be bankrupt or insolvent, or makes an assignment for the benefit of his or her creditors (collectively referred to herein as an "Event"), then to the extent necessary to divest the Spouse of any interest in the Shares of such Stockholder, within three m onths after the date of the occurrence of the Event, the Shareholder shall have the option to and must purchase such marital property interest of his or her Spouse or the estate of the deceased Spouse, as the case may be, in the Shares held by the Shareholder at a price equal to the lesser of either the value of the spouse's marital property interest in such Shares or the book value of such Shares.

(c) Marital Dissolution. Any decree of dissolution, separate maintenance agreement or other property settlement between a Shareholder and his or her Spouse shall provide that the entire marital property interest of the Spouse in the Shares of the Shareholder shall be granted to the Shareholder as part of the division of the property of the marriage and the Spouse shall release and the Shareholder shall accept any marital property interest of such Spouse in the Shares. If payment for such Shares is

FIGURE A.7 *(Continued)*

ordered by the Court or demanded by the Spouse, no consideration shall be required, but if the Shareholder volunteers consideration for said release of interest it shall be no greater than the lesser of either the value of the Spouse's marital property interest in such Shares or the book value of the Spouse's marital property interest in such Shares.

(d) Inclusion of Marital Property. Any purchase of the Shares of a Shareholder pursuant to any provision of this Agreement shall include without limitation or condition the entire marital property interest of the Spouse of such Shareholder in the Shares being purchased.

(e) Determination of Value. Book value and the value of a Spouse's interest in the Shares of a Shareholder for purposes of this Paragraph 15 shall be determined by the Shareholder. The Company and the other Shareholders shall not be responsible for the determination of the value of the marital property interest of any Spouse of a Shareholder, the determination of book value, or the purchase of or payment for such Spouse's marital property interest in the Shares of a Shareholder.

16. Insurance. The Company may, if it so desires, purchase insurance policies on the life of any Management Shareholder for the purpose of payment for stock purchases or as key man insurance. If any Shareholder on whose life the Company owns an insurance policy shall at any time during his lifetime sell all of his Shares, then that Shareholder shall have the right to purchase from the Company the insurance policy or policies on his life at the cash surrender value, if any. The Company shall deliver the policy or policies on the life of such Shareholder upon payment of the cash surrender value, if any, end shall execute any necessary instruments of transfer and change of beneficiary forms.

17. Subchapter S Election. The Company may elect to be taxed as a small business corporation under Subchapter S of the Internal Revenue Code, as amended from time to time (the "code"), or such other provisions of law as may hereafter be applicable to such an election, and for state income tax purposes, if available (hereinafter, an "Election"). Each Shareholder and the Company agree to execute and file the necessary forms for making and maintaining en Election, and each Shareholder agrees to deliver to the Company the consent of the spouse of such Shareholder if such consent is required for the Election under any community or marital property laws or otherwise. The Shareholders and the Company agree that they will take such other actions as may be deemed necessary or advisable by counsel to the Company to exercise or maintain the Election. The Shareholders shall maintain the Election unless the Management Shareholders unanimously agree otherwise or in the event that the Board of Directors requests that the Shareholders revoke the Election, in which case the Shareholders shall promptly execute and deliver to the Company such documents as may be necessary to revoke the Election. None of the Shareholders, without the consent of all of the Management Shareholders, shall take any action or position, or make any transfer or other disposition of his shares of the Company which may result in the termination or revocation of the Election. In the event of an inadvertent termination of the Election as described in Section 1362(f) of the Code or other applicable law, the Shareholders shall agree to make such adjustments as may be required to continue the Election, as provided in Section 1362(f)(4) of the Code or other applicable law.

18. Pro Rata Allocations. All items of income and loss of the Company shall be assigned pro rata to each day throughout the year. However, the Shareholders hereby consent to make an election pursuant to Section 1362(c)(3) of the Code or Section 1377(a)(2) of the Code in the event that the Board of Directors determines such elections to be in the best interest of a majority of the Shareholders.

FIGURE A.7 *(Continued)*

19. Authorization. The Company is authorized to enter into this Agreement by virtue of a resolution passed at a meeting of the Board of Directors.

20. Notices. Notices and declarations under this Agreement shall be in writing and sent by registered or certified mail, return receipt requested, postage paid, to the Company at its principal executive offices and to Shareholders at their last address as shown on the records of the Company or at such other address with respect to any party hereto as such party shall notify the other Shareholders and the Company in writing in the manner specified herein.

21. Termination. The rights and obligations of the Company and the Shareholders under this Agreement shall terminate upon written agreement of all then existing Shareholders or upon the registration or qualification of any or all of the Common stock of the Company pursuant to Paragraph 9 hereof.

22. Severability. The various provisions of this Agreement are severable from each other and from the other provisions of the Agreement, and in the event that any provision in this Agreement shall be held to be invalid or unenforceable by a court of competent jurisdiction, the remainder of this Agreement shall be fully effective, operative and enforceable.

23. Free end Clear of Encumbrances. All Shares sold pursuant to the terms of this Agreement shall be free of any and all liens and encumbrances and accompanied by stock powers duly endorsed in blank.

24. Binding Effect. This Agreement shall be binding upon and inure to the benefit of the parties hereto and their respective heirs, personal representatives, executors, administrators, successors and assigns.

25. Gender. Pronouns used herein are to be interpreted as referring to both the masculine and feminine gender.

26. Governing Law. This Agreement shall be construed and interpreted in accordance with the laws of the State of California without reference to conflict of laws principles except to the extent that the community or marital property laws of any state would otherwise be applicable to a particular situation, in which event, such community or marital property laws shall apply to the particular situation.

27. Entire Agreement. This instrument contains the entire agreement of the parties and may be changed only by an agreement in writing signed by the Company and all persons then owning Shares.

28. Counterparts. This Agreement may be executed in one or more counterparts each of which shall be deemed an original and all of which together shall be deemed to be one and the same instrument.

IN WITNESS WHEREOF, the parties hereto have duly executed this Agreement on the day and year set forth below.

_____   _____

Shareholder 1   Date

_____   _____

Shareholder 2   Date

FIGURE A.7 *(Continued)*

SPOUSAL CONSENT TO SHAREHOLDERS AGREEMENT

The undersigned being the spouse of SHAREHOLDER [#], one of the Shareholders named in the foregoing Shareholders Agreement (the "Agreement"), hereby acknowledges that:

1. I have read the foregoing Agreement in its entirety and understand that:

(A) Upon the occurrence of certain events as specified in the Agreement, the Company, my spouse, and the other Shareholders will have the right to and may be obligated to purchase Shares owned by another Shareholder at a price and on terms and conditions set forth in the Agreement;

(B) Any purchase of the Shares of any Shareholder will include his or her entire interest in such Shares and any community property interest and other marital property interest of the spouse of such Shareholder; and

(C) The Agreement imposes certain restrictions on any attempts by me to transfer any interest I may have in the Company or any Shares of the Company by virtue of my marriage and confers on my spouse the right and obligation to purchase any interest I may have in the Company or any Shares of the Company upon the occurrence of certain events.

2. I hereby approve and agree to be bound to all of the terms of the Agreement and agree that any interest (community property or otherwise) that I may have in the Company or any Shares of the Company shall be subject to the terms of this spousal consent and the Agreement.

3. l agree that my spouse may join in any future amendments or modifications to the Agreement without any notice to me and without any signature, acknowledgment, agreement or consent on my part.

4. I agree that I will transfer or bequeath any interest I may have in the Company or any Shares of the Company by my will, outright and free of trust to my spouse.

5. I acknowledge that I have been advised and have been encouraged to seek independent counsel of my own choosing to represent me in matters regarding the Shareholders Agreement and my execution of this spousal consent.

6. I hereby consent to the Company and my spouse making and maintaining the Subchapter S Election (if applicable) under the Internal Revenue Code, as amended from time to time.

_____   _____
Spouse's Signature   Date

* <u>IMPORTANT</u> *

A primary purpose of the Library has always been to provide no-cost legal information to anyone who wants or needs it. However, It's Vital that You Understand that most of our Forms are ONLY General, Generic Examples of possible formats & contents. Legal Requirements for various Business Entity related documents Can and Do Vary Greatly from State to State and can Change Often. To be Valid – and Not Create More Problems than it Solves – it MUST be Properly Drafted and Modified to fit Your Specific Location and Circumstances!

FIGURE A.7 *(Continued)*

For Up-To-Date Forms Covering Just About Every State & Situation plus Summaries of
Relevant Laws We STRONGLY SUGGEST You Check Out:

'LLL's Premium Forms 25,000+ WILLS, CONTRACTS, DEEDS, TRUSTS, LEASES ALL SUBJECTS & STATES · CLICK HERE ·

(This should open a new window. Close it when you're done and you'll be back here.)

'Lectric Law Library   'Lectric Law Library   'Lectric Law Library

We've lots of related material, so wander around & explore places like our
Business Law Topic Area and the Business Peoples's Lounge and Study of Law
Study

Our Main Forms Room
Our Law Practice Forms
Our Business & General Forms

The Library Rotunda

Our Central Hub, Directory and Index

The Reference Room

Dozens of Topic Areas & Our Law Lexicon

'Lectric Law Library   'Lectric Law Library   'Lectric Law Library

Want Forms Programs, other Legal Software & Etexts, Help with Legal Problems or Questions?

| Help with Legal Problems & Questions Legal Software, Etexts & Lots More | Join Our | GoldCard Program ***************************** | Click Here For Info |

[Last Revised 3/02]

FIGURE A.7 *(Continued)*

Form 2553

(Rev. December 2002)

Department of the Treasury
Internal Revenue Service

Election by a Small Business Corporation
(Under section 1362 of the Internal Revenue Code)

▶ See Parts II and III on back and the separate instructions.

▶ The corporation may either send or fax this form to the IRS. See page 2 of the instructions.

OMB No. 1545-0146

Notes: 1. *Do not file Form 1120S,* U.S. Income Tax Return for an S Corporation, for any tax year before the year the election takes effect.

2. *This election to be an S corporation can be accepted only if all the tests are met under Who May Elect on page 1 of the instructions; all shareholders have signed the consent statement; and the exact name and address of the corporation and other required form information are provided.*

3. *If the corporation was in existence before the effective date of this election, see Taxes an S Corporation May Owe on page 1 of the instructions.*

Part I — Election Information

Please Type or Print	Name of corporation (see instructions)	**A** Employer identification number
	Number, street, and room or suite no. (If a P.O. box, see instructions.)	**B** Date incorporated
	City or town, state, and ZIP code	**C** State of incorporation

D Check the applicable box(es) if the corporation, after applying for the EIN shown in **A** above, changed its name ☐ or address ☐

E Election is to be effective for tax year beginning (month, day, year) . . . . ▶   /   /

F Name and title of officer or legal representative who the IRS may call for more information

G Telephone number of officer or legal representative ( )

H If this election takes effect for the first tax year the corporation exists, enter month, day, and year of the **earliest** of the following: (1) date the corporation first had shareholders, (2) date the corporation first had assets, or (3) date the corporation began doing business . . . . ▶   /   /

I Selected tax year: Annual return will be filed for tax year ending (month and day) ▶ -

If the tax year ends on any date other than December 31, except for a 52–53-week tax year ending with reference to the month of December, you **must** complete Part II on the back. If the date you enter is the ending date of a 52–53-week tax year, write "52–53-week year" to the right of the date.

J Name and address of each shareholder; shareholder's spouse having a community property interest in the corporation's stock; and each tenant in common, joint tenant, and tenant by the entirety. (A husband and wife (and their estates) are counted as one shareholder in determining the number of shareholders without regard to the manner in which the stock is owned.)	K Shareholders' Consent Statement. Under penalties of perjury, we declare that we consent to the election of the above-named corporation to be an S corporation under section 1362(a) and that we have examined this consent statement, including accompanying schedules and statements, and to the best of our knowledge and belief, it is true, correct, and complete. We understand our consent is binding and may not be withdrawn after the corporation has made a valid election. (Shareholders sign and date below.)		L Stock owned		M Social security number or employer identification number (see instructions)	N Shareholder's tax year ends (month and day)
	Signature	Date	Number of shares	Dates acquired		

Under penalties of perjury, I declare that I have examined this election, including accompanying schedules and statements, and to the best of my knowledge and belief, it is true, correct, and complete.

Signature of officer ▶   Title ▶   Date ▶

For Paperwork Reduction Act Notice, see page 4 of the instructions.   Cat. No. 18629R   Form **2553** (Rev. 12-2002)

Figure A.8   IRS Form 2553 (Election by a Small Business Corporation)

Part II   Selection of Fiscal Tax Year (All corporations using this part must complete item O and item P, Q, or R.)

O   Check the applicable box to indicate whether the corporation is:

   1. ☐ A new corporation adopting the tax year entered in item I, Part I.

   2. ☐ An existing corporation retaining the tax year entered in item I, Part I.

   3. ☐ An existing corporation changing to the tax year entered in item I, Part I.

P   Complete item P if the corporation is using the automatic approval provisions of Rev. Proc. 2002-38, 2002-22 I.R.B. 1037, to request **(1)** a natural business year (as defined in section 5.05 of Rev. Proc. 2002-38) or **(2)** a year that satisfies the ownership tax year test (as defined in section 5.06 of Rev. Proc. 2002-38). Check the applicable box below to indicate the representation statement the corporation is making.

   1. Natural Business Year ► ☐ I represent that the corporation is adopting, retaining, or changing to a tax year that qualifies as its natural business year as defined in section 5.05 of Rev. Proc. 2002-38 and has attached a statement verifying that it satisfies the 25% gross receipts test (see instructions for content of statement). I also represent that the corporation is not precluded by section 4.02 of Rev. Proc. 2002-38 from obtaining automatic approval of such adoption, retention, or change in tax year.

   2. Ownership Tax Year ► ☐ I represent that shareholders (as described in section 5.06 of Rev. Proc. 2002-38) holding more than half of the shares of the stock (as of the first day of the tax year to which the request relates) of the corporation have the same tax year or are concurrently changing to the tax year that the corporation adopts, retains, or changes to per item I, Part I, and that such tax year satisfies the requirement of section 4.01(3) of Rev. Proc. 2002-38. I also represent that the corporation is not precluded by section 4.02 of Rev. Proc. 2002-38 from obtaining automatic approval of such adoption, retention, or change in tax year.

Note: *If you do not use item P and the corporation wants a fiscal tax year, complete either item Q or R below. Item Q is used to request a fiscal tax year based on a business purpose and to make a back-up section 444 election. Item R is used to make a regular section 444 election.*

Q   Business Purpose—To request a fiscal tax year based on a business purpose, you must check box Q1. See instructions for details including payment of a user fee. You may also check box Q2 and/or box Q3.

   1. Check here ► ☐ if the fiscal year entered in item I, Part I, is requested under the prior approval provisions of Rev. Proc. 2002-39, 2002-22 I.R.B. 1046. Attach to Form 2553 a statement describing the relevant facts and circumstances and, if applicable, the gross receipts from sales and services necessary to establish a business purpose. See the instructions for details regarding the gross receipts from sales and services. If the IRS proposes to disapprove the requested fiscal year, do you want a conference with the IRS National Office?
☐ Yes   ☐ No

   2. Check here ► ☐ to show that the corporation intends to make a back-up section 444 election in the event the corporation's business purpose request is not approved by the IRS. (See instructions for more information.)

   3. Check here ► ☐ to show that the corporation agrees to adopt or change to a tax year ending December 31 if necessary for the IRS to accept this election for S corporation status in the event (1) the corporation's business purpose request is not approved and the corporation makes a back-up section 444 election, but is ultimately not qualified to make a section 444 election, or (2) the corporation's business purpose request is not approved and the corporation did not make a back-up section 444 election.

R   Section 444 Election—To make a section 444 election, you must check box R1 and you may also check box R2.

   1. Check here ► ☐ to show the corporation will make, if qualified, a section 444 election to have the fiscal tax year shown in item I, Part I. To make the election, you must complete **Form 8716,** Election To Have a Tax Year Other Than a Required Tax Year, and either attach it to Form 2553 or file it separately.

   2. Check here ► ☐ to show that the corporation agrees to adopt or change to a tax year ending December 31 if necessary for the IRS to accept this election for S corporation status in the event the corporation is ultimately not qualified to make a section 444 election.

Part III   Qualified Subchapter S Trust (QSST) Election Under Section 1361(d)(2)*

Income beneficiary's name and address	Social security number
Trust's name and address	Employer identification number

Date on which stock of the corporation was transferred to the trust (month, day, year) . . . . ►   /   /

In order for the trust named above to be a QSST and thus a qualifying shareholder of the S corporation for which this Form 2553 is filed, I hereby make the election under section 1361(d)(2). Under penalties of perjury, I certify that the trust meets the definitional requirements of section 1361(d)(3) and that all other information provided in Part III is true, correct, and complete.

_____   _____
Signature of income beneficiary or signature and title of legal representative or other qualified person making the election   Date

*Use Part III to make the QSST election only if stock of the corporation has been transferred to the trust on or before the date on which the corporation makes its election to be an S corporation. The QSST election must be made and filed separately if stock of the corporation is transferred to the trust after the date on which the corporation makes the S election.

FIGURE A.8   *(Continued)*

Instructions for Form 2553

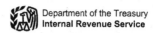

Department of the Treasury
Internal Revenue Service

(Rev. December 2002)

Election by a Small Business Corporation

Section references are to the Internal Revenue Code unless otherwise noted.

General Instructions

Purpose

To elect to be an S corporation, a corporation must file Form 2553. The election permits the income of the S corporation to be taxed to the shareholders of the corporation rather than to the corporation itself, except as noted below under **Taxes an S Corporation May Owe.**

Who May Elect

A corporation may elect to be an S corporation only if it meets all of the following tests:

1. It is a domestic corporation.

Note: *A limited liability company (LLC)* **must** *file* **Form 8832,** *Entity Classification Election, to elect to be treated as an association taxable as a corporation in order to elect to be an S corporation.*

2. It has no more than 75 shareholders. A husband and wife (and their estates) are treated as one shareholder for this requirement. All other persons are treated as separate shareholders.

3. Its only shareholders are individuals, estates, exempt organizations described in section 401(a) or 501(c)(3), or certain trusts described in section 1361(c)(2)(A). See the instructions for Part III regarding qualified subchapter S trusts (QSSTs).

A trustee of a trust wanting to make an election under section 1361(e)(3) to be an electing small business trust (ESBT) should see Notice 97-12, 1997-1 C.B. 385. However, in general, for tax years beginning after May 13, 2002, Notice 97-12 is superseded by Regulations section 1.1361-1(c)(1). Also see Rev. Proc. 98-23, 1998-1 C.B. 662, for guidance on how to convert a QSST to an ESBT. However, in general, for tax years beginning after May 13, 2002, Rev. Proc. 98-23 is superseded by Regulations section 1.1361-1(j)(12). If there was an inadvertent failure to timely file an ESBT election, see the relief provisions under Rev. Proc. 98-55, 1998-2 C.B. 643.

4. It has no nonresident alien shareholders.

5. It has only one class of stock (disregarding differences in voting rights). Generally, a corporation is treated as having only one class of stock if all outstanding shares of the corporation's stock confer identical rights to distribution and liquidation proceeds. See Regulations section 1.1361-1(l) for details.

6. It is not one of the following ineligible corporations:

a. A bank or thrift institution that uses the reserve method of accounting for bad debts under section 585,

b. An insurance company subject to tax under the rules of subchapter L of the Code,

c. A corporation that has elected to be treated as a possessions corporation under section 936, or

d. A domestic international sales corporation (DISC) or former DISC.

7. It has a permitted tax year as required by section 1378 or makes a section 444 election to have a tax year other than a permitted tax year. Section 1378 defines a permitted tax year as a tax year ending December 31, or any other tax year for which the corporation establishes a business purpose to the satisfaction of the IRS. See Part II for details on requesting a fiscal tax year based on a business purpose or on making a section 444 election.

8. Each shareholder consents as explained in the instructions for column K.

See sections 1361, 1362, and 1378 for additional information on the above tests.

A parent S corporation can elect to treat an eligible wholly-owned subsidiary as a qualified subchapter S subsidiary (QSub). If the election is made, the assets, liabilities, and items of income, deduction, and credit of the QSub are treated as those of the parent. To make the election, get **Form 8869,** Qualified Subchapter S Subsidiary Election. If the QSub election was not timely filed, the corporation may be entitled to relief under Rev. Proc. 98-55.

Taxes an S Corporation May Owe

An S corporation may owe income tax in the following instances:

1. If, at the end of any tax year, the corporation had accumulated earnings and profits, and its passive investment income under section 1362(d)(3) is more than 25% of its gross receipts, the corporation may owe tax on its excess net passive income.

2. A corporation with net recognized built-in gain (as defined in section 1374(d)(2)) may owe tax on its built-in gains.

3. A corporation that claimed investment credit before its first year as an S corporation will be liable for any investment credit recapture tax.

4. A corporation that used the LIFO inventory method for the year immediately preceding its first year as an S corporation may owe an additional tax due to LIFO recapture. The tax is paid in four equal installments, the first of which must be paid by the due date (not including extensions) of the corporation's income tax return for its last tax year as a C corporation.

For more details on these taxes, see the Instructions for Form 1120S.

Cat. No. 49978N

Figure A.9   Instructions for Form 2553

Where To File

Send the original election (no photocopies) or fax it to the Internal Revenue Service Center listed below. If the corporation files this election by fax, keep the original Form 2553 with the corporation's permanent records.

If the corporation's principal business, office, or agency is located in ▼	Use the following Internal Revenue Service Center address or fax number ▼
Connecticut, Delaware, District of Columbia, Illinois, Indiana, Kentucky, Maine, Maryland, Massachusetts, Michigan, New Hampshire, New Jersey, New York, North Carolina, Ohio, Pennsylvania, Rhode Island, South Carolina, Vermont, Virginia, West Virginia, Wisconsin	Cincinnati, OH 45999 (859) 669-5748
Alabama, Alaska, Arizona, Arkansas, California, Colorado, Florida, Georgia, Hawaii, Idaho, Iowa, Kansas, Louisiana, Minnesota, Mississippi, Missouri, Montana, Nebraska, Nevada, New Mexico, North Dakota, Oklahoma, Oregon, South Dakota, Tennessee, Texas, Utah, Washington, Wyoming	Ogden, UT 84201 (801) 620-7116

When To Make the Election

Complete and file Form 2553 **(a)** at any time before the 16th day of the 3rd month of the tax year, if filed during the tax year the election is to take effect, or **(b)** at any time during the preceding tax year. An election made no later than 2 months and 15 days after the beginning of a tax year that is less than 2½ months long is treated as timely made for that tax year. **An election made after the 15th day of the 3rd month but before the end of the tax year is effective for the next year.** For example, if a calendar tax year corporation makes the election in April 2002, it is effective for the corporation's 2003 calendar tax year.

However, an election made after the due date will be accepted as timely filed if the corporation can show that the failure to file on time was due to reasonable cause. To request relief for a late election, the corporation generally must request a private letter ruling and pay a user fee in accordance with Rev. Proc. 2002-1, 2002-1 I.R.B. 1 (or its successor). But if the election is filed within 12 months of its due date and the original due date for filing the corporation's initial Form 1120S has not passed, the ruling and user fee requirements do not apply. To request relief in this case, write "FILED PURSUANT TO REV. PROC. 98-55" at the top of page 1 of Form 2553, attach a statement explaining the reason for failing to file the election on time, and file Form 2553 as otherwise instructed. See Rev. Proc. 98-55 for more details.

See Regulations section 1.1362-6(b)(3)(iii) for how to obtain relief for an inadvertent invalid election if the corporation filed a timely election, but one or more shareholders did not file a timely consent.

Acceptance or Nonacceptance of Election

The service center will notify the corporation if its election is accepted and when it will take effect. The corporation will also be notified if its election is not accepted. The corporation should generally receive a determination on its election within 60 days after it has filed Form 2553. If box Q1 in Part II is checked on page 2, the corporation will receive a ruling letter from the IRS in Washington, DC, that either approves or denies the selected tax year. When box Q1 is checked, it will generally take an additional 90 days for the Form 2553 to be accepted.

Care should be exercised to ensure that the IRS receives the election. If the corporation is not notified of acceptance or nonacceptance of its election within 3 months of the date of filing (date mailed), or within 6 months if box Q1 is checked, take follow-up action by corresponding with the service center where the corporation filed the election.

If the IRS questions whether Form 2553 was filed, an acceptable proof of filing is **(a)** certified or registered mail receipt (timely postmarked) from the U.S. Postal Service, or its equivalent from a designated private delivery service (see Notice 2002-62, 2002-39 I.R.B. 574 (or its successor)); **(b)** Form 2553 with accepted stamp; **(c)** Form 2553 with stamped IRS received date; or **(d)** IRS letter stating that Form 2553 has been accepted.

 *Do not file Form 1120S for any tax year before the year the election takes effect. If the corporation is now required to file **Form 1120**, U.S. Corporation Income Tax Return, or any other applicable tax return, continue filing it until the election takes effect.*

End of Election

Once the election is made, it stays in effect until it is terminated. If the election is terminated in a tax year beginning after 1996, IRS consent is generally required for another election by the corporation (or a successor corporation) on Form 2553 for any tax year before the 5th tax year after the first tax year in which the termination took effect. See Regulations section 1.1362-5 for details.

FIGURE A.9 *(Continued)*

Specific Instructions

Part I (*All corporations must complete.*)

Name and Address of Corporation

Enter the true corporate name as stated in the corporate charter or other legal document creating it. If the corporation's mailing address is the same as someone else's, such as a shareholder's, enter "c/o" and this person's name following the name of the corporation. Include the suite, room, or other unit number after the street address. If the Post Office does not deliver to the street address and the corporation has a P.O. box, show the box number instead of the street address. If the corporation changed its name or address after applying for its employer identification number, be sure to check the box in item D of Part I.

Item A. Employer Identification Number (EIN)

If the corporation has applied for an EIN but has not received it, enter "applied for." If the corporation does not have an EIN, it should apply for one on **Form SS-4**, Application for Employer Identification Number. You can order Form SS-4 by calling 1-800-TAX-FORM (1-800-829-3676) or by accessing the IRS Web Site **www.irs.gov**.

Item E. Effective Date of Election

Enter the beginning effective date (month, day, year) of the tax year requested for the S corporation. Generally, this will be the beginning date of the tax year for which the ending effective date is required to be shown in item I, Part I. For a new corporation (first year the corporation exists) it will generally be the date required to be shown in item H, Part I. The tax year of a new corporation starts on the date that it has shareholders, acquires assets, or begins doing business, whichever happens first. If the effective date for item E for a newly formed corporation is later than the date in item H, the corporation should file Form 1120 or Form 1120-A for the tax period between these dates.

Column K. Shareholders' Consent Statement

Each shareholder who owns (or is deemed to own) stock at the time the election is made must consent to the election. If the election is made during the corporation's tax year for which it first takes effect, any person who held stock at any time during the part of that year that occurs before the election is made, must consent to the election, even though the person may have sold or transferred his or her stock before the election is made.

An election made during the first 2½ months of the tax year is effective for the following tax year if any person who held stock in the corporation during the part of the tax year before the election was made, and who did not hold stock at the time the election was made, did not consent to the election.

Note: *Once the election is made, a new shareholder is not required to consent to the election; a new Form 2553 will not be required.*

Each shareholder consents by signing and dating in column K or signing and dating a separate consent statement described below. The following special rules apply in determining who must sign the consent statement.

• If a husband and wife have a community interest in the stock or in the income from it, both must consent.
• Each tenant in common, joint tenant, and tenant by the entirety must consent.
• A minor's consent is made by the minor, legal representative of the minor, or a natural or adoptive parent of the minor if no legal representative has been appointed.
• The consent of an estate is made by the executor or administrator.
• The consent of an electing small business trust is made by the trustee.
• If the stock is owned by a trust (other than an electing small business trust), the deemed owner of the trust must consent. See section 1361(c)(2) for details regarding trusts that are permitted to be shareholders and rules for determining who is the deemed owner.

Continuation sheet or separate consent statement. If you need a continuation sheet or use a separate consent statement, attach it to Form 2553. The separate consent statement must contain the name, address, and EIN of the corporation and the shareholder information requested in columns J through N of Part I. If you want, you may combine all the shareholders' consents in one statement.

Column L

Enter the number of shares of stock each shareholder owns and the dates the stock was acquired. If the election is made during the corporation's tax year for which it first takes effect, do not list the shares of stock for those shareholders who sold or transferred all of their stock before the election was made. However, these shareholders must still consent to the election for it to be effective for the tax year.

Column M

Enter the social security number of each shareholder who is an individual. Enter the EIN of each shareholder that is an estate, a qualified trust, or an exempt organization.

Column N

Enter the month and day that each shareholder's tax year ends. If a shareholder is changing his or her tax year, enter the tax year the shareholder is changing to, and attach an explanation indicating the present tax year and the basis for the change (e.g., automatic revenue procedure or letter ruling request).

Signature

Form 2553 must be signed by the president, treasurer, assistant treasurer, chief accounting officer, or other corporate officer (such as tax officer) authorized to sign.

-3-

FIGURE A.9 *(Continued)*

Part II

Complete Part II if you selected a tax year ending on any date other than December 31 (other than a 52-53-week tax year ending with reference to the month of December).

Note: *In certain circumstances the corporation may not obtain automatic approval of a fiscal year under the natural business year (Box P1) or ownership tax year (Box P2) provisions if it is under examination, before an area office, or before a federal court with respect to any income tax issue and the annual accounting period is under consideration. For details, see section 4.02 of Rev. Proc. 2002-38, 2002-22 I.R.B. 1037.*

Box P1

Attach a statement showing separately for each month the amount of gross receipts for the most recent 47 months. A corporation that does not have a 47-month period of gross receipts cannot automatically establish a natural business year.

Box Q1

For examples of an acceptable business purpose for requesting a fiscal tax year, see section 5.02 of Rev. Proc. 2002-39, 2002-22 I.R.B. 1046, and Rev. Rul. 87-57, 1987-2 C.B. 117.

Attach a statement showing the relevant facts and circumstances to establish a business purpose for the requested fiscal year. For details on what is sufficient to establish a business purpose, see section 5.02 of Rev. Proc. 2002-39.

If your business purpose is based on one of the natural business year tests provided in section 5.03 of Rev. Proc. 2002-39, identify if you are using the 25% gross receipts, annual business cycle, or seasonal business test. For the 25% gross receipts test, provide a schedule showing the amount of gross receipts for each month for the most recent 47 months. For either the annual business cycle or seasonal business test, provide the gross receipts from sales and services (and inventory costs, if applicable) for each month of the short period, if any, and the three immediately preceding tax years. If the corporation has been in existence for less than three tax years, submit figures for the period of existence.

If you check box Q1, you will be charged a user fee of up to $600 (subject to change—see Rev. Proc. 2002-1 or its successor). Do not pay the fee when filing Form 2553. The service center will send Form 2553 to the IRS in Washington, DC, who, in turn, will notify the corporation that the fee is due.

Box Q2

If the corporation makes a back-up section 444 election for which it is qualified, then the election will take effect in the event the business purpose request is not approved. In some cases, the tax year requested under the back-up section 444 election may be different than the tax year requested under business purpose. See **Form 8716,** Election To Have a Tax Year Other Than a Required Tax Year, for details on making a back-up section 444 election.

Boxes Q2 and R2

If the corporation is not qualified to make the section 444 election after making the item Q2 back-up section 444 election or indicating its intention to make the election in item R1, and therefore it later files a calendar year return, it should write "Section 444 Election Not Made" in the top left corner of the first calendar year Form 1120S it files.

Part III

Certain qualified subchapter S trusts (QSSTs) may make the QSST election required by section 1361(d)(2) in Part III. Part III may be used to make the QSST election only if corporate stock has been transferred to the trust on or before the date on which the corporation makes its election to be an S corporation. However, a statement can be used instead of Part III to make the election. If there was an inadvertent failure to timely file a QSST election, see the relief provisions under Rev. Proc. 98-55.

Note: *Use Part III **only** if you make the election in Part I (i.e., Form 2553 cannot be filed with only Part III completed).*

The deemed owner of the QSST must also consent to the S corporation election in column K, page 1, of Form 2553. See section 1361(c)(2).

Paperwork Reduction Act Notice. We ask for the information on this form to carry out the Internal Revenue laws of the United States. You are required to give us the information. We need it to ensure that you are complying with these laws and to allow us to figure and collect the right amount of tax.

You are not required to provide the information requested on a form that is subject to the Paperwork Reduction Act unless the form displays a valid OMB control number. Books or records relating to a form or its instructions must be retained as long as their contents may become material in the administration of any Internal Revenue law. Generally, tax returns and return information are confidential, as required by section 6103.

The time needed to complete and file this form will depend on individual circumstances. The estimated average time is:

Recordkeeping	9 hr., 34 min.
Learning about the law or the form	3 hr., 28 min.
Preparing, copying, assembling, and sending the form to the IRS	3 hr., 47 min.

If you have comments concerning the accuracy of these time estimates or suggestions for making this form simpler, we would be happy to hear from you. You can write to the Tax Forms Committee, Western Area Distribution Center, Rancho Cordova, CA 95743-0001. **Do not** send the form to this address. Instead, see **Where To File** on page 2.

-4-

FIGURE A.9 *(Continued)*

EXAMPLES THAT COMPARE TWO TYPES OF CORPORATIONS WITH OTHER FORMS OF DOING BUSINESS

Once you decide that you should do business as a corporation or a limited liability company (LLC), you'll be faced with the filing of an income tax return at the end of your first year. While most business owners will engage a tax professional to complete a corporate tax return, you can help save your tax professional money while keeping the preparation fees lower by becoming familiar with the tax returns and what sort of information your tax professional needs from you. Therefore, I have included the initial tax forms for a hypothetical business in four formats.

First, I display an example of this business operating as a sole proprietorship (Schedule C of Form 1040). As I have noted throughout the book, operating as a sole proprietor is not something I generally recommend. However, the tax form for reporting and computing the income tax of a sole proprietorship is relatively simple. So, I hope its inclusion here makes the transition to a corporation tax return a little more understandable.

The second example illustrates the same basic facts as the first example (same income, expenses, etc.) entered on the income tax return (Form 1120) for the enterprise operating as a C corporation.

The third example (Form 1120S) is similar to the second, except for the items that reflect the operation of the enterprise as an S corporation.

The fourth example (Form 1965) reflects the operation as an LLC. Please don't be confused by the fact that the heading on the form indicates it is for use by partnerships. As most LLCs are taxed as partnerships, the partnership form is usually the proper one to use. (LLCs can also elect to be taxed as corporations, and LLCs that are owned by only one individual are taxed as sole proprietorships – but with the protection of limited liability.)

For the examples of the C corporation and the S corporation, I have included extracts of the IRS instructions that describe what numbers or other information are to be placed on which line of the form.

If you find that these forms appear complicated, that's because they are. And they are that way because Congress creates so many quirky tax rules that appear to have no logical basis.

The business we use for this example was dreamed up by Anne Who, an individual who loves cats. The business consists of selling a product called the Acme Clean Cat Device. This product is a combination of a conventional cat litter box and a built-in shower that cleans the whole cat after it uses the litter box. (Just how one convinces a cat to enter the shower after using the litter box is beyond the scope of this book.) Anne was convinced that she could create a profitable business by buying this device from the Acme Co. for $60 each and selling them for $100 each. Although she would hire two assistants who would perform clerical duties as well as pack and ship the merchandise, she felt the business would be more prosperous if she had a couple of associates to assist her in investing in the business and in the marketing of the product.

To make the numbers easier to handle, I have rounded off most of them to the nearest 100. In particular, these examples assume payroll taxes that an employer pays are 10 percent of payroll. They could be more than 10 percent on the wages of lower-paid employees and something less on higher paid managers. That means accurate computations could be rather complex, so we'll stick with the 10 percent, as that well illustrates the tax burden of income taxes and payroll taxes. (The incomes of all are below $87,000, so Social Security tax applies to all wages and salaries.)

Read and study these examples to gain an overview of what information needs to be sent off to the IRS (along with a check), when it's time to file your annual tax return. A little study now on how the tax on your business works could substantially lower the amount of that check.

Schedule C of Form 1040

The next page is an example of a Profit or Loss From Business IRS tax form. The proprietor, who we will call Anne, would report her income from her business if she operated as a sole proprietor. The net profit, shown on line 31, of $168,000 would be added to any other income she had and reported on Form 1040. Besides income tax, she would also have to pay self-employment tax (a form of Social Security tax) of 15.3% on income up to $87,000 and 2.9% on income above that level. She computes and reports that self-employment tax on Schedule SE, which is included, with Schedule C, as part of Form 1040.

SCHEDULE C
(Form 1040)

Department of the Treasury
Internal Revenue Service (99)

Profit or Loss From Business
(Sole Proprietorship)

▶ Partnerships, joint ventures, etc., must file Form 1065 or 1065-B.

▶ Attach to Form 1040 or 1041. ▶ See Instructions for Schedule C (Form 1040).

OMB No. 1545-0074

2003

Attachment
Sequence No. **09**

Name of proprietor	Social security number (SSN)
ANNE WHO	000 : 00 : 0000

A	Principal business or profession, including product or service (see page C-2 of the instructions)	B Enter code from pages C-7, 8, & 9
	SALES OF PET SUPPLIES	▶ 4 5 3 9 1 0

C	Business name. If no separate business name, leave blank.	D Employer ID number (EIN), if any
	CLEAN CAT PROCESSORS	5 5 5 5 5 5 5 5

E   Business address (including suite or room no.) ▶ 111 MAIN ST., SUITE 1, EAST OVERSHOE, VA
    City, town or post office, state, and ZIP code

F   Accounting method: (1) ☑ Cash   (2) ☐ Accrual   (3) ☐ Other (specify) ▶ ....

G   Did you "materially participate" in the operation of this business during 2003? If "No," see page C-3 for limit on losses   ☑ Yes   ☐ No

H   If you started or acquired this business during 2003, check here   .   .   .   .   ▶ ☐

Part I   Income

1	Gross receipts or sales. **Caution.** If this income was reported to you on Form W-2 and the "Statutory employee" box on that form was checked, see page C-3 and check here ▶ ☐	1	1,000,000
2	Returns and allowances	2	
3	Subtract line 2 from line 1	3	
4	Cost of goods sold (from line 42 on page 2)	4	600,000
5	**Gross profit.** Subtract line 4 from line 3	5	400,000
6	Other income, including Federal and state gasoline or fuel tax credit or refund (see page C-3) . . .	6	
7	**Gross income.** Add lines 5 and 6 . . . . ▶	7	400,000

Part II   Expenses. Enter expenses for business use of your home **only** on line 30.

8	Advertising	8	150,000	19	Pension and profit-sharing plans	19	
9	Car and truck expenses (see page C-3)	9		20	Rent or lease (see page C-5):		
				a	Vehicles, machinery, and equipment .	20a	
10	Commissions and fees . .	10		b	Other business property . .	20b	12,000
11	Contract labor (see page C-4)	11		21	Repairs and maintenance . .	21	
12	Depletion	12		22	Supplies (not included in Part III) .	22	1,000
13	Depreciation and section 179 expense deduction (not included in Part III) (see page C-4) .	13	2,000	23	Taxes and licenses . . .	23	1,000
				24	Travel, meals, and entertainment:		
				a	Travel	24a	
14	Employee benefit programs (other than on line 19) . .	14		b	Meals and entertainment		
15	Insurance (other than health) .	15	5,000	c	Enter nondeduct-ible amount in-cluded on line 24b (see page C-5) .		
16	Interest:						
a	Mortgage (paid to banks, etc.) .	16a	2,000	d	Subtract line 24c from line 24b .	24d	
b	Other	16b		25	Utilities	25	1,500
17	Legal and professional services	17	3,250	26	Wages (less employment credits) .	26	42,500
18	Office expense	18	2,500	27	Other expenses (from line 48 on page 2)	27	9,250

28	**Total expenses** before expenses for business use of home. Add lines 8 through 27 in columns . ▶	28	232,000
29	Tentative profit (loss). Subtract line 28 from line 7	29	168,000
30	Expenses for business use of your home. Attach **Form 8829**	30	
31	**Net profit or (loss).** Subtract line 30 from line 29.		
	● If a profit, enter on **Form 1040, line 12,** and **also** on **Schedule SE, line 2** (statutory employees, see page C-6). Estates and trusts, enter on Form 1041, line 3.	31	168,000
	● If a loss, you **must** go to line 32.		

32   If you have a loss, check the box that describes your investment in this activity (see page C-6).

● If you checked 32a, enter the loss on **Form 1040, line 12,** and **also** on **Schedule SE, line 2** (statutory employees, see page C-6). Estates and trusts, enter on Form 1041, line 3.

● If you checked 32b, you **must** attach **Form 6198.**

32a ☐ All investment is at risk.
32b ☐ Some investment is not at risk.

Figure A.10   Schedule C of Form 1040 (Profit or Loss From Business)

Part III   **Cost of Goods Sold** (see page C-6)

33   Method(s) used to
value closing inventory: **a** ☑ Cost   **b** ☐ Lower of cost or market   **c** ☐ Other (attach explanation)

34   Was there any change in determining quantities, costs, or valuations between opening and closing inventory? If "Yes," attach explanation . . . . ☐ Yes   ☑ No

35	Inventory at beginning of year. If different from last year's closing inventory, attach explanation . .	**35**	0
36	Purchases less cost of items withdrawn for personal use	**36**	720,000
37	Cost of labor. Do not include any amounts paid to yourself	**37**	
38	Materials and supplies	**38**	
39	Other costs	**39**	
40	Add lines 35 through 39	**40**	720,000
41	Inventory at end of year	**41**	120,000
42	**Cost of goods sold.** Subtract line 41 from line 40. Enter the result here and on page 1, line 4 . .	**42**	600,000

Part IV   **Information on Your Vehicle.** Complete this part **only** if you are claiming car or truck expenses on line 9 and are not required to file Form 4562 for this business. See the instructions for line 13 on page C-4 to find out if you must file Form 4562.

43   When did you place your vehicle in service for business purposes? (month, day, year) ▶ ..../........./....... .

44   Of the total number of miles you drove your vehicle during 2003, enter the number of miles you used your vehicle for:

a   Business ....   **b** Commuting ....   **c** Other ....

45   Do you (or your spouse) have another vehicle available for personal use? . . . . ☐ Yes   ☐ No

46   Was your vehicle available for personal use during off-duty hours? . . . . ☐ Yes   ☐ No

47a   Do you have evidence to support your deduction? . . . . ☐ Yes   ☐ No

   b   If "Yes," is the evidence written? . . . . ☐ Yes   ☐ No

Part V   **Other Expenses.** List below business expenses not included on lines 8- 26 or line 30.

TELEPHONES	5,000
PAYROLL TAX	4,250

48 **Total other expenses.** Enter here and on page 1, line 27	**48**	9,250

Figure A.10   *(Continued)*

Form 1120, U.S. Corporation Income Tax Return

This form reports the tax picture that would result if Anne elected to do business as a C corporation. For this and the following forms, let us assume that she is operating with two co-owners of the enterprise. Most of the profit is taken out by the three owners as salaries (line 12), and the remainder of the profit (line 30) is left in the business, so the corporation pays tax on that remaining $36,000, at 15% tax rate.

Note that the schedule of other deductions (page five of the form, showing Line 26) lists payroll taxes separately and divides that into payroll taxes on stockholder/employees and other employees. While it would be proper to include those taxes on line 17 of page one of the form, they are broken out separately so you can track how the government collects the Social Security tax. (The corporation pays and the employees pay.)

Given the facts in this example, the only documentation of income that the three stockholder/employees would receive is their W2 form(s). (If the Corporation also paid dividends to the stockholders, they would receive a form 1099-DIV covering those dividends.)

Form **1120**		**U.S. Corporation Income Tax Return**	OMB No. 1545-0123

Department of the Treasury
Internal Revenue Service

For calendar year 2003 or tax year beginning ...., 2003, ending ......, 20 ....
▶ Instructions are separate. See page 20 for Paperwork Reduction Act Notice.

2003

A Check if a:		Use IRS label. Other-wise, print or type.	Name		B Employer identification number
1 Consolidated return (attach Form 851) ☐			CLEAN CAT PROCESSORS, INC.		55 : 5555555
2 Personal holding co. (attach Sch. PH) ☐			Number, street, and room or suite no. (If a P.O. box, see page 7 of instructions.)		C Date incorporated
3 Personal service corp. (as defined in Regulations sec. 1.441-3(c)— see instructions) ☐			111 MAIN ST., SUITE 1		1/1/03
			City or town, state, and ZIP code		D Total assets (see page 8 of instructions)
			EAST OVERSHOE, VA 55555		

E Check applicable boxes: (1) ☑ Initial return (2) ☐ Final return (3) ☐ Name change (4) ☐ Address change $ 206,000

Income

1a	Gross receipts or sales 1,000,000 **b** Less returns and allowances **c** Bal ▶	1c	1,000,000
2	Cost of goods sold (Schedule A, line 8)	2	600,000
3	Gross profit. Subtract line 2 from line 1c	3	400,000
4	Dividends (Schedule C, line 19)	4	
5	Interest	5	
6	Gross rents	6	
7	Gross royalties	7	
8	Capital gain net income (attach Schedule D (Form 1120))	8	
9	Net gain or (loss) from Form 4797, Part II, line 18 (attach Form 4797)	9	
10	Other income (see page 9 of instructions—attach schedule)	10	
11	**Total income.** Add lines 3 through 10 ▶	11	400,000

Deductions (See instructions for limitations on deductions.)

12	Compensation of officers (Schedule E, line 4)			12	120,000
13	Salaries and wages (less employment credits)			13	42,500
14	Repairs and maintenance			14	
15	Bad debts			15	
16	Rents			16	12,000
17	Taxes and licenses			17	1,000
18	Interest			18	2,000
19	Charitable contributions (see page 11 of instructions for 10% limitation)			19	
20	Depreciation (attach Form 4562)	20	2,000		
21	Less depreciation claimed on Schedule A and elsewhere on return	21a		21b	2,000
22	Depletion			22	
23	Advertising			23	150,000
24	Pension, profit-sharing, etc., plans			24	
25	Employee benefit programs			25	
26	Other deductions (attach schedule)			26	34,500
27	**Total deductions.** Add lines 12 through 26 ▶			27	364,000
28	Taxable income before net operating loss deduction and special deductions. Subtract line 27 from line 11			28	36,000
29	**Less:** **a** Net operating loss (NOL) deduction (see page 13 of instructions)	29a			
	b Special deductions (Schedule C, line 20)	29b		29c	

Tax and Payments

30	**Taxable income.** Subtract line 29c from line 28			30	36,000
31	**Total tax** (Schedule J, line 11)			31	5,400
32	**Payments: a** 2002 overpayment credited to 2003	32a			
b	2003 estimated tax payments	32b			
c	Less 2003 refund applied for on Form 4466	32c (	) **d** Bal ▶	32d	
e	Tax deposited with Form 7004			32e	
f	Credit for tax paid on undistributed capital gains (attach Form 2439)			32f	
g	Credit for Federal tax on fuels (attach Form 4136). See instructions	32g		32h	
33	Estimated tax penalty (see page 14 of instructions). Check if Form 2220 is attached ▶ ☐			33	
34	**Tax due.** If line 32h is smaller than the total of lines 31 and 33, enter amount owed			34	5,400
35	**Overpayment.** If line 32h is larger than the total of lines 31 and 33, enter amount overpaid			35	
36	Enter amount of line 35 you want: **Credited to 2004 estimated tax** ▶ **Refunded** ▶			36	

Sign Here

Under penalties of perjury, I declare that I have examined this return, including accompanying schedules and statements, and to the best of my knowledge and belief, it is true, correct, and complete. Declaration of preparer (other than taxpayer) is based on all information of which preparer has any knowledge.

Signature of officer   Date   Title

May the IRS discuss this return with the preparer shown below (see instructions)? ☐ Yes ☐ No

Paid Preparer's Use Only

Preparer's signature ▶		Date	Check if self-employed ☐	Preparer's SSN or PTIN
Firm's name (or yours if self-employed), address, and ZIP code ▶			EIN	
			Phone no. ( )	

Cat. No. 11450Q   Form **1120** (2003)

Figure A.11   IRS Form 1120 (U.S. Corporation Income Tax Return)

Schedule A   Cost of Goods Sold (see page 14 of instructions)

1	Inventory at beginning of year **1**	0
2	Purchases **2**	720,000
3	Cost of labor **3**	
4	Additional section 263A costs (attach schedule) **4**	
5	Other costs (attach schedule) **5**	
6	**Total.** Add lines 1 through 5 . . . . **6**	720,000
7	Inventory at end of year **7**	120,000
8	**Cost of goods sold.** Subtract line 7 from line 6. Enter here and on line 2, page 1 . . . . **8**	600,000

9a Check all methods used for valuing closing inventory:

    (i) ☐ Cost as described in Regulations section 1.471-3

    (ii) ☐ Lower of cost or market as described in Regulations section 1.471-4

    (iii) ☐ Other (Specify method used and attach explanation.) ▶ ....

  b Check if there was a writedown of subnormal goods as described in Regulations section 1.471-2(c) . . . . ▶ ☐

  c Check if the LIFO inventory method was adopted this tax year for any goods (if checked, attach Form 970) . . . . ▶ ☐

  d If the LIFO inventory method was used for this tax year, enter percentage (or amounts) of closing inventory computed under LIFO   **9d**

  e If property is produced or acquired for resale, do the rules of section 263A apply to the corporation? . . . . . ☐ Yes ☑ No

  f Was there any change in determining quantities, cost, or valuations between opening and closing inventory? If "Yes," attach explanation . . . . ☐ Yes ☑ No

Schedule C   Dividends and Special Deductions (see instructions beginning on page 15)

		(a) Dividends received	(b) %	(c) Special deductions (a) × (b)
1	Dividends from less-than-20%-owned domestic corporations that are subject to the 70% deduction (other than debt-financed stock)		70	
2	Dividends from 20%-or-more-owned domestic corporations that are subject to the 80% deduction (other than debt-financed stock)		80 see instructions	
3	Dividends on debt-financed stock of domestic and foreign corporations (section 246A)			
4	Dividends on certain preferred stock of less-than-20%-owned public utilities . . .		42	
5	Dividends on certain preferred stock of 20%-or-more-owned public utilities . . .		48	
6	Dividends from less-than-20%-owned foreign corporations and certain FSCs that are subject to the 70% deduction		70	
7	Dividends from 20%-or-more-owned foreign corporations and certain FSCs that are subject to the 80% deduction		80	
8	Dividends from wholly owned foreign subsidiaries subject to the 100% deduction (section 245(b))		100	
9	**Total.** Add lines 1 through 8. See page 16 of instructions for limitation			
10	Dividends from domestic corporations received by a small business investment company operating under the Small Business Investment Act of 1958 . . .		100	
11	Dividends from certain FSCs that are subject to the 100% deduction (section 245(c)(1))		100	
12	Dividends from affiliated group members subject to the 100% deduction (section 243(a)(3))		100	
13	Other dividends from foreign corporations not included on lines 3, 6, 7, 8, or 11 . .			
14	Income from controlled foreign corporations under subpart F (attach Form(s) 5471) .			
15	Foreign dividend gross-up (section 78)			
16	IC-DISC and former DISC dividends not included on lines 1, 2, or 3 (section 246(d)) .			
17	Other dividends			
18	Deduction for dividends paid on certain preferred stock of public utilities			
19	**Total dividends.** Add lines 1 through 17. Enter here and on line 4, page 1 . . . ▶			
20	**Total special deductions.** Add lines 9, 10, 11, 12, and 18. Enter here and on line 29b, page 1 . . . . . . ▶			

Schedule E   Compensation of Officers (see instructions for line 12, page 1, on page 10 of instructions)

Note: *Complete Schedule E only if total receipts (line 1a plus lines 4 through 10 on page 1) are $500,000 or more.*

	(a) Name of officer	(b) Social security number	(c) Percent of time devoted to business	Percent of corporation stock owned (d) Common	(e) Preferred	(f) Amount of compensation
1	ANNE WHO	000-00-0000	100 %	33.3 %	%	40,000
	BAXTER WHEN	111-11-1111	100 %	33.3 %	%	40,000
	CAROL WHAT	222-22-2222	100 %	33.3 %	%	40,000
			%	%	%	
			%	%	%	
2	Total compensation of officers					120,000
3	Compensation of officers claimed on Schedule A and elsewhere on return					
4	Subtract line 3 from line 2. Enter the result here and on line 12, page 1					120,000

Form **1120** (2003)

Figure A.11 *(Continued)*

Schedule J   Tax Computation (see page 17 of instructions)

1	Check if the corporation is a member of a controlled group (see sections 1561 and 1563) . . . . ▶ ☐		
	Important: Members of a controlled group, see instructions on page 17.		
2a	If the box on line 1 is checked, enter the corporation's share of the $50,000, $25,000, and $9,925,000 taxable income brackets (in that order):		
	(1) ⌊$ ⌋ **(2)** ⌊$ ⌋ **(3)** ⌊$		
b	Enter the corporation's share of: **(1)** Additional 5% tax (not more than $11,750) ⌊$		
	(2) Additional 3% tax (not more than $100,000) ⌊$		
3	Income tax. Check if a qualified personal service corporation under section 448(d)(2) (see page 17) . ▶ ☐	**3**	5,400
4	Alternative minimum tax (attach Form 4626)	**4**	
5	Add lines 3 and 4	**5**	5,400
6a	Foreign tax credit (attach Form 1118)	**6a**	
b	Possessions tax credit (attach Form 5735)	**6b**	
c	Check: ☐ Nonconventional source fuel credit ☐ QEV credit (attach Form 8834)	**6c**	
d	General business credit. Check box(es) and indicate which forms are attached.		
	☐ Form 3800 ☐ Form(s) (specify) ▶	**6d**	
e	Credit for prior year minimum tax (attach Form 8827)	**6e**	
f	Qualified zone academy bond credit (attach Form 8860)	**6f**	
7	**Total credits.** Add lines 6a through 6f	**7**	
8	Subtract line 7 from line 5	**8**	
9	Personal holding company tax (attach Schedule PH (Form 1120))	**9**	
10	Other taxes. Check if from: ☐ Form 4255 ☐ Form 8611 ☐ Form 8697		
	☐ Form 8866 ☐ Other (attach schedule)	**10**	
11	**Total tax.** Add lines 8 through 10. Enter here and on line 31, page 1	**11**	5,400

Schedule K   Other Information (see page 19 of instructions)

		Yes	No
1	Check method of accounting: **a** ☑ Cash		
	b ☐ Accrual **c** ☐ Other (specify) ▶		
2	See page 21 of the instructions and enter the:		
a	Business activity code no. ▶ 453910		
b	Business activity ▶ SALES		
c	Product or service ▶ PET SUPPLIES		
3	At the end of the tax year, did the corporation own, directly or indirectly, 50% or more of the voting stock of a domestic corporation? (For rules of attribution, see section 267(c).)		✓
	If "Yes," attach a schedule showing: **(a)** name and employer identification number (EIN), **(b)** percentage owned, and **(c)** taxable income or (loss) before NOL and special deductions of such corporation for the tax year ending with or within your tax year.		
4	Is the corporation a subsidiary in an affiliated group or a parent-subsidiary controlled group?		✓
	If "Yes," enter name and EIN of the parent corporation ▶		
5	At the end of the tax year, did any individual, partnership, corporation, estate, or trust own, directly or indirectly, 50% or more of the corporation's voting stock? (For rules of attribution, see section 267(c).)		✓
	If "Yes," attach a schedule showing name and identifying number. (Do not include any information already entered in **4** above.) Enter percentage owned ▶		
6	During this tax year, did the corporation pay dividends (other than stock dividends and distributions in exchange for stock) in excess of the corporation's current and accumulated earnings and profits? (See sections 301 and 316.) . . .		✓
	If "Yes," file **Form 5452,** Corporate Report of Nondividend Distributions.		
	If this is a consolidated return, answer here for the parent corporation and on **Form 851,** Affiliations Schedule, for each subsidiary.		

		Yes	No
7	At any time during the tax year, did one foreign person own, directly or indirectly, at least 25% of **(a)** the total voting power of all classes of stock of the corporation entitled to vote or **(b)** the total value of all classes of stock of the corporation?		✓
	If "Yes," enter: **(a)** Percentage owned ▶		
	and **(b)** Owner's country ▶		
c	The corporation may have to file **Form 5472,** Information Return of a 25% Foreign-Owned U.S. Corporation or a Foreign Corporation Engaged in a U.S. Trade or Business. Enter number of Forms 5472 attached ▶		
8	Check this box if the corporation issued publicly offered debt instruments with original issue discount . . ▶ ☐		
	If checked, the corporation may have to file **Form 8281,** Information Return for Publicly Offered Original Issue Discount Instruments.		
9	Enter the amount of tax-exempt interest received or accrued during the tax year ▶ $		
10	Enter the number of shareholders at the end of the tax year (if 75 or fewer) ▶ ....3..........		
11	If the corporation has an NOL for the tax year and is electing to forego the carryback period, check here ▶ ☐		
	If the corporation is filing a consolidated return, the statement required by Temporary Regulations section 1.1502-21T(b)(3)(i) or (ii) must be attached or the election will not be valid.		
12	Enter the available NOL carryover from prior tax years (Do not reduce it by any deduction on line 29a.) ▶ $		
13	Are the corporation's total receipts (line 1a plus lines 4 through 10 on page 1) for the tax year **and** its total assets at the end of the tax year less than $250,000? . . .		✓
	If "Yes," the corporation is not required to complete Schedules L, M-1, and M-2 on page 4. Instead, enter the total amount of cash distributions and the book value of property distributions (other than cash) made during the tax year. ▶ $		

Note: *If the corporation, at any time during the tax year, had assets or operated a business in a foreign country or U.S. possession, it may be required to attach* **Schedule N (Form 1120),** *Foreign Operations of U.S. Corporations, to this return. See Schedule N for details.*

Form **1120** (2003)

Figure A.11   *(Continued)*

Note: *The corporation is not required to complete Schedules L, M-1, and M-2 if Question 13 on Schedule K is answered "Yes."*

Schedule L — Balance Sheets per Books

	Assets	Beginning of tax year (a)	(b)	End of tax year (c)	(d)
1	Cash		FIRST YEAR		28,000
2a	Trade notes and accounts receivable			50,000	
b	Less allowance for bad debts	( )		( )	50,000
3	Inventories				120,000
4	U.S. government obligations				
5	Tax-exempt securities (see instructions)				
6	Other current assets (attach schedule)				
7	Loans to shareholders				
8	Mortgage and real estate loans				
9	Other investments (attach schedule)				
10a	Buildings and other depreciable assets			10,000	
b	Less accumulated depreciation	( )		(2,000)	8,000
11a	Depletable assets				
b	Less accumulated depletion	( )		( )	
12	Land (net of any amortization)				
13a	Intangible assets (amortizable only)				
b	Less accumulated amortization	( )		( )	
14	Other assets (attach schedule)				
15	Total assets				206,000
	Liabilities and Shareholders' Equity				
16	Accounts payable				55,000
17	Mortgages, notes, bonds payable in less than 1 year				
18	Other current liabilities (attach schedule)				5,400
19	Loans from shareholders				
20	Mortgages, notes, bonds payable in 1 year or more				40,000
21	Other liabilities (attach schedule)				
22	Capital stock: **a** Preferred stock				
	b Common stock			75,000	75,000
23	Additional paid-in capital				
24	Retained earnings- Appropriated (attach schedule)				
25	Retained earnings- Unappropriated				30,600
26	Adjustments to shareholders' equity (attach schedule)				
27	Less cost of treasury stock		( )		( )
28	Total liabilities and shareholders' equity				206,000

Schedule M-1 — Reconciliation of Income (Loss) per Books With Income per Return (see page 20 of instructions)

1	Net income (loss) per books	30,600	7	Income recorded on books this year not included on this return (itemize):	
2	Federal income tax per books	5,400		Tax-exempt interest $	
3	Excess of capital losses over capital gains			....	
4	Income subject to tax not recorded on books this year (itemize):			....	
	....		8	Deductions on this return not charged against book income this year (itemize):	
5	Expenses recorded on books this year not deducted on this return (itemize):		**a**	Depreciation . . . $	
a	Depreciation . . . $		**b**	Charitable contributions $	
b	Charitable contributions $			....	
c	Travel and entertainment $		9	Add lines 7 and 8	
6	Add lines 1 through 5	36,000	10	Income (line 28, page 1)- line 6 less line 9	36,000

Schedule M-2 — Analysis of Unappropriated Retained Earnings per Books (Line 25, Schedule L)

1	Balance at beginning of year	0	5	Distributions: **a** Cash	
2	Net income (loss) per books	30,600		**b** Stock	
3	Other increases (itemize):			**c** Property	
	....		6	Other decreases (itemize):	
	....		7	Add lines 5 and 6	
4	Add lines 1, 2, and 3	30,600	8	Balance at end of year (line 4 less line 7)	30,600

Figure A.11   *(Continued)*

Form 1120   page 5

CLEAN CAT PROCESSORS, INC.

Employer Identification Number 55-5555555

Form 1120, year ended 12/31/2003

Line 26, Other deductions

Professional services	$ 3,250
Office expense	2,500
Supplies	1,000
Insurance	5,000
Telephone	5,000
Payroll tax, regular employees	4,250
Payroll tax, stockholder/employees	12,000
Utilities	1,500
	$34,500

Specific Instructions

Subchapter T Cooperative

To ensure that Form 1120 or Form 1120-A is timely and properly processed, a corporation that is a cooperative should write "SUBCHAPTER T COOPERATIVE" at the top of page 1 of the form.

Period Covered

File the 2003 return for calendar year 2003 and fiscal years that begin in 2003 and end in 2004. For a fiscal year return, fill in the tax year space at the top of the form.

Note: *The 2003 Form 1120 may also be used if:*
* *The corporation has a tax year of less than 12 months that begins and ends in 2004 and*
* *The 2004 Form 1120 is not available at the time the corporation is required to file its return.*

The corporation must show its 2004 tax year on the 2003 Form 1120 and take into account any tax law changes that are effective for tax years beginning after December 31, 2003.

Name

Use the preprinted label on the tax package information form (Form 8160-A) or the Form 1120 package that was mailed to the corporation. Cross out any errors and print the correct information on the label. If the corporation did not receive a label, print or type the corporation's true name (as set forth in the charter or other legal document creating it), address, and EIN on the appropriate lines.

Address

Include the suite, room, or other unit number after the street address. If a preaddressed label is used, include this information on the label. If the Post Office does not deliver mail to the street address and the corporation has a P.O. box, show the box number instead.

Item A

Consolidated Return (Form 1120 Only)

Corporations filing a consolidated return must attach Form 851 and other supporting statements to the return. For details, see **Other Forms and Statements That May Be Required** on page 3, and **Statements** on page 5.

Personal Holding Company (Form 1120 Only)

A personal holding company must attach to Form 1120 a **Schedule PH (Form 1120),** U.S. Personal Holding Company (PHC) Tax. See the instructions for that form for details.

Personal Service Corporation

A personal service corporation is a corporation whose principal activity (defined on page 8) for the testing period for the tax year is the performance of personal services. The services must be substantially performed by employee-owners. Employee-owners must own more than 10% of the fair market value of the corporation's outstanding stock on the last day of the testing period.

Testing period. Generally, the testing period for a tax year is the prior tax year. The testing period for a new corporation starts with the first day of its first tax year and ends on the **earlier** of:
* The last day of its first tax year or

Figure A.12   Instructions for Form 1120

- The last day of the calendar year in which the first tax year began.

Principal activity. The principal activity of a corporation is considered to be the performance of personal services if, during the testing period, the corporation's compensation costs for the performance of personal services (defined below) are more than 50% of its total compensation costs.

Performance of personal services. The term "performance of personal services" includes any activity involving the performance of personal services in the field of: health, law, engineering, architecture, accounting, actuarial science, performing arts, or consulting (as defined in Temporary Regulations section 1.448-1T(e)).

Substantial performance by employee-owners. Personal services are substantially performed by employee-owners if, for the testing period, more than 20% of the corporation's compensation costs for the performance of personal services are for services performed by employee-owners.

Employee-owner. A person is considered to be an employee-owner if the person:
- Is an employee of the corporation on any day of the testing period **and**
- Owns any outstanding stock of the corporation on any day of the testing period. Stock ownership is determined under the attribution rules of section 318, except that "any" is substituted for "50% or more in value" in section 318(a)(2)(C).

Accounting period. A personal service corporation must use a calendar tax year unless:
- It elects to use a 52-53-week tax year that ends with reference to the calendar year or tax year elected under section 444;
- It can establish a business purpose for a different tax year and obtains the approval of the IRS (see Form 1128 and Pub. 538); or
- It elects under section 444 to have a tax year other than a calendar year. To make the election, use **Form 8716,** Election To Have a Tax Year Other Than a Required Tax Year.

If a corporation makes the section 444 election, its deduction for certain amounts paid to employee-owners may be limited. See **Schedule H (Form 1120),** Section 280H Limitations for a Personal Service Corporation (PSC), to figure the maximum deduction.

If a section 444 election is terminated and the termination results in a short tax year, type or print at the top of the first page of Form 1120 or 1120-A for the short tax year "SECTION 444 ELECTION TERMINATED." See Temporary Regulations section 1.444-1T(a)(5) for more information.

Personal service corporations that want to change their tax year must file Form 1128 to get IRS consent. For more information about personal service corporations, see Regulations section 1.441-3. For rules and procedures on adopting, changing, or retaining an accounting period for a personal service corporation, see Form 1128 and Pub. 538.

Other rules. For other rules that apply to personal service corporations, see **Passive activity limitations** on page 10 and

Contributions of property other than **cash** on page 11.

Item B
Employer Identification Number (EIN)

Enter the corporation's EIN. If the corporation does not have an EIN, it must apply for one. An EIN may be applied for:
- Online—Click on the EIN link at **www.irs.gov/businesses/small.** The EIN is issued immediately once the application information is validated.
- By telephone at 1-800-829-4933 from 7:30 a.m. to 5:30 p.m. in the corporation's local time zone.
- By mailing or faxing **Form SS-4,** Application for Employer Identification Number.

If the corporation has not received its EIN by the time the return is due, write "Applied for" in the space for the EIN. For more details, see Pub. 583.

Note: *The online application process is not yet available for corporations with addresses in foreign countries or Puerto Rico.*

Item D
Total Assets

Enter the corporation's total assets (as determined by the accounting method regularly used in keeping the corporation's books and records) at the end of the tax year. If there are no assets at the end of the tax year, enter -0-.

Item E
Initial Return, Final Return, Name Change, or Address Change

- If this is the corporation's first return, check the "Initial return" box.
- If the corporation ceases to exist, file Form 1120 and check the "Final return" box. Do not file Form 1120-A.
- If the corporation changed its name since it last filed a return, check the box for "Name change." Generally, a corporation also must have amended its articles of incorporation and filed the amendment with the state in which it was incorporated.
- If the corporation has changed its address since it last filed a return, check the box for "Address change."

Note: *If a change in address occurs after the return is filed, use Form 8822, Change of Address, to notify the IRS of the new address.*

Income

Except as otherwise provided in the Internal Revenue Code, gross income includes all income from whatever source derived. Gross income, however, does not include **extraterritorial income** that is qualifying foreign trade income. Use **Form 8873,** Extraterritorial Income Exclusion, to figure the exclusion. Include the exclusion in the total for "Other deductions" on line 26, Form 1120 (line 22, Form 1120-A).

Line 1
Gross Receipts

Enter gross receipts or sales from all business operations except those that must be reported on lines 4 through 10. In general, advance payments are reported in the year of receipt. To report income from long-term contracts, see section 460. For special rules for reporting certain advance payments for goods and long-term contracts, see Regulations section 1.451-5. For permissible methods for reporting advance payments for services by an accrual method corporation, see Rev. Proc. 71-21, 1971-2 C.B. 549.

Installment sales. Generally, the installment method cannot be used for dealer dispositions of property. A "dealer disposition" is: **(a)** any disposition of personal property by a person who regularly sells or otherwise disposes of personal property of the same type on the installment plan or **(b)** any disposition of real property held for sale to customers in the ordinary course of the taxpayer's trade or business.

These restrictions on using the installment method do not apply to dispositions of property used or produced in a farming business or sales of timeshares and residential lots for which the corporation elects to pay interest under section 453(l)(3).

For sales of timeshares and residential lots reported under the installment method, the corporation's income tax is increased by the interest payable under section 453(l)(3). To report this addition to the tax, see the instructions for line 10, Schedule J, Form 1120.

Enter on line 1 (and carry to line 3), the gross profit on collections from installment sales for any of the following:
- Dealer dispositions of property before March 1, 1986.
- Dispositions of property used or produced in the trade or business of farming.
- Certain dispositions of timeshares and residential lots reported under the installment method.

Attach a schedule showing the following information for the current and the 3 preceding years: **(a)** gross sales, **(b)** cost of goods sold, **(c)** gross profits, **(d)** percentage of gross profits to gross sales, **(e)** amount collected, and **(f)** gross profit on the amount collected.

Nonaccrual experience method. Corporations that qualify to use the nonaccrual experience method (described on page 6) should attach a schedule showing total gross receipts, the amount not accrued as a result of the application of section 448(d)(5), and the net amount accrued. Enter the net amount on line 1a.

Line 2
Cost of Goods Sold

Enter the cost of goods sold on line 2, page 1. Before making this entry, a Form 1120 filer must complete Schedule A on page 2 of Form 1120. See the Schedule A instructions on page 14. Form 1120-A filers may use the worksheet on page 14 to figure the amount to enter on line 2.

Instructions for Forms 1120 and 1120-A

Figure A.12 *(Continued)*

Line 4

Dividends

Form 1120 filers. See the instructions for Schedule C on page 15. Then, complete Schedule C and enter on line 4 the amount from Schedule C, line 19.

Form 1120-A filers. Enter the total dividends received (that are not from debt-financed stock) from domestic corporations that qualify for the 70% dividends-received deduction.

Line 5

Interest

Enter taxable interest on U.S. obligations and on loans, notes, mortgages, bonds, bank deposits, corporate bonds, tax refunds, etc. Do not offset interest expense against interest income. Special rules apply to interest income from certain below-market-rate loans. See section 7872 for more information.

Line 6

Gross Rents

Enter the gross amount received for the rental of property. Deduct expenses such as repairs, interest, taxes, and depreciation on the proper lines for deductions. A rental activity held by a closely held corporation or a personal service corporation may be subject to the passive activity loss rules. See Form 8810 and its instructions.

Line 8

Capital Gain Net Income

Every sale or exchange of a capital asset must be reported in detail on **Schedule D (Form 1120),** Capital Gains and Losses, even if there is no gain or loss.

Line 9

Net Gain or (Loss)

Enter the net gain or (loss) from line 18, Part II, **Form 4797,** Sales of Business Property.

Line 10

Other Income

Enter any other taxable income not reported on lines 1 through 9. List the type and amount of income on an attached schedule. If the corporation has only one item of other income, describe it in parentheses on line 10. Examples of other income to report on line 10 are:
• Recoveries of bad debts deducted in prior years under the specific charge-off method.
• The amount of credit for alcohol used as fuel (determined without regard to the limitation based on tax) entered on **Form 6478,** Credit for Alcohol Used as Fuel.
• Refunds of taxes deducted in prior years to the extent they reduced income subject to tax in the year deducted (see section 111). Do not offset current year taxes against tax refunds.
• The amount of any deduction previously taken under section 179A that is subject to recapture. The corporation must recapture the benefit of any allowable deduction for clean-fuel vehicle property (or clean-fuel

vehicle refueling property) if the property later ceases to qualify. See Regulations section 1.179A-1 for details.
• Ordinary income from trade or business activities of a partnership (from Schedule K-1 (Form 1065 or 1065-B)). Do not offset ordinary losses against ordinary income. Instead, include the losses on line 26, Form 1120 (line 22, Form 1120-A). Show the partnership's name, address, and EIN on a separate statement attached to this return. If the amount entered is from more than one partnership, identify the amount from each partnership.
• Any **LIFO recapture amount** under section 1363(d). The corporation may have to include a LIFO recapture amount in income if it:

1. Used the LIFO inventory method for its last tax year before the first tax year for which it elected to become an S corporation or

2. Transferred LIFO inventory assets to an S corporation in a nonrecognition transaction in which those assets were transferred basis property.

The LIFO recapture amount is the amount by which the C corporation's inventory under the FIFO method exceeds the inventory amount under the LIFO method at the close of the corporation's last tax year as a C corporation (or for the year of the transfer, if **2** above applies). For more information, see Regulations section 1.1363-2 and Rev. Proc. 94-61, 1994-2 C.B. 775. Also see the instructions for Schedule J, line 11.

Deductions

Limitations on Deductions

Section 263A uniform capitalization rules. The uniform capitalization rules of section 263A require corporations to capitalize, or include in inventory, certain costs incurred in connection with:
• The production of real property and tangible personal property held in inventory or held for sale in the ordinary course of business.
• Real property or personal property (tangible and intangible) acquired for resale.
• The production of real property and tangible personal property by a corporation for use in its trade or business or in an activity engaged in for profit.

Tangible personal property produced by a corporation includes a film, sound recording, videotape, book, or similar property.

Corporations subject to the section 263A uniform capitalization rules are required to capitalize:

1. Direct costs and
2. An allocable part of most indirect costs (including taxes) that **(a)** benefit the assets produced or acquired for resale or **(b)** are incurred by reason of the performance of production or resale activities.

For inventory, some of the **indirect expenses** that must be capitalized are:
• Administration expenses.
• Taxes.
• Depreciation.
• Insurance.

• Compensation paid to officers attributable to services.
• Rework labor.
• Contributions to pension, stock bonus, and certain profit-sharing, annuity, or deferred compensation plans.

Regulations section 1.263A-1(e)(3) specifies other indirect costs that relate to production or resale activities that must be capitalized and those that may be currently deductible.

Interest expense paid or incurred during the production period of designated property must be capitalized and is governed by special rules. For more details, see Regulations sections 1.263A-8 through 1.263A-15.

The costs required to be capitalized under section 263A are not deductible until the property (to which the costs relate) is sold, used, or otherwise disposed of by the corporation.

Exceptions. Section 263A **does not** apply to:
• Personal property acquired for resale if the corporation's average annual gross receipts for the 3 prior tax years were $10 million or less.
• Timber.
• Most property produced under a long-term contract.
• Certain property produced in a farming business.
• Research and experimental costs under section 174.
• Intangible drilling costs for oil, gas, and geothermal property.
• Mining exploration and development costs.
• Inventoriable items accounted for in the same manner as materials and supplies that are not incidental. See **Cost of Goods Sold** on page 14 for details.

For more details on the uniform capitalization rules, see Regulations sections 1.263A-1 through 1.263A-3. See Regulations section 1.263A-4 for rules for property produced in a farming business.

Transactions between related taxpayers. Generally, an accrual basis taxpayer may only deduct business expenses and interest owed to a related party in the year the payment is included in the income of the related party. See sections 163(e)(3),163(j), and 267 for limitations on deductions for unpaid interest and expenses.

Section 291 limitations. Corporations may be required to adjust deductions for depletion of iron ore and coal, intangible drilling and exploration and development costs, certain deductions for financial institutions, and the amortizable basis of pollution control facilities. See section 291 to determine the amount of the adjustment. Also see section 43.

Golden parachute payments. A portion of the payments made by a corporation to key personnel that exceeds their usual compensation may not be deductible. This occurs when the corporation has an agreement (golden parachute) with these key employees to pay them these excess amounts if control of the corporation changes. See section 280G.

Business startup expenses. Business startup expenses must be capitalized unless an election is made to amortize them over a

Instructions for Forms 1120 and 1120-A   -9-

Figure A.12   *(Continued)*

period of 60 months. See section 195 and Regulations section 1.195-1.

Passive activity limitations. Limitations on passive activity losses and credits under section 469 apply to personal service corporations (see **Personal Service Corporation** on page 7) and closely held corporations (see below).

Generally, the two kinds of passive activities are:
• Trade or business activities in which the corporation did not materially participate for the tax year and
• Rental activities, regardless of its participation.

For exceptions, see Form 8810.
An activity is a trade or business activity if it is not a rental activity and:
• The activity involves the conduct of a trade or business (i.e., deductions from the activity would be allowable under section 162 if other limitations, such as the passive loss rules, did not apply) or
• The activity involves research and experimental costs that are deductible under section 174 (or would be deductible if the corporation chose to deduct rather than capitalize them).

Corporations subject to the passive activity limitations must complete Form 8810 to compute their allowable passive activity loss and credit. Before completing Form 8810, see Temporary Regulations section 1.163-8T, which provides rules for allocating interest expense among activities. If a passive activity is also subject to the earnings stripping rules of section 163(j) or the at-risk rules of section 465, those rules apply before the passive loss rules. For more information, see section 469, the related regulations, and **Pub. 925**, Passive Activity and At-Risk Rules.

Closely held corporations. A corporation is a closely held corporation if:
• At any time during the last half of the tax year more than 50% in value of its outstanding stock is owned, directly or indirectly, by or for not more than five individuals and
• The corporation is not a personal service corporation.

Certain organizations are treated as individuals for purposes of this test. See section 542(a)(2). For rules for determining stock ownership, see section 544 (as modified by section 465(a)(3)).

Reducing certain expenses for which credits are allowable. For each credit listed below, the corporation must reduce the otherwise allowable deductions for expenses used to figure the credit by the amount of the current year credit.
• Work opportunity credit.
• Research credit.
• Enhanced oil recovery credit.
• Disabled access credit.
• Empowerment zone and renewal community employment credit.
• Indian employment credit.
• Employer credit for social security and Medicare taxes paid on certain employee tips.
• Orphan drug credit.
• Welfare-to-work credit.
• New York Liberty Zone business employee credit.

If the corporation has any of these credits, figure each current year credit

before figuring the deduction for expenses on which the credit is based.

Line 12

Compensation of Officers

Enter deductible officers' compensation on line 12. Form 1120 filers must complete Schedule E if their total receipts (line 1a, plus lines 4 through 10) are $500,000 or more. Do not include compensation deductible elsewhere on the return, such as amounts included in cost of goods sold, elective contributions to a section 401(k) cash or deferred arrangement, or amounts contributed under a salary reduction SEP agreement or a SIMPLE IRA plan.

Include only the deductible part of each officer's compensation on Schedule E. See **Disallowance of deduction for employee compensation in excess of $1 million** below. Complete Schedule E, line 1, columns (a) through (f), for all officers. The corporation determines who is an officer under the laws of the state where it is incorporated.

If a consolidated return is filed, each member of an affiliated group must furnish this information.

Disallowance of deduction for employee compensation in excess of $1 million. Publicly held corporations may not deduct compensation to a "covered employee" to the extent that the compensation exceeds $1 million. Generally, a covered employee is:
• The chief executive officer of the corporation (or an individual acting in that capacity) as of the end of the tax year or
• An employee whose total compensation must be reported to shareholders under the Securities Exchange Act of 1934 because the employee is among the four highest compensated officers for that tax year (other than the chief executive officer).

For this purpose, compensation does not include the following:
• Income from certain employee trusts, annuity plans, or pensions and
• Any benefit paid to an employee that is excluded from the employee's income.
The deduction limit does not apply to:
• Commissions based on individual performance,
• Qualified performance-based compensation, and
• Income payable under a written, binding contract in effect on February 17, 1993.
The $1-million limit is reduced by amounts disallowed as excess parachute payments under section 280G.

For details, see section 162(m) and Regulations section 1.162-27.

Line 13

Salaries and Wages

Enter the amount of salaries and wages paid for the tax year, reduced by the current year credits claimed on:
• **Form 5884**, Work Opportunity Credit,
• **Form 8844**, Empowerment Zone and Renewal Community Employment Credit,
• **Form 8845**, Indian Employment Credit,
• **Form 8861**, Welfare-to-Work Credit, and
• **Form 8884**, New York Liberty Zone Business Employee Credit.

See the instructions for these forms for more information. Do not include salaries and wages deductible elsewhere on the return, such as amounts included in cost of goods sold, elective contributions to a section 401(k) cash or deferred arrangement, or amounts contributed under a salary reduction SEP agreement or a SIMPLE IRA plan.

 If the corporation provided taxable fringe benefits to its employees, such as personal use of a car, do not deduct as wages the amount allocated for depreciation and other expenses claimed on lines 20 and 26, Form 1120 (lines 20 and 22, Form 1120-A).

Line 14

Repairs and Maintenance

Enter the cost of incidental repairs and maintenance not claimed elsewhere on the return, such as labor and supplies, that do not add to the value of the property or appreciably prolong its life. New buildings, machinery, or permanent improvements that increase the value of the property are not deductible. They must be depreciated or amortized.

Line 15

Bad Debts

Enter the total debts that became worthless in whole or in part during the tax year. A small bank or thrift institution using the reserve method of section 585 should attach a schedule showing how it figured the current year's provision. A cash basis taxpayer may not claim a bad debt deduction unless the amount was previously included in income.

Line 16

Rents

If the corporation rented or leased a vehicle, enter the total annual rent or lease expense paid or incurred during the year. Also complete Part V of **Form 4562**, Depreciation and Amortization. If the corporation leased a vehicle for a term of 30 days or more, the deduction for vehicle lease expense may have to be reduced by an amount called the **inclusion amount.** The corporation may have an inclusion amount if:

The lease term began:	And the vehicle's FMV on the first day of the lease exceeded:
After 12/31/02 and before 1/1/04	$18,000
After 12/31/98 but before 1/1/03	$15,500
After 12/31/96 but before 1/1/99	$15,800
After 12/31/94 but before 1/1/97	$15,500
After 12/31/93 but before 1/1/95	$14,600

If the lease term began before January 1, 1994, see **Pub. 463**, Travel, Entertainment, Gift, and Car Expenses, to find out if the corporation has an inclusion amount. The inclusion amount for lease terms beginning in 2004 will be published in the Internal Revenue Bulletin in early 2004.

See Pub. 463 for instructions on figuring the inclusion amount.

-10-

Instructions for Forms 1120 and 1120-A

Figure A.12 *(Continued)*

158

Line 17

Taxes and Licenses

Enter taxes paid or accrued during the tax year, but do not include the following.
- Federal income taxes.
- Foreign or U.S. possession income taxes if a tax credit is claimed (however, see the Instructions for Form 5735 for special rules for possession income taxes).
- Taxes not imposed on the corporation.
- Taxes, including state or local sales taxes, that are paid or incurred in connection with an acquisition or disposition of property (these taxes must be treated as a part of the cost of the acquired property or, in the case of a disposition, as a reduction in the amount realized on the disposition).
- Taxes assessed against local benefits that increase the value of the property assessed (such as for paving, etc.).
- Taxes deducted elsewhere on the return, such as those reflected in cost of goods sold.

See section 164(d) for apportionment of taxes on real property between seller and purchaser.

Line 18

Interest

Note: *The deduction for interest is limited when the corporation is a policyholder or beneficiary with respect to a life insurance, endowment, or annuity contract issued after June 8, 1997. For details, see section 264(f). Attach a statement showing the computation of the deduction.*

The corporation must make an interest allocation if the proceeds of a loan were used for more than one purpose (e.g., to purchase a portfolio investment and to acquire an interest in a passive activity). See Temporary Regulations section 1.163-8T for the interest allocation rules.

Mutual savings banks, building and loan associations, and cooperative banks can deduct the amounts paid or credited to the accounts of depositors as dividends, interest, or earnings. See section 591.

Do not deduct the following interest.
- Interest on indebtedness incurred or continued to purchase or carry obligations if the interest is wholly exempt from income tax. For exceptions, see section 265(b).
- For cash basis taxpayers, prepaid interest allocable to years following the current tax year (e.g., a cash basis calendar year taxpayer who in 2003 prepaid interest allocable to any period after 2003 can deduct only the amount allocable to 2003).
- Interest and carrying charges on straddles. Generally, these amounts must be capitalized. See section 263(g).
- Interest on debt allocable to the production of designated property by a corporation for its own use or for sale. The corporation must capitalize this interest. Also capitalize any interest on debt allocable to an asset used to produce the property. See section 263A(f) and Regulations sections 1.263A-8 through 1.263A-15 for definitions and more information.

Special rules apply to:
- Interest on which no tax is imposed (see section 163(j)).

- Foregone interest on certain below-market-rate loans (see section 7872).
- Original issue discount on certain high-yield discount obligations. (See section 163(e) to figure the disqualified portion.)

Line 19

Charitable Contributions

Enter contributions or gifts actually paid within the tax year to or for the use of charitable and governmental organizations described in section 170(c) and any unused contributions carried over from prior years.

Corporations reporting taxable income on the accrual method may elect to treat as paid during the tax year any contributions paid by the 15th day of the 3rd month after the end of the tax year if the contributions were authorized by the board of directors during the tax year. Attach a declaration to the return stating that the resolution authorizing the contributions was adopted by the board of directors during the tax year. The declaration must include the date the resolution was adopted.

Limitation on deduction. The total amount claimed may not be more than 10% of taxable income (line 30, Form 1120, or line 26, Form 1120-A) computed without regard to the following:
- Any deduction for contributions,
- The special deductions on line 29b, Form 1120 (line 25b, Form 1120-A),
- The deduction allowed under section 249,
- Any net operating loss (NOL) carryback to the tax year under section 172, and
- Any capital loss carryback to the tax year under section 1212(a)(1).

Carryover. Charitable contributions over the 10% limitation may not be deducted for the tax year but may be carried over to the next 5 tax years.

Special rules apply if the corporation has an NOL carryover to the tax year. In figuring the charitable contributions deduction for the tax year, the 10% limit is applied using the taxable income after taking into account any deduction for the NOL.

To figure the amount of any remaining NOL carryover to later years, taxable income must be modified (see section 172(b)). To the extent that contributions are used to reduce taxable income for this purpose and increase an NOL carryover, a contributions carryover is not allowed. See section 170(d)(2)(B).

Substantiation requirements. Generally, no deduction is allowed for any contribution of $250 or more unless the corporation gets a written acknowledgment from the donee organization that shows the amount of cash contributed, describes any property contributed, and, either gives a description and a good faith estimate of the value of any goods or services provided in return for the contribution or states that no goods or services were provided in return for the contribution. The acknowledgment must be obtained by the due date (including extensions) of the corporation's return, or, if earlier, the date the return is filed. Do not attach the acknowledgment to the tax return, but keep it with the corporation's records. These rules apply in addition to the filing requirements for **Form 8283**, Noncash Charitable Contributions, described below.

For more information on substantiation and recordkeeping requirements, see the regulations under section 170 and **Pub. 526,** Charitable Contributions.

Contributions to organizations conducting lobbying activities. Contributions made to an organization that conducts lobbying activities are not deductible if:
- The lobbying activities relate to matters of direct financial interest to the donor's trade or business and
- The principal purpose of the contribution was to avoid Federal income tax by obtaining a deduction for activities that would have been nondeductible under the lobbying expense rules if conducted directly by the donor.

Contributions of property other than cash. If a corporation (other than a closely held or personal service corporation) contributes property other than cash and claims over a $500 deduction for the property, it must attach a schedule to the return describing the kind of property contributed and the method used to determine its fair market value (FMV). Closely held corporations and personal service corporations must complete Form 8283 and attach it to their returns. All other corporations generally must complete and attach Form 8283 to their returns for contributions of property (other than money) if the total claimed deduction for all property contributed was more than $5,000.

If the corporation made a "qualified conservation contribution" under section 170(h), also include the FMV of the underlying property before and after the donation, as well as the type of legal interest contributed, and describe the conservation purpose benefited by the donation. If a contribution carryover is included, show the amount and how it was determined.

Reduced deduction for contributions of certain property. For a charitable contribution of property, the corporation must reduce the contribution by the sum of:
- The ordinary income and short-term capital gain that would have resulted if the property were sold at its FMV and
- For certain contributions, the long-term capital gain that would have resulted if the property were sold at its FMV.

The reduction for the long-term capital gain applies to:
- Contributions of tangible personal property for use by an exempt organization for a purpose or function unrelated to the basis for its exemption and
- Contributions of any property to or for the use of certain private foundations except for stock for which market quotations are readily available (section 170(e)(5)).

Larger deduction. A larger deduction is allowed for certain contributions of:
- Inventory and other property to certain organizations for use in the care of the ill, needy, or infants (see section 170(e)(3) and Regulations section 1.170A-4A);
- Scientific equipment used for research to institutions of higher learning or to certain scientific research organizations (other than by personal holding companies and service organizations) (see section 170(e)(4)); and
- Computer technology and equipment for educational purposes.

Figure A.12 *(Continued)*

Contributions of computer technology and equipment for educational purposes. A corporation may take an increased deduction under section 170(e)(6) for qualified contributions of computer technology or equipment for educational purposes. **Computer technology or equipment** means computer software, computer or peripheral equipment, and fiber optic cable related to computer use. A contribution is a qualified contribution if:
* It is made to an eligible donee (see below);
* Substantially all of the donee property's use is:
   1. Related to the purpose or function of the donee,
   2. For use within the United States, and
   3. For educational purposes.
* The contribution is made not later than 3 years after the date the taxpayer acquired or substantially completed the construction of the property;
* The original use of the property is by the donor or the donee;
* The property is not transferred by the donee for money, services, or other property, except for shipping, transfer, and installation costs;
* The property fits productively into the donee's education plan; and
* The property meets standards, if any, that may be prescribed by future regulations, to assure it meets minimum functionality and suitability for educational purposes.

Eligible donee. The term "eligible donee" means:
* An educational organization that normally maintains a regular faculty and curriculum and has a regularly enrolled body of pupils in attendance at the place where its educational activities are regularly conducted,
* A section 501(c)(3) entity organized primarily for purposes of supporting elementary and secondary education, or
* A public library (as described in section 170(e)(6)(B)(i)(III)).

Exceptions. The following exceptions apply to the above rules for computer technology and equipment:
* Contributions to private foundations may qualify if the foundation contributes the property to an eligible donee within 30 days after the contribution and notifies the donor of the contribution. For more details, see section 170(e)(6)(C).
* For contributions of property reacquired by the manufacturer of the property, the 3-year period begins on the date that the original construction of the property was substantially completed. Also, the original use of the property may be by someone other than the donor or the donee.

Line 20

Depreciation

Besides depreciation, include on line 20 the part of the cost that the corporation elected to expense under section 179 for certain tangible property placed in service during tax year 2003 or carried over from 2002. See Form 4562 and its instructions.

Line 22 (Form 1120 Only)

Depletion

See sections 613 and 613A for percentage depletion rates applicable to natural deposits. Also, see section 291 for the limitation on the depletion deduction for iron ore and coal (including lignite).

Attach **Form T (Timber),** Forest Activities Schedule, if a deduction for depletion of timber is taken.

Foreign intangible drilling costs and foreign exploration and development costs must either be added to the corporation's basis for cost depletion purposes or be deducted ratably over a 10-year period. See sections 263(i), 616, and 617 for details.

Line 24 (Form 1120 Only)

Pension, Profit-Sharing, etc., Plans

Enter the deduction for contributions to qualified pension, profit-sharing, or other funded deferred compensation plans. Employers who maintain such a plan generally must file one of the forms listed below, even if the plan is not a qualified plan under the Internal Revenue Code. The filing requirement applies even if the corporation does not claim a deduction for the current tax year. There are penalties for failure to file these forms on time and for overstating the pension plan deduction. See sections 6652(e) and 6662(f).

Form 5500, Annual Return/Report of Employee Benefit Plan. File this form for a plan that is not a one-participant plan (see below).

Form 5500-EZ, Annual Return of One-Participant (Owners and Their Spouses) Retirement Plan. File this form for a plan that only covers the owner (or the owner and his or her spouse) but only if the owner (or the owner and his or her spouse) owns the entire business.

Line 25 (Form 1120 Only)

Employee Benefit Programs

Enter contributions to employee benefit programs not claimed elsewhere on the return (e.g., insurance, health and welfare programs, etc.) that are not an incidental part of a pension, profit-sharing, etc., plan included on line 24.

Line 26, Form 1120 (Line 22, Form 1120-A)

Other Deductions

Attach a schedule, listing by type and amount, all allowable deductions that are not deductible elsewhere on Form 1120 or Form 1120-A. Form 1120-A filers should include amounts described in the instructions above for lines 22, 24, and 25 of Form 1120. Enter the total of other deductions on line 26, Form 1120 (line 22, Form 1120-A).

Examples of other deductions include:
* Amortization of pollution control facilities, organization expenses, etc. (see Form 4562).
* Insurance premiums.
* Legal and professional fees.

* Supplies used and consumed in the business.
* Utilities.
* Ordinary losses from trade or business activities of a partnership (from Schedule K-1 (Form 1065 or 1065-B)). Do not offset ordinary income against ordinary losses. Instead, include the income on line 10. Show the partnership's name, address, and EIN on a separate statement attached to this return. If the amount is from more than one partnership, identify the amount from each partnership.
* Extraterritorial income exclusion (from Form 8873, line 52).
* Dividends paid in cash on stock held by an employee stock ownership plan. However, a deduction may only be taken if, according to the plan, the dividends are:
   1. Paid in cash directly to the plan participants or beneficiaries;
   2. Paid to the plan, which distributes them in cash to the plan participants or their beneficiaries no later than 90 days after the end of the plan year in which the dividends are paid;
   3. At the election of such participants or their beneficiaries **(a)** payable as provided under **1** or **2** above or **(b)** paid to the plan and reinvested in qualifying employer securities; or
   4. Used to make payments on a loan described in section 404(a)(9).

See section 404(k) for more details and the limitation on certain dividends.

Also see **Special rules** below for limits on certain other deductions.

Do not deduct:
* Fines or penalties paid to a government for violating any law.
* Any amount that is allocable to a class of exempt income. See section 265(b) for exceptions.

Special rules apply to the following expenses:

Travel, meals, and entertainment. Subject to limitations and restrictions discussed below, a corporation can deduct ordinary and necessary travel, meals, and entertainment expenses paid or incurred in its trade or business. Also, special rules apply to deductions for gifts, skybox rentals, luxury water travel, convention expenses, and entertainment tickets. See section 274 and Pub. 463 for more details.

Travel. The corporation cannot deduct travel expenses of any individual accompanying a corporate officer or employee, including a spouse or dependent of the officer or employee, unless:
* That individual is an employee of the corporation and
* His or her travel is for a bona fide business purpose and would otherwise be deductible by that individual.

Meals and entertainment. Generally, the corporation can deduct only 50% of the amount otherwise allowable for meals and entertainment expenses paid or incurred in its trade or business. In addition (subject to exceptions under section 274(k)(2)):
* Meals must not be lavish or extravagant;
* A bona fide business discussion must occur during, immediately before, or immediately after the meal; and
* An employee of the corporation must be present at the meal.

-12-

Figure A.12 *(Continued)*

See section 274(n)(3) for a special rule that applies to expenses for meals consumed by individuals subject to the hours of service limits of the Department of Transportation.

Membership dues. The corporation may deduct amounts paid or incurred for membership dues in civic or public service organizations, professional organizations (such as bar and medical associations), business leagues, trade associations, chambers of commerce, boards of trade, and real estate boards. However, no deduction is allowed if a principal purpose of the organization is to entertain, or provide entertainment facilities for, members or their guests. In addition, corporations may not deduct membership dues in any club organized for business, pleasure, recreation, or other social purpose. This includes country clubs, golf and athletic clubs, airline and hotel clubs, and clubs operated to provide meals under conditions favorable to business discussion.

Entertainment facilities. The corporation cannot deduct an expense paid or incurred for a facility (such as a yacht or hunting lodge) used for an activity usually considered entertainment, amusement, or recreation.

Note: *The corporation may be able to deduct otherwise nondeductible meals, travel, and entertainment expenses if the amounts are treated as compensation and reported on Form W-2 for an employee or on Form 1099-MISC for an independent contractor.*

Deduction for clean-fuel vehicles and certain refueling property. Section 179A allows a deduction for part of the cost of qualified clean-fuel vehicle property and qualified clean-fuel vehicle refueling property placed in service during the tax year. For more information, see Pub. 535.

Lobbying expenses. Generally, lobbying expenses are not deductible. These expenses include:
- Amounts paid or incurred in connection with influencing Federal or state legislation (but not local legislation) or
- Amounts paid or incurred in connection with any communication with certain Federal executive branch officials in an attempt to influence the official actions or positions of the officials. See Regulations section 1.162-29 for the definition of "influencing legislation."

Dues and other similar amounts paid to certain tax-exempt organizations may not be deductible. See section 162(e)(3). If certain in-house lobbying expenditures do not exceed $2,000, they are deductible. For information on contributions to charitable organizations that conduct lobbying activities, see the instructions for line 19. For more information on lobbying expenses, see section 162(e).

Line 28, Form 1120
(Line 24, Form 1120-A)

Taxable Income Before NOL Deduction and Special Deductions

At-risk rules. Generally, special at-risk rules under section 465 apply to closely held corporations (see **Passive activity limitations** on page 10) engaged in any activity as a trade or business or for the production of income. These corporations may have to adjust the amount on line 28, Form 1120, or line 24, Form 1120-A. (See below.)

The at-risk rules do not apply to:
- Holding real property placed in service by the taxpayer before 1987;
- Equipment leasing under sections 465(c)(4), (5), and (6); or
- Any qualifying business of a qualified corporation under section 465(c)(7).

However, the at-risk rules do apply to the holding of mineral property.

If the at-risk rules apply, adjust the amount on this line for any section 465(d) losses. These losses are limited to the amount for which the corporation is at risk for each separate activity at the close of the tax year. If the corporation is involved in one or more activities, any of which incurs a loss for the year, report the losses for each activity separately. Attach **Form 6198,** At-Risk Limitations, showing the amount at risk and gross income and deductions for the activities with the losses.

If the corporation sells or otherwise disposes of an asset or its interest (either total or partial) in an activity to which the at-risk rules apply, determine the net profit or loss from the activity by combining the gain or loss on the sale or disposition with the profit or loss from the activity. If the corporation has a net loss, it may be limited because of the at-risk rules.

Treat any loss from an activity not allowed for the tax year as a deduction allocable to the activity in the next tax year.

Line 29a, Form 1120
(Line 25a, Form 1120-A)

Net Operating Loss Deduction

A corporation may use the NOL incurred in one tax year to reduce its taxable income in another tax year. Enter on line 29a (line 25a, Form 1120-A), the total NOL carryovers from other tax years, but do not enter more than the corporation's taxable income (after special deductions). Attach a schedule showing the computation of the NOL deduction. Form 1120 filers must also complete item 12 on Schedule K.

The following special rules apply.
- A personal service corporation may not carry back an NOL to or from any tax year to which an election under section 444 to have a tax year other than a required tax year applies.
- A corporate equity reduction interest loss may not be carried back to a tax year preceding the year of the equity reduction transaction (see section 172(b)(1)(E)).
- If an ownership change occurs, the amount of the taxable income of a loss corporation that may be offset by the pre-change NOL carryovers may be limited (see section 382 and the related regulations). A loss corporation must file an information statement with its income tax return for each tax year that certain ownership shifts occur (see Temporary Regulations section 1.382-2T(a)(2)(ii) for details). See Regulations section 1.382-6(b) for details on how to make the closing-of-the-books election.

- If a corporation acquires control of another corporation (or acquires its assets in a reorganization), the amount of pre-acquisition losses that may offset recognized built-in gain may be limited (see section 384).

For details on the NOL deduction, see Pub. 542, section 172, and **Form 1139,** Corporation Application for Tentative Refund.

Line 29b, Form 1120
(Line 25b, Form 1120-A)

Special Deductions

Form 1120 filers. See the instructions for Schedule C on page 15.

Form 1120-A filers. Generally, enter 70% of line 4, page 1, on line 25b. However, this deduction may not be more than 70% of line 24, page 1. Compute line 24 without regard to any adjustment under section 1059 and without regard to any capital loss carryback to the tax year under section 1212(a)(1).

In a year in which an NOL occurs, this 70% limitation does not apply even if the loss is created by the dividends-received deduction. See sections 172(d) and 246(b).

Line 30, Form 1120
(Line 26, Form 1120-A)

Taxable Income

Net operating loss (NOL). If line 30 is zero or less, the corporation may have an NOL that can be carried back or forward as a deduction to other tax years. Generally, a corporation first carries back an NOL 2 tax years (pending legislation may change the period to 5 tax years—see Pub. 553). However, the corporation may elect to waive the carryback period and instead carry the NOL forward to future tax years. To make the election, see the instructions for Schedule K, item 11, on page 20.

See Form 1139 for details, including other elections that may be available, which must be made no later than 6 months after the due date (excluding extensions) of the corporation's tax return.

Capital construction fund. To take a deduction for amounts contributed to a capital construction fund (CCF), reduce the amount that would otherwise be entered on line 30 (line 26, Form 1120-A) by the amount of the deduction. On the dotted line next to the entry space, write "CCF" and the amount of the deduction. For more information, see **Pub. 595,** Tax Highlights for Commercial Fishermen.

Line 32b, Form 1120
(Line 28b, Form 1120-A)

Estimated Tax Payments

Enter any estimated tax payments the corporation made for the tax year.

Beneficiaries of trusts. If the corporation is the beneficiary of a trust, and the trust makes a section 643(g) election to credit its estimated tax payments to its beneficiaries, include the corporation's share of the payment in the total for line 32b, Form 1120 (line 28b, Form 1120-A). Write "T" and the amount on the dotted line next to the entry space.

Instructions for Forms 1120 and 1120-A

Figure A.12 *(Continued)*

Special estimated tax payments for certain life insurance companies. If the corporation is required to make or apply special estimated tax payments (SETP) under section 847 in addition to its regular estimated tax payments, enter on line 32b (line 28b, Form 1120-A), the corporation's total estimated tax payments. In the margin near line 32b, write "Form 8816" and the amount. Attach a schedule showing your computation of estimated tax payments. See sections 847(2) and 847(8) and **Form 8816,** Special Loss Discount Account and Special Estimated Tax Payments for Insurance Companies, for more information.

Line 32f, Form 1120 (Line 28f, Form 1120-A)

Enter the credit (from **Form 2439,** Notice to Shareholder of Undistributed Long-Term Capital Gains) for the corporation's share of the tax paid by a regulated investment company (RIC) or a real estate investment trust (REIT) on undistributed long-term capital gains included in the corporation's income. Attach Form 2439 to Form 1120 or 1120-A.

Line 32g, Form 1120 (Line 28g, Form 1120-A)

Credit for Federal Tax on Fuels

Enter the credit from **Form 4136,** Credit for Federal Tax Paid on Fuels, if the corporation qualifies to take this credit. Attach Form 4136 to Form 1120 or 1120-A.

Credit for tax on ozone-depleting chemicals. Include on line 32g (line 28g, Form 1120-A) any credit the corporation is claiming under section 4682(g)(2) for tax on ozone-depleting chemicals. Write "ODC" to the left of the entry space.

Line 32h, Form 1120 (Line 28h, Form 1120-A)

Total Payments

On Form 1120, add the amounts on lines 32d through 32g and enter the total on line 32h. On Form 1120-A, add the amounts on lines 28d through 28g and enter the total on line 28h.

Backup withholding. If the corporation had Federal income tax withheld from any payments it received because, for example, it failed to give the payer its correct EIN, include the amount withheld in the total for line 32h, Form 1120 (line 28h, Form 1120-A). On Form 1120, write the amount withheld and the words "Backup Withholding" in the blank space above line 32h. On Form 1120-A, show the amount withheld on the dotted line to the left of line 28h, and write "Backup Withholding."

Line 33, Form 1120 (Line 29, Form 1120-A)

Estimated Tax Penalty

A corporation that does not make estimated tax payments when due may be subject to an underpayment penalty for the period of underpayment. Generally, a corporation is subject to the penalty if its tax liability is $500 or more and it did not timely pay the smaller of:
• Its tax liability for 2003 or

• Its prior year's tax.
See section 6655 for details and exceptions, including special rules for large corporations.

Use **Form 2220,** Underpayment of Estimated Tax by Corporations, to see if the corporation owes a penalty and to figure the amount of the penalty. Generally, the corporation does not have to file this form because the IRS can figure the amount of any penalty and bill the corporation for it. However, even if the corporation does not owe the penalty, complete and attach Form 2220 if:
• The annualized income or adjusted seasonal installment method is used or
• The corporation is a large corporation computing its first required installment based on the prior year's tax. (See the Instructions for Form 2220 for the definition of a large corporation.)

If Form 2220 is attached, check the box on line 33, Form 1120 (line 29, Form 1120-A), and enter the amount of any penalty on this line.

Line 36, Form 1120 (Line 32, Form 1120-A)

Direct Deposit of Refund

If the corporation wants its refund directly deposited into its checking or savings account at any U.S. bank or other financial institution instead of having a check sent to the corporation, complete Form 8050 and attach it to the corporation's tax return.

Schedule A, Form 1120 (Worksheet, Form 1120-A)

Cost of Goods Sold

Generally, inventories are required at the beginning and end of each tax year if the production, purchase, or sale of merchandise is an income-producing factor. See Regulations section 1.471-1.

However, if the corporation is a qualifying taxpayer or a qualifying small business taxpayer, it may adopt or change its accounting method to account for inventoriable items in the same manner as materials and supplies that are not

incidental (unless its business is a tax shelter (as defined in section 448(d)(3))).

A **qualifying taxpayer** is a taxpayer that, for each prior tax year ending after December 16, 1998, has average annual gross receipts of $1 million or less for the 3-tax-year period ending with that prior tax year. See Rev. Proc. 2001-10, 2001-2 I.R.B. 272, for details.

A **qualifying small business taxpayer** is a taxpayer (a) that, for each prior tax year ending on or after December 31, 2000, has average annual gross receipts of $10 million or less for the 3-tax-year period ending with that prior tax year and (b) whose principal business activity is not an ineligible activity. See Rev. Proc. 2002-28, 2002-18 I.R.B. 815, for details.

Under this accounting method, inventory costs for raw materials purchased for use in producing finished goods and merchandise purchased for resale are deductible in the year the finished goods or merchandise are sold (but not before the year the corporation paid for the raw materials or merchandise, if it is also using the cash method). For additional guidance on this method of accounting for inventoriable items, see Pub. 538.

Enter amounts paid for all raw materials and merchandise during the tax year on line 2. The amount the corporation can deduct for the tax year is figured on line 8.

All filers not using the cash method of accounting should see **Section 263A uniform capitalization rules** on page 9 before completing Schedule A or the worksheet. The instructions for lines 1 through 7 that follow apply to Schedule A (Form 1120) and the worksheet for Form 1120-A below.

Line 1

Inventory at Beginning of Year

If the corporation is changing its method of accounting for the current tax year, it must refigure last year's closing inventory using its new method of accounting and enter the result on line 1. If there is a difference between last year's closing inventory and the refigured amount, attach an explanation and take it into account when figuring the corporation's section 481(a) adjustment (explained on page 6).

Cost of Goods Sold Worksheet

Form 1120-A
(keep for your records)

1. Inventory at beginning of year. Enter here and in Part III, line 3, column (a), Form 1120-A	1. _____
2. Purchases. Enter here and in Part II, line 5a(1), Form 1120-A .	2. _____
3. Cost of labor. Enter here and include in total in Part II, line 5a(3), Form 1120-A	3. _____
4. Additional section 263A costs. Enter here and include in Part II, line 5a(2), Form 1120-A (see instructions for line 4)	4. _____
5. Other costs. Enter here and include in Part II, line 5a(3), Form 1120-A	5. _____
6. **Total.** Add lines 1 through 5	6. _____
7. Inventory at end of year. Enter here and in Part III, line 3, column (b), Form 1120-A	7. _____
8. **Cost of goods sold.** Subtract line 7 from line 6. Enter the result here and on page 1, line 2, Form 1120-A	8. _____

-14-　　　　　　　　　　　　　　　Instructions for Forms 1120 and 1120-A

Figure A.12 *(Continued)*

162

Line 4

Additional Section 263A Costs

An entry is required on this line only for corporations that have elected a simplified method of accounting.

For corporations that have elected the **simplified production method**, additional section 263A costs are generally those costs, other than interest, that were not capitalized under the corporation's method of accounting immediately prior to the effective date of section 263A but are now required to be capitalized under section 263A. For details, see Regulations section 1.263A-2(b).

For corporations that have elected the **simplified resale method**, additional section 263A costs are generally those costs incurred with respect to the following categories.
• Off-site storage or warehousing.
• Purchasing; handling, such as processing, assembling, repackaging, and transporting.
• General and administrative costs (mixed service costs).

For details, see Regulations section 1.263A-3(d).

Enter on line 4 the balance of section 263A costs paid or incurred during the tax year not includible on lines 2, 3, and 5.

Line 5

Other Costs

Enter on line 5 any costs paid or incurred during the tax year not entered on lines 2 through 4.

Line 7

Inventory at End of Year

See Regulations sections 1.263A-1 through 1.263A-3 for details on figuring the amount of additional section 263A costs to be included in ending inventory. If the corporation accounts for inventoriable items in the same manner as materials and supplies that are not incidental, enter on line 7 the portion of its raw materials and merchandise purchased for resale that is included on line 6 and was not sold during the year.

Lines 9a Through 9f (Schedule A)

Inventory Valuation Methods

Inventories can be valued at:
• Cost;
• Cost or market value (whichever is lower); or
• Any other method approved by the IRS that conforms to the requirements of the applicable regulations cited below.

However, if the corporation is using the cash method of accounting, it is required to use cost.

Corporations that account for inventoriable items in the same manner as materials and supplies that are not incidental may currently deduct expenditures for direct labor and all indirect costs that would otherwise be included in inventory costs.

The average cost (rolling average) method of valuing inventories generally does not conform to the requirements of the regulations. See Rev. Rul. 71-234, 1971-1 C.B. 148.

Corporations that use erroneous valuation methods must change to a method permitted for Federal income tax purposes. Use Form 3115 to make this change.

On line 9a, check the method(s) used for valuing inventories. Under lower of cost or market, the term "market" (for normal goods) means the current bid price prevailing on the inventory valuation date for the particular merchandise in the volume usually purchased by the taxpayer. For a manufacturer, market applies to the basic elements of cost—raw materials, labor, and burden. If section 263A applies to the taxpayer, the basic elements of cost must reflect the current bid price of all direct costs and all indirect costs properly allocable to goods on hand at the inventory date.

Inventory may be valued below cost when the merchandise is unsalable at normal prices or unusable in the normal way because the goods are subnormal due to damage, imperfections, shopwear, etc., within the meaning of Regulations section 1.471-2(c). The goods may be valued at the current bona fide selling price, minus direct cost of disposition (but not less than scrap value) if such a price can be established.

If this is the first year the Last-in, First-out (LIFO) inventory method was either adopted or extended to inventory goods not previously valued under the LIFO method provided in section 472, attach **Form 970,** Application To Use LIFO Inventory Method, or a statement with the information required by Form 970. Also check the LIFO box on line 9c. On line 9d, enter the amount or the percent of total closing inventories covered under section 472. Estimates are acceptable.

If the corporation changed or extended its inventory method to LIFO and had to write up the opening inventory to cost in the year of election, report the effect of the write-up as other income (line 10, page 1), proportionately over a 3-year period that begins with the year of the LIFO election (section 472(d)).

Note: *Corporations using the LIFO method that make an S corporation election or transfer LIFO inventory to an S corporation in a nonrecognition transaction may be subject to an additional tax attributable to the LIFO recapture amount. See the instructions for line 11, Schedule J, on page 19, and for line 10,* **Other Income,** *on page 9.*

For more information on inventory valuation methods, see Pub. 538.

Schedule C (Form 1120 Only)

For purposes of the 20% ownership test on lines 1 through 7, the percentage of stock owned by the corporation is based on voting power and value of the stock. Preferred stock described in section 1504(a)(4) is not taken into account. Corporations filing a consolidated return should see Regulations

sections 1.1502-13, 1.1502-26, and 1.1502-27 before completing Schedule C.

Line 1, Column (a)

Enter dividends (except those received on debt-financed stock acquired after July 18, 1984 – see section 246A) that:
• Are received from less-than-20%-owned domestic corporations subject to income tax and
• Qualify for the 70% deduction under section 243(a)(1).

Also include on line 1:
• Taxable distributions from an IC-DISC or former DISC that are designated as eligible for the 70% deduction and certain dividends of Federal Home Loan Banks. See section 246(a)(2).
• Dividends (except those received on debt-financed stock acquired after July 18, 1984) from a regulated investment company (RIC). The amount of dividends eligible for the dividends-received deduction under section 243 is limited by section 854(b). The corporation should receive a notice from the RIC specifying the amount of dividends that qualify for the deduction.

Report so-called dividends or earnings received from mutual savings banks, etc., as interest. Do not treat them as dividends.

Line 2, Column (a)

Enter on line 2:
• Dividends (except those received on debt-financed stock acquired after July 18, 1984) that are received from 20%-or-more-owned domestic corporations subject to income tax and that are subject to the 80% deduction under section 243(c) and
• Taxable distributions from an IC-DISC or former DISC that are considered eligible for the 80% deduction.

Line 3, Column (a)

Enter dividends that are:
• Received on debt-financed stock acquired after July 18, 1984, from domestic and foreign corporations subject to income tax that would otherwise be subject to the dividends-received deduction under section 243(a)(1), 243(c), or 245(a). Generally, debt-financed stock is stock that the corporation acquired by incurring a debt (e.g., it borrowed money to buy the stock).
• Received from a RIC on debt-financed stock. The amount of dividends eligible for the dividends-received deduction is limited by section 854(b). The corporation should receive a notice from the RIC specifying the amount of dividends that qualify for the deduction.

Line 3, Columns (b) and (c)

Dividends received on debt-financed stock acquired after July 18, 1984, are not entitled to the full 70% or 80% dividends-received deduction. The 70% or 80% deduction is reduced by a percentage that is related to the amount of debt incurred to acquire the stock. See section 246A. Also, see section 245(a) before making this computation for an additional limitation that applies to dividends received from foreign corporations. Attach a schedule to Form 1120 showing how the amount on line 3, column (c), was figured.

Figure A.12 *(Continued)*

Line 4, Column (a)

Enter dividends received on the preferred stock of a less-than-20%-owned public utility that is subject to income tax and is allowed the deduction provided in section 247 for dividends paid.

Line 5, Column (a)

Enter dividends received on preferred stock of a 20%-or-more-owned public utility that is subject to income tax and is allowed the deduction provided in section 247 for dividends paid.

Line 6, Column (a)

Enter the U.S.-source portion of dividends that:
- Are received from less-than-20%-owned foreign corporations and
- Qualify for the 70% deduction under section 245(a). To qualify for the 70% deduction, the corporation must own at least 10% of the stock of the foreign corporation by vote and value.

Also include dividends received from a less-than-20%-owned FSC that:
- Are attributable to income treated as effectively connected with the conduct of a trade or business within the United States (excluding foreign trade income) and
- Qualify for the 70% deduction provided in section 245(c)(1)(B).

Line 7, Column (a)

Enter the U.S.-source portion of dividends that are received from 20%-or-more-owned foreign corporations that qualify for the 80% deduction under section 245(a). Also include dividends received from a 20%-or-more-owned FSC that:
- Are attributable to income treated as effectively connected with the conduct of a trade or business within the United States (excluding foreign trade income) and
- Qualify for the 80% deduction provided in section 245(c)(1)(B).

Line 8, Column (a)

Enter dividends received from wholly owned foreign subsidiaries that are eligible for the 100% deduction provided in section 245(b).

In general, the deduction under section 245(b) applies to dividends paid out of the earnings and profits of a foreign corporation for a tax year during which:
- All of its outstanding stock is owned (directly or indirectly) by the domestic corporation receiving the dividends and
- All of its gross income from all sources is effectively connected with the conduct of a trade or business within the United States.

Line 9, Column (c)

Generally, line 9, column (c), may not exceed the amount from the worksheet below. However, in a year in which an NOL occurs, this limitation does not apply even if the loss is created by the dividends-received deduction. See sections 172(d) and 246(b).

Line 10, Columns (a) and (c)

Small business investment companies operating under the Small Business Investment Act of 1958 (see 15 U.S.C. 661 and following) must enter dividends that are received from domestic corporations subject to income tax even though a deduction is allowed for the entire amount of those dividends. To claim the 100% deduction on line 10, column (c), the company must file with its return a statement that it was a Federal licensee under the Small Business Investment Act of 1958 at the time it received the dividends.

Line 11, Column (a)

Enter dividends from FSCs that are attributable to foreign trade income and that are eligible for the 100% deduction provided in section 245(c)(1)(A).

Line 12, Columns (a) and (c)

Enter only those dividends that qualify under section 243(b) for the 100% dividends-received deduction described in section 243(a)(3). Corporations taking this

deduction are subject to the provisions of section 1561.

The 100% deduction does not apply to affiliated group members that are joining in the filing of a consolidated return.

Line 13, Column (a)

Enter foreign dividends not reportable on lines 3, 6, 7, 8, or 11 of column (a). Include on line 13 the corporation's share of the ordinary earnings of a qualified electing fund from Form 8621, line 1c. Exclude distributions of amounts constructively taxed in the current year or in prior years under subpart F (sections 951 through 964).

Line 14, Column (a)

Include income constructively received from controlled foreign corporations under subpart F. This amount should equal the total subpart F income reported on Schedule I, Form 5471.

Line 15, Column (a)

Include gross-up for taxes deemed paid under sections 902 and 960.

Line 16, Column (a)

Enter taxable distributions from an IC-DISC or former DISC that are designated as not eligible for a dividends-received deduction.

No deduction is allowed under section 243 for a dividend from an IC-DISC or former DISC (as defined in section 992(a)) to the extent the dividend:
- Is paid out of the corporation's accumulated IC-DISC income or previously taxed income or
- Is a deemed distribution under section 995(b)(1).

Line 17, Column (a)

Include the following:
1. Dividends (other than capital gain distributions reported on Schedule D (Form 1120) and exempt-interest dividends) that are received from RICs and that are not subject to the 70% deduction.
2. Dividends from tax-exempt organizations.
3. Dividends (other than capital gain distributions) received from a REIT that, for the tax year of the trust in which the dividends are paid, qualifies under sections 856 through 860.
4. Dividends not eligible for a dividends-received deduction because of the holding period of the stock or an obligation to make corresponding payments with respect to similar stock.

Two situations in which the dividends-received deduction will not be allowed on any share of stock are:
- If the corporation held it less than 46 days during the 90-day period beginning 45 days before the stock became ex-dividend with respect to the dividend (see section 246(c)(1)(A)) or
- To the extent the corporation is under an obligation to make related payments for substantially similar or related property.
5. Any other taxable dividend income not properly reported above (including distributions under section 936(h)(4)).

If patronage dividends or per-unit retain allocations are included on line 17, identify

---

Worksheet for Schedule C, line 9

(keep for your records)

1. Refigure line 28, page 1, Form 1120, without any adjustment under section 1059 and without any capital loss carryback to the tax year under section 1212(a)(1) . . . . 1. _____
2. Complete lines 10, 11, and 12, column (c), and enter the total here 2. _____
3. Subtract line 2 from line 1 . . . . 3. _____
4. Multiply line 3 by 80% . . . . 4. _____
5. Add lines 2, 5, 7, and 8, column (c), and the part of the deduction on line 3, column (c), that is attributable to dividends from 20%-or-more-owned corporations . . . . 5. _____
6. Enter the smaller of line 4 or 5. If line 5 is greater than line 4, stop here; enter the amount from line 6 on line 9, column (c), and do not complete the rest of this worksheet . . . . 6. _____
7. Enter the total amount of dividends from 20%-or-more-owned corporations that are included on lines 2, 3, 5, 7, and 8, column (a) 7. _____
8. Subtract line 7 from line 3 . . . . 8. _____
9. Multiply line 8 by 70% . . . . 9. _____
10. Subtract line 5 above from line 9, column (c). . . . . . . 10. _____
11. Enter the smaller of line 9 or line 10 . . . . 11. _____
12. **Dividends-received deduction after limitation** (sec. 246(b)). Add lines 6 and 11. Enter the result here and on line 9, column (c) . 12. _____

Instructions for Forms 1120 and 1120-A

Figure A.12 *(Continued)*

the total of these amounts in a schedule attached to Form 1120.

Line 18, Column (c)

Section 247 allows public utilities a deduction of 40% of the smaller of (a) dividends paid on their preferred stock during the tax year or (b) taxable income computed without regard to this deduction. In a year in which an NOL occurs, compute the deduction without regard to section 247(a)(1)(B). See section 172(d).

Schedule J, Form 1120 (Part I, Form 1120-A)

Lines 1 and 2 (Form 1120 Only)

Members of a controlled group. A member of a controlled group, as defined in section 1563, must check the box on line 1 and complete lines 2a and 2b of Schedule J, Form 1120.

Line 2a. Members of a controlled group are entitled to one $50,000, one $25,000, and one $9,925,000 taxable income bracket amount (in that order) on line 2a.

When a controlled group adopts or later amends an apportionment plan, each member must attach to its tax return a copy of its consent to this plan. The copy (or an attached statement) must show the part of the amount in each taxable income bracket apportioned to that member. See Regulations section 1.1561-3(b) for other requirements and for the time and manner of making the consent.

Unequal apportionment plan. Members of a controlled group may elect an unequal apportionment plan and divide the taxable income brackets as they want. There is no need for consistency among taxable income brackets. Any member may be entitled to all, some, or none of the taxable income bracket. However, the total amount for all members cannot be more than the total amount in each taxable income bracket.

Equal apportionment plan. If no apportionment plan is adopted, members of a controlled group must divide the amount in each taxable income bracket equally among themselves. For example, Controlled Group AB consists of Corporation A and Corporation B. They do not elect an apportionment plan. Therefore, each corporation is entitled to:
- $25,000 (one-half of $50,000) on line 2a(1),
- $12,500 (one-half of $25,000) on line 2a(2), and
- $4,962,500 (one-half of $9,925,000) on line 2a(3).

Line 2b. Members of a controlled group are treated as one group to figure the applicability of the additional 5% tax and the additional 3% tax. If an additional tax applies, each member will pay that tax based on the part of the amount used in each taxable income bracket to reduce that member's tax. See section 1561(a). If an additional tax applies, attach a schedule showing the taxable income of the entire group and how the corporation figured its share of the additional tax.

Instructions for Forms 1120 and 1120-A

Tax Computation Worksheet for Members of a Controlled Group
(keep for your records)

Note: *Each member of a controlled group (except a qualified personal service corporation) must compute the tax using this worksheet.*

1. Enter taxable income (line 30, page 1, Form 1120)	1. _____
2. Enter line 1 or the corporation's share of the $50,000 taxable income bracket, whichever is less	2. _____
3. Subtract line 2 from line 1	3. _____
4. Enter line 3 or the corporation's share of the $25,000 taxable income bracket, whichever is less	4. _____
5. Subtract line 4 from line 3	5. _____
6. Enter line 5 or the corporation's share of the $9,925,000 taxable income bracket, whichever is less	6. _____
7. Subtract line 6 from line 5	7. _____
8. Multiply line 2 by 15%	8. _____
9. Multiply line 4 by 25%	9. _____
10. Multiply line 6 by 34%	10. _____
11. Multiply line 7 by 35%	11. _____
12. If the taxable income of the controlled group exceeds $100,000, enter this member's share of the smaller of: 5% of the taxable income in excess of $100,000, or $11,750 (see the instructions for Schedule J, line 2b)	12. _____
13. If the taxable income of the controlled group exceeds $15 million, enter this member's share of the smaller of: 3% of the taxable income in excess of $15 million, or $100,000 (see the instructions for Schedule J, line 2b)	13. _____
14. **Total.** Add lines 8 through 13. Enter here and on line 3, Schedule J, Form 1120	14. _____

Line 2b(1). Enter the corporation's share of the additional 5% tax on line 2b(1).

Line 2b(2). Enter the corporation's share of the additional 3% tax on line 2b(2).

Line 3, Form 1120 (Line 1, Form 1120-A)

Members of a controlled group should use the worksheet above to figure the tax for the group. In addition, members of a controlled group **must** attach to Form 1120 a statement showing the computation of the tax entered on line 3.

Most corporations not filing a consolidated return figure their tax by using the Tax Rate Schedule below. Qualified personal service corporations should see the instructions below.

Tax Rate Schedule

If taxable income (line 30, Form 1120, or line 26, Form 1120-A) on page 1 is:

Over—	But not over—	Tax is:	Of the amount over—
$0	$50,000	15%	$0
50,000	75,000	$ 7,500 + 25%	50,000
75,000	100,000	13,750 + 34%	75,000
100,000	335,000	22,250 + 39%	100,000
335,000	10,000,000	113,900 + 34%	335,000
10,000,000	15,000,000	3,400,000 + 35%	10,000,000
15,000,000	18,333,333	5,150,000 + 38%	15,000,000
18,333,333	- - - - -	35%	0

Qualified personal service corporation. A qualified personal service corporation is taxed at a flat rate of 35% on taxable income. If the corporation is a qualified personal service corporation, check the box on line 3, Schedule J, Form 1120 (line 1, Part I, Form 1120-A) even if the corporation has no tax liability.

A corporation is a qualified personal service corporation if it meets **both** of the following tests:
- Substantially all of the corporation's activities involve the performance of services in the fields of health, law, engineering, architecture, accounting, actuarial science, performing arts, or consulting and
- At least 95% of the corporation's stock, by value, is owned, directly or indirectly, by (a) employees performing the services, (b) retired employees who had performed the services listed above, (c) any estate of an employee or retiree described above, or (d) any person who acquired the stock of the corporation as a result of the death of an employee or retiree (but only for the 2-year period beginning on the date of the employee or retiree's death). See Temporary Regulations section 1.448-1T(e) for details.

Mutual savings bank conducting life insurance business. The tax under section 594 consists of the sum of (a) a partial tax computed on Form 1120 on the taxable income of the bank determined without regard to income or deductions allocable to the life insurance department and (b) a partial tax on the taxable income computed on Form 1120-L of the life insurance department. Enter the combined tax on line 3 of Schedule J, Form 1120. Attach Form 1120-L as a schedule (and identify it as such) or a statement showing the computation of the taxable income of the life insurance department.

Deferred tax under section 1291. If the corporation was a shareholder in a passive foreign investment company (PFIC) and received an excess distribution or disposed of its investment in the PFIC during the year, it must include the increase in taxes due under section 1291(c)(2) in the total for line

-17-

Figure A.12 *(Continued)*

3, Schedule J, Form 1120. On the dotted line next to line 3, write "Section 1291" and the amount.

Do not include on line 3 any interest due under section 1291(c)(3). Instead, show the amount of interest owed in the bottom margin of page 1, Form 1120, and write "Section 1291 interest." For details, see **Form 8621,** Return by a Shareholder of a Passive Foreign Investment Company or Qualified Electing Fund.

Additional tax under section 197(f). A corporation that elects to pay tax on the gain from the sale of an intangible under the related person exception to the anti-churning rules should include any additional tax due under section 197(f)(9)(B) in the total for line 3. On the dotted line next to line 3, write "Section 197" and the amount. For more information, see **Pub. 535,** Business Expenses.

Line 4 (Form 1120 Only)

Note: *A corporation that is not a small corporation exempt from the AMT (see below) may be required to file Form 4626 if it claims certain credits, even though it does not owe any AMT. See Form 4626 for details.*

Unless the corporation is treated as a small corporation exempt from the AMT, it may owe the AMT if it has any of the adjustments and tax preference items listed on Form 4626. The corporation must file Form 4626 if its taxable income (or loss) before the NOL deduction, combined with these adjustments and tax preference items is more than the smaller of $40,000 or the corporation's allowable exemption amount (from Form 4626).

For this purpose, taxable income does not include the NOL deduction. See Form 4626 for details.

Exemption for small corporations. A corporation is treated as a small corporation exempt from the AMT for its tax year beginning in 2003 if that year is the corporation's first tax year in existence (regardless of its gross receipts) **or:**

1. It was treated as a small corporation exempt from the AMT for all prior tax years beginning after 1997 **and**

2. Its average annual gross receipts for the 3-tax-year period (or portion thereof during which the corporation was in existence) ending before its tax year beginning in 2003 did not exceed $7.5 million ($5 million if the corporation had only 1 prior tax year).

Line 6a (Form 1120 Only)

To find out when a corporation can take the credit for payment of income tax to a foreign country or U.S. possession, see **Form 1118,** Foreign Tax Credit—Corporations.

Line 6b (Form 1120 Only)

The Small Business Job Protection Act of 1996 repealed the possessions credit. However, existing credit claimants may qualify for a credit under the transitional rules. See **Form 5735,** Possessions Corporation Tax Credit (Under Sections 936 and 30A).

Line 6c (Form 1120 Only)

If the corporation can take either of the following credits, check the appropriate box(es) and include the amount of the credits in the total for line 6c.

Nonconventional source fuel credit. A credit is allowed for the sale of qualified fuels produced from a nonconventional source. Section 29 contains a definition of qualified fuels, provisions for figuring the credit, and other special rules. Attach a separate schedule to the return showing the computation of the credit.

Qualified electric vehicle (QEV) credit. Use **Form 8834,** Qualified Electric Vehicle Credit, if the corporation can claim a credit for the purchase of a new qualified electric vehicle. Vehicles that qualify for this credit are not eligible for the deduction for clean-fuel vehicles under section 179A.

Line 6d, Form 1120 (Line 2a, Form 1120-A)

Enter on line 6d (line 2a of Form 1120-A) the corporation's total general business credit.

If the corporation is filing Form 8844 (Empowerment Zone and Renewal Community Employment Credit) or Form 8884 (New York Liberty Zone Business Employee Credit), check the "Form(s)" box, write the form number in the space provided, and include the allowable credit on line 6d (line 2a of Form 1120-A).

If the corporation is required to file **Form 3800,** General Business Credit, check the "Form 3800" box and include the allowable credit on line 6d (line 2a of Form 1120-A).

If the corporation is not required to file Form 3800, check the "Form(s)" box, write the form number in the space provided, and include on line 6d (line 2a of Form 1120-A) the allowable credit from the applicable form listed below.

- Investment Credit (Form 3468).
- Work Opportunity Credit (Form 5884).
- Credit for Alcohol Used as Fuel (Form 6478).
- Credit for Increasing Research Activities (Form 6765).
- Low-Income Housing Credit (Form 8586).
- Orphan Drug Credit (Form 8820).
- Disabled Access Credit (Form 8826).
- Enhanced Oil Recovery Credit (Form 8830).
- Renewable Electricity Production Credit (Form 8835).
- Indian Employment Credit (Form 8845).
- Credit for Employer Social Security and Medicare Taxes Paid on Certain Employee Tips (Form 8846).
- Credit for Contributions to Selected Community Development Corporations (Form 8847).
- Welfare-to-Work Credit (Form 8861).
- New Markets Credit (Form 8874).
- Credit for Small Employer Pension Plan Startup Costs (Form 8881).
- Credit for Employer-Provided Childcare Facilities and Services (Form 8882).

Line 6e, Form 1120 (Line 2b, Form 1120-A)

To figure the minimum tax credit and any carryforward of that credit, use **Form 8827,** Credit for Prior Year Minimum Tax—

Corporations. Also see Form 8827 if any of the corporation's 2002 nonconventional source fuel credit or qualified electric vehicle credit was disallowed solely because of the tentative minimum tax limitation. See section 53(d).

Line 6f (Form 1120 Only)

Enter the amount of any credit from **Form 8860,** Qualified Zone Academy Bond Credit.

Line 9 (Form 1120 Only)

A corporation is taxed as a personal holding company under section 542 if:
- At least 60% of its adjusted ordinary gross income for the tax year is personal holding company income and
- At any time during the last half of the tax year more than 50% in value of its outstanding stock is owned, directly or indirectly, by five or fewer individuals.

See Schedule PH (Form 1120) for definitions and details on how to figure the tax.

Line 10, Form 1120 (Line 5, Form 1120-A)

Include any of the following taxes and interest in the total on line 10 (line 5, Part I, Form 1120-A). Check the appropriate box(es) for the form, if any, used to compute the total.

Recapture of investment credit. If the corporation disposed of investment credit property or changed its use before the end of its useful life or recovery period, it may owe a tax. See **Form 4255,** Recapture of Investment Credit, for details.

Recapture of low-income housing credit. If the corporation disposed of property (or there was a reduction in the qualified basis of the property) for which it took the low-income housing credit, it may owe a tax. See **Form 8611,** Recapture of Low-Income Housing Credit.

Interest due under the look-back methods. If the corporation used the look-back method for certain long-term contracts, see Form 8697 for information on figuring the interest the corporation may have to include. The corporation may also have to include interest due under the look-back method for property depreciated under the income forecast method. See Form 8866.

Other. Additional taxes and interest amounts may be included in the total entered on line 10 (line 5, Part I, Form 1120-A). Check the box for "Other" if the corporation includes any of the taxes and interest discussed below. See *How to report* on page 19 for details on reporting these amounts on an attached schedule.
- Recapture of qualified electric vehicle (QEV) credit. The corporation must recapture part of the QEV credit it claimed in a prior year if, within 3 years of the date the vehicle was placed in service, it ceases to qualify for the credit. See Regulations section 1.30-1 for details on how to figure the recapture.
- Recapture of Indian employment credit. Generally, if an employer terminates the employment of a qualified employee less than 1 year after the date of initial employment, any Indian employment credit allowed for a prior tax year because of

-18-

Figure A.12 *(Continued)*

wages paid or incurred to that employee must be recaptured. For details, see Form 8845 and section 45A.

• Recapture of new markets credit (see Form 8874).

• Recapture of employer-provided childcare facilities and services credit (see Form 8882).

• Tax and interest on a nonqualified withdrawal from a capital construction fund (section 7518).

• Interest on deferred tax attributable to (a) installment sales of certain timeshares and residential lots (section 453(l)(3)) and (b) certain nondealer installment obligations (section 453A(c)).

• Interest due on deferred gain (section 1260(b)).

How to report. If the corporation checked the "Other" box, attach a schedule showing the computation of each item included in the total for line 10 (line 5, Part I, Form 1120-A) and identify the applicable Code section and the type of tax or interest.

Line 11 (Form 1120 Only)

Include any deferred tax on the termination of a section 1294 election applicable to shareholders in a qualified electing fund in the amount entered on line 11. See Form 8621, Part V, and **How to report,** below.

Subtract the following amounts from the total for line 11.

• Deferred tax on the corporation's share of undistributed earnings of a qualified electing fund (see Form 8621, Part II).

• Deferred LIFO recapture tax (section 1363(d)). This tax is the part of the LIFO recapture tax that will be deferred and paid with Form 1120S in the future. To figure the deferred tax, first figure the total LIFO recapture tax. Follow the steps below to figure the total LIFO recapture tax and the deferred amount. Also see the instructions regarding LIFO recapture amount under **Line 10, Other Income,** on page 9.

Step 1. Figure the tax on the corporation's income including the LIFO recapture amount. (Complete Schedule J through line 10, but do not enter a total on line 11 yet.)

Step 2. Using a separate worksheet, complete Schedule J again, but **do not** include the LIFO recapture amount in the corporation's taxable income.

Step 3. Compare the tax in Step 2 to the tax in Step 1. (The difference between the two is the **LIFO recapture tax.**)

Step 4. Multiply the amount figured in Step 3 by 75%. (The result is the **deferred LIFO recapture tax.**)

How to report. Attach a schedule showing the computation of each item included in, or subtracted from, the total for line 11. On the dotted line next to line 11, specify (a) the applicable Code section, (b) the type of tax, and (c) enter the amount of tax. For example, if the corporation is deferring $100 LIFO recapture tax, subtract this amount from the total on line 11, then enter "Section 1363-Deferred Tax-$100" on the dotted line next to line 11.

Schedule K, Form 1120 (Part II, Form 1120-A)

The following instructions apply to Form 1120, page 3, Schedule K, or Form 1120-A, page 2, Part II. Be sure to complete all the items that apply to the corporation.

Question 4 (Form 1120 Only)

Check the "Yes" box for question 4 if:

• The corporation is a subsidiary in an affiliated group (defined below), but is not filing a consolidated return for the tax year with that group or

• The corporation is a subsidiary in a parent-subsidiary controlled group (defined below).

Any corporation that meets either of the requirements above should check the "Yes" box. This applies even if the corporation is a subsidiary member of one group and the parent corporation of another.

Note: *If the corporation is an "excluded member" of a controlled group (see section 1563(b)(2)), it is still considered a member of a controlled group for this purpose.*

Affiliated group. The term "affiliated group" means one or more chains of includible corporations (section 1504(a)) connected through stock ownership with a common parent corporation. The common parent must be an includible corporation and the following requirements **must** be met:

1. The common parent must own directly stock that represents at least 80% of the total voting power and at least 80% of the total value of the stock of at least one of the other includible corporations and

2. Stock that represents at least 80% of the total voting power and at least 80% of the total value of the stock of each of the other corporations (except for the common parent) must be owned directly by one or more of the other includible corporations.

For this purpose, the term "stock" generally does not include any stock that (a) is nonvoting, (b) is nonconvertible, (c) is limited and preferred as to dividends and does not participate significantly in corporate growth, and (d) has redemption and liquidation rights that do not exceed the issue price of the stock (except for a reasonable redemption or liquidation premium). See section 1504(a)(4).

Parent-subsidiary controlled group. The term "parent-subsidiary controlled group" means one or more chains of corporations connected through stock ownership (section 1563(a)(1)). Both of the following requirements **must** be met:

1. At least 80% of the total combined voting power of all classes of voting stock, or at least 80% of the total value of all classes of stock of each corporation in the group (except the parent) must be owned by one or more of the other corporations in the group and

2. The common parent must own at least 80% of the total combined voting power of all classes of stock entitled to vote or at least 80% of the total value of all classes of stock of one or more of the other corporations in the group. Stock owned directly by other members of the group is not counted when computing the voting power or value.

-19-

See section 1563(d)(1) for the definition of "stock" for purposes of determining stock ownership above.

Question 6 (Form 1120-A Only)

Foreign financial accounts. Check the "Yes" box for question 6 if either **1** or **2** below applies to the corporation. Otherwise, check the "No" box:

1. At any time during the 2003 calendar year, the corporation had an interest in or signature or other authority over a bank, securities, or other financial account in a foreign country (see **Form TD F 90-22.1,** Report of Foreign Bank and Financial Accounts); and

• The combined value of the accounts was more than $10,000 at any time during the calendar year and

• The account was **not** with a U.S. military banking facility operated by a U.S. financial institution.

2. The corporation owns more than 50% of the stock in any corporation that would answer "Yes" to item **1** above.

If the "Yes" box is checked for the question:

• Enter the name of the foreign country or countries. Attach a separate sheet if more space is needed.

• File Form TD F 90-22.1 by June 30, 2004, with the Department of the Treasury at the address shown on the form. Because Form TD F 90-22.1 is not a tax form, do not file it with Form 1120-A. You can order Form TD F 90-22.1 by calling 1-800-TAX-FORM (1-800-829-3676) or you can download it from the IRS website at **www.irs.gov.**

Question 7 (Form 1120 Only)

Check the "Yes" box if one foreign person owned at least 25% of **(a)** the total voting power of all classes of stock of the corporation entitled to vote or **(b)** the total value of all classes of stock of the corporation.

The constructive ownership rules of section 318 apply in determining if a corporation is foreign owned. See section 6038A(c)(5) and the related regulations.

Enter on line 7a the percentage owned by the foreign person specified in question 7. On line 7b, write the name of the owner's country.

Note: *If there is more than one 25%-or-more foreign owner, complete lines 7a and 7b for the foreign person with the highest percentage of ownership.*

Foreign person. The term "foreign person" means:

• A foreign citizen or nonresident alien.

• An individual who is a citizen of a U.S. possession (but who is not a U.S. citizen or resident).

• A foreign partnership.

• A foreign corporation.

• Any foreign estate or trust within the meaning of section 7701(a)(31).

• A foreign government (or one of its agencies or instrumentalities) to the extent that it is engaged in the conduct of a commercial activity as described in section 892.

Owner's country. For individuals, the term "owner's country" means the country of residence. For all others, it is the country

Figure A.12 *(Continued)*

167

where incorporated, organized, created, or administered.

Requirement to file Form 5472. If the corporation checked "Yes," it may have to file Form 5472. Generally, a 25% foreign-owned corporation that had a reportable transaction with a foreign or domestic related party during the tax year must file Form 5472.

See Form 5472 for filing instructions and penalties for failure to file.

Item 9, Form 1120
(Item 3, Form 1120-A)

Show any **tax-exempt interest** received or accrued. Include any exempt-interest dividends received as a shareholder in a mutual fund or other RIC.

Item 11 (Form 1120 Only)

If the corporation has an NOL for its 2003 tax year, it may elect under section 172(b)(3) to waive the entire carryback period for the NOL and instead carry the NOL forward to future tax years. To do so, check the box on line 11 and file the tax return by its due date, including extensions (do not attach the statement described in Temporary Regulations section 301.9100-12T). Once made, the election is irrevocable. See Pub. 542, section 172, and Form 1139 for more details.

Corporations filing a **consolidated return** must also attach the statement required by Temporary Regulations section 1.1502-21T(b)(3)(i) or (ii).

Item 12 (Form 1120 Only)

Enter the amount of the NOL carryover to the tax year from prior years, even if some of the loss is used to offset income on this return. The amount to enter is the total of all NOLs generated in prior years but not used to offset income (either as a carryback or carryover) to a tax year prior to 2003. Do not reduce the amount by any NOL deduction reported on line 29a.

Schedule L, Form 1120
(Part III, Form 1120-A)

The balance sheet should agree with the corporation's books and records. Include certificates of deposit as cash on line 1, Schedule L.

Line 5

Include on this line:
- State and local government obligations, the interest on which is excludable from gross income under section 103(a) and
- Stock in a mutual fund or other RIC that distributed exempt-interest dividends during the tax year of the corporation.

Line 26, Form 1120
(Line 21, Form 1120-A)

Some examples of adjustments to report on this line include:
- Unrealized gains and losses on securities held "available for sale."
- Foreign currency translation adjustments.
- The excess of additional pension liability over unrecognized prior service cost.
- Guarantees of employee stock (ESOP) debt.
- Compensation related to employee stock award plans.

If the total adjustment to be entered on line 26 (line 21, Form 1120-A) is a negative amount, enter the amount in parentheses.

Schedule M-1, Form 1120
(Part IV, Form 1120-A)

Line 5c, Form 1120
(Line 5, Form 1120-A)

Include any of the following:
- Meal and entertainment expenses not deductible under section 274(n).
- Expenses for the use of an entertainment facility.
- The part of business gifts over $25.
- Expenses of an individual over $2,000, which are allocable to conventions on cruise ships.
- Employee achievement awards over $400.
- The cost of entertainment tickets over face value (also subject to 50% limit under section 274(n)).
- The cost of skyboxes over the face value of nonluxury box seat tickets.
- The part of luxury water travel expenses not deductible under section 274(m).
- Expenses for travel as a form of education.
- Other nondeductible travel and entertainment expenses.

For more information, see Pub. 542.

Line 7, Form 1120
(Line 6, Form 1120-A)

Include as interest on line 7 (line 6, Form 1120-A), any exempt-interest dividends received as a shareholder in a mutual fund or other RIC.

Paperwork Reduction Act Notice. We ask for the information on these forms to carry out the Internal Revenue laws of the United States. You are required to give us the information. We need it to ensure that you are complying with these laws and to allow us to figure and collect the right amount of tax.

You are not required to provide the information requested on a form that is subject to the Paperwork Reduction Act unless the form displays a valid OMB control number. Books or records relating to a form or its instructions must be retained as long as their contents may become material in the administration of any Internal Revenue law. Generally, tax returns and return information are confidential, as required by section 6103.

The time needed to complete and file the following forms will vary depending on individual circumstances. The estimated average times are:

Form	Recordkeeping	Learning about the law or the form	Preparing the form	Copying, assembling, and sending the form to the IRS
1120	70 hr., 47 min.	42 hr., 1 min.	72 hr., 56 min.	8 hr., 2 min.
1120-A	43 hr., 45 min.	24 hr., 34 min.	49 hr., 3 min.	5 hr., 5 min.
Sch. D (1120)	6 hr., 56 min.	3 hr., 55 min.	6 hr., 3 min.	32 min.
Sch. H (1120)	5 hr., 58 min.	35 min.	43 min.	- - - - -
Sch. N (1120)	3 hr., 35 min.	1 hr., 7 min.	3 hr., 6 min.	32 min.
Sch. PH (1120)	15 hr., 18 min.	6 hr., 12 min.	8 hr., 35 min.	32 min.

If you have comments concerning the accuracy of these time estimates or suggestions for making this form and related schedules simpler, we would be happy to hear from you. You can write to the Tax Products Coordinating Committee, Western Area Distribution Center, Rancho Cordova, CA 95743-0001. **Do not** send the tax form to this address. Instead, see **Where To File** on page 3.

Instructions for Forms 1120 and 1120-A

Figure A.12   *(Continued)*

Form 1120S, U.S. Income Tax Return for an S Corporation

This form looks much like the tax form for C corporations, and it is. The difference is how the $36,000 of ordinary income on line 21 is handled. As we are dealing with the ordinary income of an S corporation, the corporation does not pay tax on it, but the stockholders pay tax on the $36,000 whether or not those earnings are paid over to the stockholders.

In this case, the stockholders not only receive forms W-2 for their salaries of $40,000 each, but they also receive a Form K-1 reporting $12,000 of additional income on which they get to pay income tax. (Only one Form K-1 is reproduced here, but as each of these three stockholders own 33.3 percent of the corporation, each would receive an identical Form K-1.) There is some savings on Social Security tax, however. While the wages are subject to Social Security tax, the stockholders do not pay Social Security tax on the additional $12,000 each, whether or not they actually receive that in cash payments.

The S corporation also made a $1000 contribution to an eligible charity. This item is not deducted in computing the income shared by the stockholders, but one third of that amount is listed separately on the K-1 that each stockholder receives. That stockholder then lists that $333 contribution on his or her individual income tax return as an itemized deduction. (If the stockholder does not itemized deductions, the tax benefit of the charitable contribution is lost to that stockholder.)

While you're looking at Form K-1, glance through the list of income, deduction, and credit items that are listed. Generally, all of those are reported by stockholders as separate items on their individual income tax returns. (This treatment of certain items is often referred to as those items "flowing through" from the corporation to the stockholder's individual tax return.)

Department of the Treasury
Internal Revenue Service

U.S. Income Tax Return for an S Corporation

▶ Do not file this form unless the corporation has timely filed
Form 2553 to elect to be an S corporation.
▶ See separate instructions.

OMB No. 1545-0130

2003

For calendar year 2003, or tax year beginning _____, 2003, and ending _____, 20 ___

A Effective date of election as an S corporation	Use the IRS label. Other- wise, print or type.	Name **CLEAN CAT PROCESSORS, INC.**	C Employer identification number **55 : 5555555**
1/1/03		Number, street, and room or suite no. (If a P.O. box, see page 12 of the instructions.) **111 MAIN ST., SUITE 1**	D Date incorporated **1/1/03**
B Business code number (see pages 31–33 of the insts.) **453910**		City or town, state, and ZIP code **EAST OVERSHOE, VA 55555**	E Total assets (see page 12 of instructions) $ **190,000**

F Check applicable boxes: (1) ☑ Initial return (2) ☐ Final return (3) ☐ Name change (4) ☐ Address change (5) ☐ Amended return
G Enter number of shareholders in the corporation at end of the tax year . . . . ▶

Caution: *Include* **only** *trade or business income and expenses on lines 1a through 21. See page 12 of the instructions for more information.*

Income

1a Gross receipts or sales	**1,000,000**	b Less returns and allowances	c Bal ▶	**1c**	**1,000,000**
2 Cost of goods sold (Schedule A, line 8)			**2**	**600,000**
3 Gross profit. Subtract line 2 from line 1c			**3**	**400,000**
4 Net gain (loss) from Form 4797, Part II, line 18 (attach Form 4797)			**4**	
5 Other income (loss) (attach schedule)			**5**	
6 **Total income (loss).** Add lines 3 through 5. . . . . ▶			**6**	**400,000**

Deductions (see page 13 of the instructions for limitations)

7 Compensation of officers	**7**	**120,000**
8 Salaries and wages (less employment credits)	**8**	**42,500**
9 Repairs and maintenance	**9**	
10 Bad debts	**10**	
11 Rents.	**11**	**12,000**
12 Taxes and licenses	**12**	**1,000**
13 Interest	**13**	**2,000**
14a Depreciation (Attach Form 4562)	14a	**2,000**		
b Depreciation claimed on Schedule A and elsewhere on return . .	14b			
c Subtract line 14b from line 14a			**14c**	**2,000**
15 Depletion **(Do not deduct oil and gas depletion.)**			**15**	
16 Advertising			**16**	**150,000**
17 Pension, profit-sharing, etc., plans			**17**	
18 Employee benefit programs.			**18**	
19 Other deductions (attach schedule)			**19**	**34,500**
20 **Total deductions.** Add the amounts shown in the far right column for lines 7 through 19. ▶			**20**	**364,000**
21 Ordinary income (loss) from trade or business activities. Subtract line 20 from line 6. . . .			**21**	**36,000**

Tax and Payments

22 **Tax: a** Excess net passive income tax (attach schedule) . . .	22a			
b Tax from Schedule D (Form 1120S)	22b			
c Add lines 22a and 22b (see page 17 of the instructions for additional taxes)			**22c**	
23 **Payments: a** 2003 estimated tax payments and amount applied from 2002 return	23a			
b Tax deposited with Form 7004.	23b			
c Credit for Federal tax paid on fuels (attach Form 4136) . . .	23c			
d Add lines 23a through 23c			**23d**	
24 Estimated tax penalty (See page 17 of instructions). Check if Form 2220 is attached . ▶ ☐			**24**	
25 **Tax due.** If line 23d is smaller than the total of lines 22c and 24, enter amount owed. . .			**25**	**0**
26 **Overpayment.** If line 23d is larger than the total of lines 22c and 24, enter amount overpaid .			**26**	
27 Enter amount of line 26 you want: **Credited to 2004 estimated tax** ▶		Refunded ▶	**27**	

Sign Here

Under penalties of perjury, I declare that I have examined this return, including accompanying schedules and statements, and to the best of my knowledge and belief, it is true, correct, and complete. Declaration of preparer (other than taxpayer) is based on all information of which preparer has any knowledge.

▶ Signature of officer ___ Date ___ ▶ Title ___

May the IRS discuss this return with the preparer shown below (see instructions)? ☐ Yes ☐ No

Paid Preparer's Use Only

Preparer's signature ▶	Date	Check if self-employed ☐	Preparer's SSN or PTIN
Firm's name (or yours if self-employed), address, and ZIP code ▶		EIN	
		Phone no. ( )	

For Paperwork Reduction Act Notice, see the separate instructions.   Cat. No. 11510H   Form **1120S** (2003)

Figure A.13   IRS Form 1120S (U.S. Income Tax Return for an S Corporation)

Schedule A   Cost of Goods Sold (see page 18 of the instructions)

1	Inventory at beginning of year	1	0
2	Purchases	2	720,000
3	Cost of labor	3	
4	Additional section 263A costs (attach schedule)	4	
5	Other costs (attach schedule)	5	
6	**Total.** Add lines 1 through 5	6	720,000
7	Inventory at end of year	7	120,000
8	**Cost of goods sold.** Subtract line 7 from line 6. Enter here and on page 1, line 2	8	600,000

9a Check all methods used for valuing closing inventory: *(i)* ☑ Cost as described in Regulations section 1.471-3

     (ii) ☐ Lower of cost or market as described in Regulations section 1.471-4

     (iii) ☐ Other (specify method used and attach explanation) ▶ ....

  b Check if there was a writedown of subnormal goods as described in Regulations section 1.471-2(c)   ▶ ☐

  c Check if the LIFO inventory method was adopted this tax year for any goods (if checked, attach Form 970)   ▶ ☐

  d If the LIFO inventory method was used for this tax year, enter percentage (or amounts) of closing inventory computed under LIFO | **9d** |

  e If property is produced or acquired for resale, do the rules of Section 263A apply to the corporation?   ☐ Yes   ☑ No

  f Was there any change in determining quantities, cost, or valuations between opening and closing inventory?   ☐ Yes   ☑ No
     If "Yes," attach explanation.

Schedule B   Other Information (see page 19 of instructions)

		Yes	No
1	Check method of accounting: **(a)** ☑ Cash **(b)** ☐ Accrual **(c)** ☐ Other (specify) ▶		
2	See pages 31 through 33 of the instructions and enter the: **(a)** Business activity ▶ **SALES** .... **(b)** Product or service ▶ **PET SUPPLIES**		
3	At the end of the tax year, did the corporation own, directly or indirectly, 50% or more of the voting stock of a domestic corporation? (For rules of attribution, see section 267(c).) If "Yes," attach a schedule showing: **(a)** name, address, and employer identification number and **(b)** percentage owned		✔
4	Was the corporation a member of a controlled group subject to the provisions of section 1561?		✔
5	Check this box if the corporation has filed or is required to file **Form 8264,** Application for Registration of a Tax Shelter ▶ ☐		
6	Check this box if the corporation issued publicly offered debt instruments with original issue discount ▶ ☐		
	If checked, the corporation may have to file **Form 8281,** Information Return for Publicly Offered Original Issue Discount Instruments.		
7	If the corporation: **(a)** was a C corporation before it elected to be an S corporation **or** the corporation acquired an asset with a basis determined by reference to its basis (or the basis of any other property) in the hands of a C corporation **and (b)** has net unrealized built-in gain (defined in section 1374(d)(1)) in excess of the net recognized built-in gain from prior years, enter the net unrealized built-in gain reduced by net recognized built-in gain from prior years ▶ $		
8	Check this box if the corporation had accumulated earnings and profits at the close of the tax year ▶ ☐		
9	Are the corporation's total receipts (see page 19 of the instructions) for the tax year **and** its total assets at the end of the tax year less than $250,000? If "Yes," the corporation is not required to complete Schedules L and M-1.		

Note: *If the corporation had assets or operated a business in a foreign country or U.S. possession, it may be required to attach* **Schedule N (Form 1120),** *Foreign Operations of U.S. Corporations, to its return. See Schedule N for details.*

Schedule K   Shareholders' Shares of Income, Credits, Deductions, etc.

	(a) Pro rata share items		(b) Total amount
1	Ordinary income (loss) from trade or business activities (page 1, line 21)	1	36,000
2	Net income (loss) from rental real estate activities (attach Form 8825)	2	
3a	Gross income from other rental activities **3a**		
b	Expenses from other rental activities (attach schedule) **3b**		
c	Net income (loss) from other rental activities. Subtract line 3b from line 3a	3c	
4	Portfolio income (loss):		
a	Interest income	4a	
b	Dividends: **(1)** Qualified dividends ▶ .... **(2)** Total ordinary dividends ▶	4b(2)	
c	Royalty income	4c	
d	Net short-term capital gain (loss): **(1)** Post-May 5, 2003 ▶ .... **(2)** Entire year ▶	4d(2)	
e	Net long-term capital gain (loss): **(1)** Post-May 5, 2003 ▶ .... **(2)** Entire year ▶	4e(2)	
f	Other portfolio income (loss) (attach schedule)	4f	
5	Net section 1231 gain (loss) (attach Form 4797): **(a)** Post-May 5, 2003 ▶ .... **(b)** Entire year ▶	5(b)	
6	Other income (loss) (attach schedule)	6	

Income (Loss)

Form **1120S** (2003)

FIGURE A.13   *(Continued)*

Schedule K   **Shareholders' Shares of Income, Credits, Deductions, etc.** *(continued)*

		(a) Pro rata share items		(b) Total amount
Deductions	7	Charitable contributions (attach schedule)	7	1,000
	8	Section 179 expense deduction (attach Form 4562)	8	
	9	Deductions related to portfolio income (loss) (itemize)	9	
	10	Other deductions (attach schedule)	10	
Investment Interest	11a	Interest expense on investment debts	11a	
	b (1)	Investment income included on lines 4a, 4b(2), 4c, and 4f on page 2	11b(1)	
	(2)	Investment expenses included on line 9 above	11b(2)	
Credits	12a	Credit for alcohol used as a fuel (attach Form 6478)	12a	
	b	Low-income housing credit:		
	(1)	From partnerships to which section 42(j)(5) applies	12b(1)	
	(2)	Other than on line 12b(1)	12b(2)	
	c	Qualified rehabilitation expenditures related to rental real estate activities (attach Form 3468)	12c	
	d	Credits (other than credits shown on lines 12b and 12c) related to rental real estate activities	12d	
	e	Credits related to other rental activities	12e	
	13	Other credits	13	
Adjustments and Tax Preference Items	14a	Depreciation adjustment on property placed in service after 1986	14a	
	b	Adjusted gain or loss	14b	
	c	Depletion (other than oil and gas)	14c	
	d (1)	Gross income from oil, gas, or geothermal properties	14d(1)	
	(2)	Deductions allocable to oil, gas, or geothermal properties	14d(2)	
	e	Other adjustments and tax preference items (attach schedule)	14e	
Foreign Taxes	15a	Name of foreign country or U.S. possession ▶		
	b	Gross income from all sources	15b	
	c	Gross income sourced at shareholder level	15c	
	d	Foreign gross income sourced at corporate level:		
	(1)	Passive	15d(1)	
	(2)	Listed categories (attach schedule)	15d(2)	
	(3)	General limitation	15d(3)	
	e	Deductions allocated and apportioned at shareholder level:		
	(1)	Interest expense	15e(1)	
	(2)	Other	15e(2)	
	f	Deductions allocated and apportioned at corporate level to foreign source income:		
	(1)	Passive	15f(1)	
	(2)	Listed categories (attach schedule)	15f(2)	
	(3)	General limitation	15f(3)	
	g	Total foreign taxes (check one): ▶ ☐ Paid ☐ Accrued	15g	
	h	Reduction in taxes available for credit (attach schedule)	15h	
Other	16	Section 59(e)(2) expenditures: **a** Type ▶ .... **b** Amount ▶	16b	
	17	Tax-exempt interest income	17	
	18	Other tax-exempt income	18	
	19	Nondeductible expenses	19	
	20	Total property distributions (including cash) other than dividends reported on line 22 below	20	
	21	Other items and amounts required to be reported separately to shareholders (attach schedule)		
	22	Total dividend distributions paid from accumulated earnings and profits	22	
	23	**Income (loss).** (Required only if Schedule M-1 must be completed.) Combine lines 1 through 6 in column (b). From the result, subtract the sum of lines 7 through 11a, 15g, and 16b	23	35,000

FIGURE A.13   *(Continued)*

Note: The corporation is not required to complete Schedules L and M-1 if question 9 of Schedule B is answered "Yes."

Schedule L	Balance Sheets per Books	Beginning of tax year		End of tax year	
	Assets	(a)	(b)	(c)	(d)
1	Cash		FIRST YEAR		12,000
2a	Trade notes and accounts receivable			50,000	
b	Less allowance for bad debts				50,000
3	Inventories				120,000
4	U.S. government obligations				
5	Tax-exempt securities				
6	Other current assets (attach schedule)				
7	Loans to shareholders				
8	Mortgage and real estate loans				
9	Other investments (attach schedule)				
10a	Buildings and other depreciable assets			10,000	
b	Less accumulated depreciation			2,000	8,000
11a	Depletable assets				
b	Less accumulated depletion				
12	Land (net of any amortization)				
13a	Intangible assets (amortizable only)				
b	Less accumulated amortization				
14	Other assets (attach schedule)				
15	Total assets				190,000
	Liabilities and Shareholders' Equity				
16	Accounts payable				55,000
17	Mortgages, notes, bonds payable in less than 1 year				
18	Other current liabilities (attach schedule)				
19	Loans from shareholders				
20	Mortgages, notes, bonds payable in 1 year or more				40,000
21	Other liabilities (attach schedule)				
22	Capital stock				75,000
23	Additional paid-in capital				
24	Retained earnings				20,000
25	Adjustments to shareholders' equity (attach schedule)				
26	Less cost of treasury stock		( )		( )
27	Total liabilities and shareholders' equity				190,000

Schedule M-1	Reconciliation of Income (Loss) per Books With Income (Loss) per Return			
1	Net income (loss) per books	36,000	5 Income recorded on books this year not included on Schedule K, lines 1 through 6 (itemize):	
2	Income included on Schedule K, lines 1 through 6, not recorded on books this year (itemize):		a Tax-exempt interest $	
3	Expenses recorded on books this year not included on Schedule K, lines 1 through 11a, 15g, and 16b (itemize):		6 Deductions included on Schedule K, lines 1 through 11a, 15g, and 16b, not charged against book income this year (itemize):	
a	Depreciation $		a Depreciation $	
b	Travel and entertainment $		7 Add lines 5 and 6	
4	Add lines 1 through 3	36,000	8 Income (loss) (Schedule K, line 23). Line 4 less line 7	36,000

Schedule M-2	Analysis of Accumulated Adjustments Account, Other Adjustments Account, and Shareholders' Undistributed Taxable Income Previously Taxed (see page 29 of the instructions)	(a) Accumulated adjustments account	(b) Other adjustments account	(c) Shareholders' undistributed taxable income previously taxed
1	Balance at beginning of tax year	0		
2	Ordinary income from page 1, line 21	36,000		
3	Other additions			
4	Loss from page 1, line 21	( )		
5	Other reductions	( )	( )	
6	Combine lines 1 through 5	36,000		
7	Distributions other than dividend distributions	15,000		
8	Balance at end of tax year. Subtract line 7 from line 6	21,000		

Form **1120S** (2003)

FIGURE A.13 *(Continued)*

6711

Shareholder's Share of Income, Credits, Deductions, etc.

▶ See separate instructions.

OMB No. 1545-0130

Department of the Treasury
Internal Revenue Service

For calendar year 2003 or tax year
beginning _____ , 2003, and ending _____ , 20 ____

2003

Shareholder's identifying number ▶	000-00-0000	Corporation's identifying number ▶	55 : 5555555

Shareholder's name, address, and ZIP code	Corporation's name, address, and ZIP code
ANNE WHO 234 CAT COURT EAST OVERSHOE, VA 55555	CLEAN CAT PROCESSORS, INC. 111 MAIN ST, SUITE 1 EAST OVERSHOE, VA 55555

A Shareholder's percentage of stock ownership for tax year (see instructions for Schedule K-1) . . . . ▶ ___33.3___ %

B Internal Revenue Service Center where corporation filed its return ▶ **CINCINNATI, OH**

C Tax shelter registration number (see instructions for Schedule K-1) . . . . ▶ _____

D Check applicable boxes: **(1)** ☐ Final K-1 **(2)** ☐ Amended K-1

	(a) Pro rata share items		(b) Amount	(c) Form 1040 filers enter the amount in column (b) on:
Income (Loss)	1 Ordinary income (loss) from trade or business activities . . .	1	12,000	See page 4 of the Shareholder's Instructions for Schedule K-1 (Form 1120S).
	2 Net income (loss) from rental real estate activities	2		
	3 Net income (loss) from other rental activities	3		
	4 Portfolio income (loss):			
	a Interest income	4a		Form 1040, line 8a
	b (1) Qualified dividends	4b(1)		Form 1040, line 9b
	(2) Total ordinary dividends	4b(2)		Form 1040, line 9a
	c Royalty income	4c		Sch. E, Part I, line 4
	d (1) Net short-term capital gain (loss) (post-May 5, 2003) . . .	4d(1)		Sch. D, line 5, col. (g)
	(2) Net short-term capital gain (loss) (entire year)	4d(2)		Sch. D, line 5, col. (f)
	e (1) Net long-term capital gain (loss) (post-May 5, 2003) . . .	4e(1)		Sch. D, line 12, col. (g)
	(2) Net long-term capital gain (loss) (entire year)	4e(2)		Sch. D, line 12, col. (f)
	f Other portfolio income (loss) (attach schedule)	4f		(Enter on applicable line of your return.)
	5a Net section 1231 gain (loss) (post-May 5, 2003)	5a		See Shareholder's Instructions for Schedule K-1 (Form 1120S).
	b Net section 1231 gain (loss) (entire year)	5b		
	6 Other income (loss) (attach schedule)	6		(Enter on applicable line of your return.)
Deductions	7 Charitable contributions (attach schedule)	7	333	Sch. A, line 15 or 16
	8 Section 179 expense deduction	8		See page 5 of the Shareholder's Instructions for Schedule K-1 (Form 1120S).
	9 Deductions related to portfolio income (loss) (attach schedule) .	9		
	10 Other deductions (attach schedule)	10		
Investment Interest	11a Interest expense on investment debts	11a		Form 4952, line 1
	b (1) Investment income included on lines 4a, 4b(2), 4c, and 4f above	11b(1)		See Shareholder's Instructions for Schedule K-1 (Form 1120S).
	(2) Investment expenses included on line 9 above	11b(2)		
Credits	12a Credit for alcohol used as fuel	12a		Form 6478, line 10
	b Low-income housing credit:			
	(1) From section 42(j)(5) partnerships	12b(1)		Form 8586, line 5
	(2) Other than on line 12b(1)	12b(2)		
	c Qualified rehabilitation expenditures related to rental real estate activities	12c		See pages 6 and 7 of the Shareholder's Instructions for Schedule K-1 (Form 1120S).
	d Credits (other than credits shown on lines 12b and 12c) related to rental real estate activities	12d		
	e Credits related to other rental activities.	12e		
	13 Other credits	13		

For Paperwork Reduction Act Notice, see the Instructions for Form 1120S.   Cat. No. 11520D   **Schedule K-1 (Form 1120S) 2003**

Figure A.14 Schedule K-1 (Shareholder's Share of Income, Credits, Deductions, etc.)

	(a) Pro rata share items		(b) Amount	(c) Form 1040 filers enter the amount in column (b) on:
Adjustments and Tax Preference Items	**14a** Depreciation adjustment on property placed in service after 1986	**14a**		See page 6 of the Shareholder's Instructions for Schedule K-1 (Form 1120S) and Instructions for Form 6251
	b Adjusted gain or loss	**14b**		
	c Depletion (other than oil and gas)	**14c**		
	d (1) Gross income from oil, gas, or geothermal properties . .	**14d(1)**		
	(2) Deductions allocable to oil, gas, or geothermal properties .	**14d(2)**		
	e Other adjustments and tax preference items (attach schedule) .	**14e**		
Foreign Taxes	**15a** Name of foreign country or U.S. possession ▶			Form 1116, Part I
	b Gross income from all sources	**15b**		
	c Gross income sourced at shareholder level	**15c**		
	d Foreign gross income sourced at corporate level:			
	(1) Passive	**15d(1)**		
	(2) Listed categories (attach schedule)	**15d(2)**		
	(3) General limitation	**15d(3)**		
	e Deductions allocated and apportioned at shareholder level:			
	(1) Interest expense.	**15e(1)**		
	(2) Other	**15e(2)**		
	f Deductions allocated and apportioned at corporate level to foreign source income:			
	(1) Passive	**15f(1)**		
	(2) Listed categories (attach schedule)	**15f(2)**		
	(3) General limitation	**15f(3)**		
	g Total foreign taxes (check one): ▶ ☐ Paid ☐ Accrued . .	**15g**		Form 1116, Part II
	h Reduction in taxes available for credit (attach schedule) . . .	**15h**		See Instructions for Form 1116
Other	**16** Section 59(e)(2) expenditures: **a** Type ▶			See Shareholder's Instructions for Schedule K-1 (Form 1120S).
	b Amount	**16b**		
	17 Tax-exempt interest income	**17**		Form 1040, line 8b
	18 Other tax-exempt income	**18**		
	19 Nondeductible expenses	**19**		See page 7 of the Shareholder's Instructions for Schedule K-1 (Form 1120S).
	20 Property distributions (including cash) other than dividend distributions reported to you on Form 1099-DIV	**20**		
	21 Amount of loan repayments for "Loans From Shareholders" . .	**21**		
	22 Recapture of low-income housing credit:			
	a From section 42(j)(5) partnerships	**22a**		Form 8611, line 8
	b Other than on line 22a	**22b**		
Supplemental Information	**23** Supplemental information required to be reported separately to each shareholder (attach additional schedules if more space is needed):			

FIGURE A.14   *(Continued)*

SCHEDULE K-1
(Form 1120S)

Department of the Treasury
Internal Revenue Service

Shareholder's Share of Income, Credits, Deductions, etc.

▶ See separate instructions.

For calendar year 2003 or tax year
beginning _____, 2003, and ending _____, 20____

OMB No. 1545-0130

2003

Shareholder's identifying number ▶	111-11-1111	Corporation's identifying number ▶	55 : 5555555

Shareholder's name, address, and ZIP code	Corporation's name, address, and ZIP code
BAXTER WHEN 345 CAT AVENUE EAST OVERSHOE, VA 55555	CLEAN CAT PROCESSORS, INC. 111 MAIN ST, SUITE 1 EAST OVERSHOE, VA 55555

A Shareholder's percentage of stock ownership for tax year (see instructions for Schedule K-1) . . . . ▶ __33.3__ %

B Internal Revenue Service Center where corporation filed its return ▶ CINCINNATI, OH

C Tax shelter registration number (see instructions for Schedule K-1) . . . . ▶ ....

D Check applicable boxes: **(1)** ☐ Final K-1 **(2)** ☐ Amended K-1

	(a) Pro rata share items		(b) Amount	(c) Form 1040 filers enter the amount in column (b) on:
Income (Loss)	**1** Ordinary income (loss) from trade or business activities . . .	**1**	12,000	See page 4 of the Shareholder's Instructions for Schedule K-1 (Form 1120S).
	2 Net income (loss) from rental real estate activities	**2**		
	3 Net income (loss) from other rental activities	**3**		
	4 Portfolio income (loss):			
	a Interest income	**4a**		Form 1040, line 8a
	b (1) Qualified dividends	**4b(1)**		Form 1040, line 9b
	(2) Total ordinary dividends	**4b(2)**		Form 1040, line 9a
	c Royalty income	**4c**		Sch. E, Part I, line 4
	d (1) Net short-term capital gain (loss) (post-May 5, 2003) . . .	**4d(1)**		Sch. D, line 5, col. (g)
	(2) Net short-term capital gain (loss) (entire year)	**4d(2)**		Sch. D, line 5, col. (f)
	e (1) Net long-term capital gain (loss) (post-May 5, 2003) . .	**4e(1)**		Sch. D, line 12, col. (g)
	(2) Net long-term capital gain (loss) (entire year)	**4e(2)**		Sch. D, line 12, col. (f)
	f Other portfolio income (loss) (attach schedule)	**4f**		(Enter on applicable line of your return.)
	5a Net section 1231 gain (loss) (post-May 5, 2003)	**5a**		See Shareholder's Instructions for Schedule K-1 (Form 1120S).
	b Net section 1231 gain (loss) (entire year)	**5b**		
	6 Other income (loss) (attach schedule)	**6**		(Enter on applicable line of your return.)
Deductions	**7** Charitable contributions (attach schedule)	**7**	333	Sch. A, line 15 or 16
	8 Section 179 expense deduction	**8**		See page 5 of the Shareholder's Instructions for Schedule K-1 (Form 1120S).
	9 Deductions related to portfolio income (loss) (attach schedule) .	**9**		
	10 Other deductions (attach schedule)	**10**		
Investment Interest	**11a** Interest expense on investment debts	**11a**		Form 4952, line 1
	b (1) Investment income included on lines 4a, 4b(2), 4c, and 4f above	**11b(1)**		See Shareholder's Instructions for Schedule K-1 (Form 1120S).
	(2) Investment expenses included on line 9 above	**11b(2)**		
Credits	**12a** Credit for alcohol used as fuel	**12a**		Form 6478, line 10
	b Low-income housing credit:			
	(1) From section 42(j)(5) partnerships	**12b(1)**		Form 8586, line 5
	(2) Other than on line 12b(1)	**12b(2)**		
	c Qualified rehabilitation expenditures related to rental real estate activities	**12c**		See pages 6 and 7 of the Shareholder's Instructions for Schedule K-1 (Form 1120S).
	d Credits (other than credits shown on lines 12b and 12c) related to rental real estate activities	**12d**		
	e Credits related to other rental activities.	**12e**		
	13 Other credits	**13**		

For Paperwork Reduction Act Notice, see the Instructions for Form 1120S.   Cat. No. 11520D   **Schedule K-1 (Form 1120S) 2003**

FIGURE A.14 *(Continued)*

SCHEDULE K-1
(Form 1120S)

Department of the Treasury
Internal Revenue Service

Shareholder's Share of Income, Credits, Deductions, etc.

▶ See separate instructions.

For calendar year 2003 or tax year
beginning _____, 2003, and ending _____, 20 ___

OMB No. 1545-0130

2003

Shareholder's identifying number ▶ 222-22-2222	Corporation's identifying number ▶ 55 : 5555555
Shareholder's name, address, and ZIP code CAROL WHAT 678 FELINE FREEWAY EAST OVERSHOE, VA 55555	Corporation's name, address, and ZIP code CLEAN CAT PROCESSORS, INC. 111 MAIN ST, SUITE 1 EAST OVERSHOE, VA 55555

A Shareholder's percentage of stock ownership for tax year (see instructions for Schedule K-1) . . . . . . ▶ ___33.3___ %
B Internal Revenue Service Center where corporation filed its return ▶ CINCINATTI, OH
C Tax shelter registration number (see instructions for Schedule K-1) . . . . ▶ _____
D Check applicable boxes: **(1)** ☐ Final K-1 **(2)** ☐ Amended K-1

		(a) Pro rata share items		(b) Amount	(c) Form 1040 filers enter the amount in column (b) on:
Income (Loss)	1	Ordinary income (loss) from trade or business activities . . .	1	12,000	See page 4 of the Shareholder's Instructions for Schedule K-1 (Form 1120S).
	2	Net income (loss) from rental real estate activities	2		
	3	Net income (loss) from other rental activities	3		
	4	Portfolio income (loss):			
	a	Interest income	4a		Form 1040, line 8a
	b	**(1)** Qualified dividends	4b(1)		Form 1040, line 9b
		(2) Total ordinary dividends	4b(2)		Form 1040, line 9a
	c	Royalty income	4c		Sch. E, Part I, line 4
	d	**(1)** Net short-term capital gain (loss) (post-May 5, 2003) . . .	4d(1)		Sch. D, line 5, col. (g)
		(2) Net short-term capital gain (loss) (entire year)	4d(2)		Sch. D, line 5, col. (f)
	e	**(1)** Net long-term capital gain (loss) (post-May 5, 2003) . . .	4e(1)		Sch. D, line 12, col. (g)
		(2) Net long-term capital gain (loss) (entire year)	4e(2)		Sch. D, line 12, col. (f)
	f	Other portfolio income (loss) (attach schedule)	4f		(Enter on applicable line of your return.)
	5a	Net section 1231 gain (loss) (post-May 5, 2003)	5a		See Shareholder's Instructions for Schedule K-1 (Form 1120S).
	b	Net section 1231 gain (loss) (entire year)	5b		
	6	Other income (loss) (attach schedule)	6		(Enter on applicable line of your return.)
Deductions	7	Charitable contributions (attach schedule)	7	333	Sch. A, line 15 or 16
	8	Section 179 expense deduction	8		See page 5 of the Shareholder's Instructions for Schedule K-1 (Form 1120S).
	9	Deductions related to portfolio income (loss) (attach schedule) .	9		
	10	Other deductions (attach schedule)	10		
Investment Interest	11a	Interest expense on investment debts	11a		Form 4952, line 1
	b	**(1)** Investment income included on lines 4a, 4b(2), 4c, and 4f above	11b(1)		See Shareholder's Instructions for Schedule K-1 (Form 1120S).
		(2) Investment expenses included on line 9 above	11b(2)		
Credits	12a	Credit for alcohol used as fuel	12a		Form 6478, line 10
	b	Low-income housing credit:			
		(1) From section 42(j)(5) partnerships	12b(1)		Form 8586, line 5
		(2) Other than on line 12b(1)	12b(2)		
	c	Qualified rehabilitation expenditures related to rental real estate activities	12c		See pages 6 and 7 of the Shareholder's Instructions for Schedule K-1 (Form 1120S).
	d	Credits (other than credits shown on lines 12b and 12c) related to rental real estate activities	12d		
	e	Credits related to other rental activities	12e		
	13	Other credits	13		

For Paperwork Reduction Act Notice, see the Instructions for Form 1120S.   Cat. No. 11520D   **Schedule K-1 (Form 1120S) 2003**

FIGURE A.14 *(Continued)*

- By mailing or faxing **Form SS-4,** Application for Employer Identification Number.

If the corporation has not received its EIN by the time the return is due, write "Applied for" in the space for the EIN. For more details, see **Pub. 583,** Starting a Business and Keeping Records. Please call the toll-free Business and Specialty Tax Line at 1-800-829-4933 for assistance in applying for an EIN.

Item E. Total Assets

Enter the corporation's total assets at the end of the tax year, as determined by the accounting method regularly used in maintaining the corporation's books and records. If there were no assets at the end of the tax year, enter "0". If the S election terminated during the tax year, see the instructions for Schedule L on page 28 for special rules that may apply when figuring the corporation's year-end assets.

Item F. Initial Return, Final Return, Name Change, Address Change, and Amended Return

- If this is the corporation's first return, check the "Initial return" box.
- If the corporation has ceased to exist, file Form 1120S and check the "Final return" box. Also check box D(1) on each Schedule K-1 to indicate that it is a final Schedule K-1.
- If the corporation changed its name since it last filed a return, check the box for "Name change." Generally, a corporation must also have amended its articles of incorporation and filed the amendment with the state in which it is incorporated.
- If the corporation has changed its address since it last filed a return, check the box for "Address change."

Note: *If a change in address occurs after the return is filed, use **Form 8822,** Change of Address, to notify the IRS of the new address.*

- If this amends a previously filed return, check the box for "Amended return." If Schedules K-1 are also being amended, check box D(2) on each Schedule K-1.

Income

⚠️ CAUTION *Report only trade or business activity income or loss on lines 1a through 6. **Do not report rental activity income or portfolio income or loss on these lines.** (See **Passive Activity Limitations** beginning on page 8 for definitions of rental income and portfolio income.) Rental activity income and portfolio income are reported on Schedules K and K-1 (rental real estate activities are also reported on Form 8825).*

Tax-exempt income. Do not include any tax-exempt income on lines 1 through 5. A corporation that receives any exempt income other than interest, or holds any

property or engages in an activity that produces exempt income, reports this income on line 18 of Schedules K and K-1.

Report tax-exempt interest income, including exempt-interest dividends received as a shareholder in a mutual fund or other regulated investment company, on line 17 of Schedules K and K-1.

See **Deductions** beginning on page 13 for information on how to report expenses related to tax-exempt income.

Cancelled debt exclusion. If the S corporation has had debt discharged resulting from a title 11 bankruptcy proceeding, or while insolvent, see **Form 982,** Reduction of Tax Attributes Due to Discharge of Indebtedness, and **Pub. 908,** Bankruptcy Tax Guide.

Line 1. Gross Receipts or Sales

Enter gross receipts or sales from all trade or business operations except those that must be reported on lines 4 and 5. In general, advance payments are reported in the year of receipt. To report income from long-term contracts, see section 460. For special rules for reporting certain advance payments for goods and long-term contracts, see Regulations section 1.451-5. For permissible methods for reporting certain advance payments for services by an accrual method corporation, see Rev. Proc. 71-21,1971-2 C.B. 549.

Installment sales. Generally, the installment method cannot be used for dealer dispositions of property. A "dealer disposition" is any disposition of **(a)** personal property by a person who regularly sells or otherwise disposes of personal property of the same type on the installment plan or **(b)** real property held for sale to customers in the ordinary course of the taxpayer's trade or business.

Exception. These restrictions on using the installment method do not apply to dispositions of property used or produced in a farming business or sales of timeshares and residential lots for which the corporation elects to pay interest under section 453(I)(3).

Enter on line 1a the gross profit on collections from installment sales for any of the following:
- Dealer dispositions of property before March 1, 1986.
- Dispositions of property used or produced in the trade or business of farming.
- Certain dispositions of timeshares and residential lots reported under the installment method.

Attach a schedule showing the following information for the current and the 3 preceding years:
- Gross sales.
- Cost of goods sold.
- Gross profits.
- Percentage of gross profits to gross sales.
- Amount collected.
- Gross profit on the amount collected.

-12-

Specific Instructions

Name

If the corporation did not receive a label, print or type the corporation's true name (as set forth in the corporate charter or other legal document creating it).

Address

Include the suite, room, or other unit number after the street address. If a preaddressed label is used, include the information on the label. If the Post Office does not deliver to the street address and the corporation has a P.O. box, show the box number instead of the street address.

Item B. Business Code No.

See the **Codes for Principal Business Activity** on pages 31 through 33 of these instructions.

Item C. Employer Identification Number (EIN)

Enter the corporation's EIN. If the corporation does not have an EIN, it must apply for one. An EIN may be applied for:
- Online—Click on the EIN link at **www.irs.gov/businesses/small.** The EIN is issued immediately once the application information is validated.
- By telephone at 1-800-829-4933 from 7:30am to 5:30pm in the corporation's local time zone.

FIGURE A.15   Instructions for Form K-1

Line 2. Cost of Goods Sold

See the instructions for Schedule A on page 17.

Line 4. Net Gain (Loss) From Form 4797

 Include only ordinary gains or losses from the sale, exchange, or involuntary conversion of assets used in a trade or business activity. Ordinary gains or losses from the sale, exchange, or involuntary conversions of assets used in rental activities are reported separately on Schedule K as part of the net income (loss) from the rental activity in which the property was used.

A corporation that is a partner in a partnership must include on **Form 4797,** Sales of Business Property, its share of ordinary gains (losses) from sales, exchanges, or involuntary or compulsory conversions (other than casualties or thefts) of the partnership's trade or business assets.

If the corporation sold or otherwise disposed of business property for which the corporation passed through a section 179 expense deduction to its shareholders, the disposition must be reported separately on line 23 of Schedule K-1 instead of being reported on Form 4797.

Line 5. Other Income (Loss)

Enter on line 5 trade or business income (loss) that is not included on lines 1a through 4. List the type and amount of income on an attached schedule. If the corporation has only one item of other income, describe it in parentheses on line 5. Examples of other income include:
- Interest income derived in the ordinary course of the corporation's trade or business, such as interest charged on receivable balances.
- Recoveries of bad debts deducted in prior years under the specific charge-off method.
- Taxable income from insurance proceeds.
- The amount of credit figured on **Form 6478,** Credit for Alcohol Used as Fuel.

The corporation must also include in other income the:
- Recapture amount under section 280F if the business use of listed property drops to 50% or less. To figure the recapture amount, the corporation must complete Part IV of Form 4797.
- Recapture of any deduction previously taken under section 179A. The S corporation may have to recapture part or all of the benefit of any allowable deduction for qualified clean-fuel vehicle property (or clean-fuel vehicle refueling property), if the property ceases to qualify for the deduction within 3 years after the date it was placed in service. See **Pub. 535,** Business Expenses, for details on how to figure the recapture.

If "other income" consists of only one item, identify it by showing the account caption in parentheses on line 5. A

separate schedule need not be attached to the return in this case.

Do not net any expense item (such as interest) with a similar income item. Report all trade or business expenses on lines 7 through 19.

Do not include items requiring separate computations by shareholders that must be reported on Schedules K and K-1. See the instructions for Schedules K and K-1 beginning on page 19.

Ordinary Income (Loss) From a Partnership, Estate, or Trust

Enter the ordinary trade or business income (loss) from a partnership shown on Schedule K-1 (Form 1065), from an estate or trust shown on Schedule K-1 (Form 1041), or from a foreign partnership, estate, or trust. Show the partnership's, estate's, or trust's name, address, and EIN (if any) on a separate statement attached to this return. If the amount entered is from more than one source, identify the amount from each source.

Do not include portfolio income or rental activity income (loss) from a partnership, estate, or trust on this line. Instead, report these amounts on the applicable lines of Schedules K and K-1, or on line 20a of Form 8825 if the amount is from a rental real estate activity.

Ordinary income or loss from a partnership that is a publicly traded partnership is not reported on this line. Instead, report the amount separately on line 6 of Schedules K and K-1.

Treat shares of other items separately reported on Schedule K-1 issued by the other entity as if the items were realized or incurred by the S corporation.

If there is a loss from a partnership, the amount of the loss that may be claimed is subject to the at-risk and basis limitations as appropriate.

If the tax year of the S corporation does not coincide with the tax year of the partnership, estate, or trust, include the ordinary income (loss) from the other entity in the tax year in which the other entity's tax year ends.

Deductions

 Report only trade or business activity expenses on lines 7 through 19.

Do not report rental activity expenses or deductions allocable to portfolio income on these lines. Rental activity expenses are separately reported on Form 8825 or line 3 of Schedules K and K-1. Deductions allocable to portfolio income are separately reported on line 9 of Schedules K and K-1. See **Passive Activity Limitations** beginning on page 8 for more information on rental activities and portfolio income.

Do not report any nondeductible amounts (such as expenses connected with the production of tax-exempt income) on lines 7 through 19. Instead, report

nondeductible expenses on line 19 of Schedules K and K-1. If an expense is connected with both taxable income and nontaxable income, allocate a reasonable part of the expense to each kind of income.

Limitations on Deductions

Section 263A uniform capitalization rules. The uniform capitalization rules of section 263A require corporations to capitalize or include in inventory costs certain costs incurred in connection with:
- The production of real and tangible personal property held in inventory or held for sale in the ordinary course of business.
- Real property or personal property (tangible and intangible) acquired for resale.
- The production of real property and tangible personal property by a corporation for use in its trade or business or in an activity engaged in for profit.

The costs required to be capitalized under section 263A are not deductible until the property to which the costs relate is sold, used, or otherwise disposed of by the corporation.

Exceptions. Section 263A **does not** apply to:
- Personal property acquired for resale if the taxpayer's average annual gross receipts for the 3 prior tax years are $10 million or less.
- Timber.
- Most property produced under a long-term contract.
- Certain property produced in a farming business. See **Special rules for certain corporations engaged in farming** on page 14.

The corporation must report the following costs separately to the shareholders for purposes of determinations under section 59(e):
- Research and experimental costs under section 174.
- Intangible drilling costs for oil, gas, and geothermal property.
- Mining exploration and development costs.
- Inventoriable items accounted for in the same manner as materials and supplies that are not incidental. See **Schedule A. Cost of Goods Sold** on page 17 for details.

Tangible personal property produced by a corporation includes a film, sound recording, video tape, book, or similar property.

Indirect costs. Corporations subject to the rules are required to capitalize not only direct costs but an allocable portion of most indirect costs (including taxes) that benefit the assets produced or acquired for resale or are incurred by reason of the performance of production or resale activities.

For inventory, some of the *indirect costs* that must be capitalized are:
- Administration expenses.
- Taxes.
- Depreciation.
- Insurance.

-13-

FIGURE A.15 *(Continued)*

- Compensation paid to officers attributable to services.
- Rework labor.
- Contributions to pension, stock bonus, and certain profit-sharing, annuity, or deferred compensation plans.

Regulations section 1.263A-1(e)(3) specifies other indirect costs that relate to production or resale activities that must be capitalized and those that may be currently deducted.

Interest expense paid or incurred during the production period of designated property must be capitalized and is governed by special rules. For more details, see Regulations sections 1.263A-8 through 1.263A-15.

For more details on the uniform capitalization rules, see Regulations sections 1.263A-1 through 1.263A-3.

Special rules for certain corporations engaged in farming. For S corporations not required to use the accrual method of accounting, the rules of section 263A **do not** apply to expenses of raising any:
- Animal or
- Plant that has a preproductive period of 2 years or less.

Shareholders of S corporations not required to use the accrual method of accounting may elect to currently deduct the preproductive period expenses of certain plants that have a preproductive period of more than 2 years. Because each shareholder makes the election to deduct these expenses, the corporation should not capitalize them. Instead, the corporation should report the expenses separately on line 21 of Schedule K and each shareholder's pro rata share on line 23 of Schedule K-1.

See sections 263A(d) and (e) and Regulations section 1.263A-4 for definitions and other details.

Transactions between related taxpayers. Generally, an accrual basis S corporation may deduct business expenses and interest owed to a related party (including any shareholder) **only** in the tax year of the corporation that includes the day on which the payment is includible in the income of the related party. See section 267 for details.

Section 291 limitations. If the S corporation was a C corporation for any of the 3 immediately preceding years, the corporation may be required to adjust deductions allowed to the corporation for depletion of iron ore and coal, and the amortizable basis of pollution control facilities. See section 291 to determine the amount of the adjustment.

Business start-up expenses. Business start-up expenses must be capitalized. An election may be made to amortize them over a period of not less than 60 months. See section 195 and Regulations section 1.195-1.

Reducing certain expenses for which credits are allowable. For each credit listed below, the corporation must reduce the otherwise allowable deductions for expenses used to figure the credit by the amount of the current year credit.

- The work opportunity credit,
- The welfare-to-work credit,
- The credit for increasing research activities,
- The enhanced oil recovery credit,
- The disabled access credit,
- The empowerment zone and renewal community employment credit,
- The Indian employment credit,
- The credit for employer social security and Medicare taxes paid on certain employee tips,
- The orphan drug credit, and
- The New York Liberty Zone business employee credit.

If the corporation has any of these credits, be sure to figure each current year credit before figuring the deductions for expenses on which the credit is based.

Line 7. Compensation of Officers and Line 8—Salaries and Wages

 Distributions and other payments by an S corporation to a corporate officer must be treated as wages to the extent the amounts are reasonable compensation for services to the corporation.

Enter on line 7 the total compensation of all officers paid or incurred in the trade or business activities of the corporation. Enter on line 8 the amount of salaries and wages paid or incurred to employees (other than officers) during the tax year in the trade or business activities of the corporation.

Do not include amounts reported elsewhere on the return, such as salaries and wages included in cost of goods sold, elective contributions to a section 401(k) cash or deferred arrangement, or amounts contributed under a salary reduction SEP agreement or a SIMPLE IRA plan.

Reduce the amounts on lines 7 and 8 by any applicable employment credits from:
- **Form 5884,** Work Opportunity Credit,
- **Form 8861,** Welfare-to-Work Credit,
- **Form 8844,** Empowerment Zone and Renewable Community Employment Credit,
- **Form 8845,** Indian Employment Credit, and
- **Form 8884,** New York Liberty Zone Business Employee Credit.

See the instructions for these forms for more information.

Include fringe benefit expenditures made on behalf of officers and employees owning more than 2% of the corporation's stock. Also report these fringe benefits as wages in box 1 of Form W-2. Do not include amounts paid or incurred for fringe benefits of officers and employees owning 2% or less of the corporation's stock. These amounts are reported on line 18, page 1, of Form 1120S. See the instructions for that line for information on the types of expenditures that are treated as fringe benefits and for the stock ownership rules.

Report amounts paid for health insurance coverage for a more than 2% shareholder (including that shareholder's spouse and dependents) as an information item in box 14 of that shareholder's Form W-2. For 2003, a more-than-2% shareholder may be allowed to deduct up to 100% of such amounts on Form 1040, line 29.

If a shareholder or a member of the family of one or more shareholders of the corporation renders services or furnishes capital to the corporation for which reasonable compensation is not paid, the IRS may make adjustments in the items taken into account by such individuals and the value of such services or capital. See section 1366(e).

Line 9. Repairs and Maintenance

Enter the costs of incidental repairs and maintenance, such as labor and supplies, that do not add to the value of the property or appreciably prolong its life, but only to the extent that such costs relate to a trade or business activity and are not claimed elsewhere on the return. New buildings, machinery, or permanent improvements that increase the value of the property are not deductible. They are chargeable to capital accounts and may be depreciated or amortized.

Line 10. Bad Debts

Enter the total debts that became worthless in whole or in part during the year, but only to the extent such debts relate to a trade or business activity. Report deductible nonbusiness bad debts as a short-term capital loss on Schedule D (Form 1120S).

 Cash method taxpayers may not claim a bad debt deduction unless the amount was previously included in income.

Line 11. Rents

If the corporation rented or leased a vehicle, enter the total annual rent or lease expense paid or incurred in the trade or business activities of the corporation. Also complete Part V of **Form 4562,** Depreciation and Amortization. If the corporation leased a vehicle for a term of 30 days or more, the deduction for vehicle lease expense may have to be reduced by an amount called the **inclusion amount.** The corporation may have an inclusion amount if:

The lease term began:

After 12/31/02 and before 1/1/04	$18,000
After 12/31/98 and before 1/1/03	$15,500
After 12/31/96 but before 1/1/99	$15,800
After 12/31/94 but before 1/1/97	$15,500
After 12/31/93 but before 1/1/95	$14,600

If the lease term began before January 1, 1994, see **Pub. 463,** Travel, Entertainment, Gift, and Car Expenses, to find out if the corporation has an inclusion amount and how to figure it.

-14-

FIGURE A.15 *(Continued)*

Line 12. Taxes and Licenses

Enter taxes and licenses paid or incurred in the trade or business activities of the corporation, if not reflected in cost of goods sold. Federal import duties and Federal excise and stamp taxes are deductible only if paid or incurred in carrying on the trade or business of the corporation.

Do not deduct the following taxes on line 12:
• Federal income taxes (except for the portion of built-in gains tax allocable to ordinary income), or taxes reported elsewhere on the return.
• Section 901 foreign taxes. Report these taxes separately on line 15g, Schedule K.
• Taxes allocable to a rental activity. Taxes allocable to a rental real estate activity are reported on Form 8825. Taxes allocable to a rental activity other than a rental real estate activity are reported on line 3b of Schedule K.
• Taxes allocable to portfolio income. Report these taxes separately on line 9 of Schedules K and K-1.
• Taxes paid or incurred for the production or collection of income, or for the management, conservation, or maintenance of property held to produce income. Report these taxes separately on line 10 of Schedules K and K-1.

See section 263A(a) for information on capitalization of allocable costs (including taxes) for any property.

• Taxes not imposed on the corporation.
• Taxes, including state or local sales taxes, that are paid or incurred in connection with an acquisition or disposition of property (these taxes must be treated as a part of the cost of the acquired property or, in the case of a disposition, as a reduction in the amount realized on the disposition).
• Taxes assessed against local benefits that increase the value of the property assessed (such as for paving, etc.).
• Taxes deducted elsewhere on the return, such as those reflected in cost of goods sold.

See section 164(d) for apportionment of taxes on real property between seller and purchaser.

Line 13. Interest

Include on line 13 only interest incurred in the trade or business activities of the corporation that is not claimed elsewhere on the return. **Do not** include interest expense:
• On debt used to purchase rental property or debt used in a rental activity. Interest allocable to a rental real estate activity is reported on Form 8825 and is used in arriving at net income (loss) from rental real estate activities on line 2 of Schedules K and K-1. Interest allocable to a rental activity other than a rental real estate activity is included on line 3b of Schedule K and is used in arriving at net income (loss) from a rental activity (other than a rental real estate activity). This net amount is reported on line 3c of Schedule K and line 3 of Schedule K-1.

• Clearly and directly allocable to portfolio or investment income. This interest expense is reported separately on line 11a of Schedule K.
• On debt proceeds allocated to distributions made to shareholders during the tax year. Instead, report such interest on line 10 of Schedules K and K-1. To determine the amount to allocate to distributions to shareholders, see Notice 89-35, 1989-1 C.B. 675.
• On debt required to be allocated to the production of designated property. Interest allocable to designated property produced by an S corporation for its own use or for sale must instead be capitalized. The corporation must also capitalize any interest on debt allocable to an asset used to produce designated property. A shareholder may have to capitalize interest that the shareholder incurs during the tax year for the production expenditures of the S corporation. Similarly, interest incurred by an S corporation may have to be capitalized by a shareholder for the shareholder's own production expenditures. The information required by the shareholder to properly capitalize interest for this purpose must be provided by the corporation on an attachment for line 23 of Schedule K-1. See section 263A(f) and Regulations sections 1.263A-8 through 1.263A-15 for additional information, including the definition of "designated property."

Special rules apply to:
• Allocating interest expense among activities so that the limitations on passive activity losses, investment interest, and personal interest can be properly figured. Generally, interest expense is allocated in the same manner as debt is allocated. Debt is allocated by tracing disbursements of the debt proceeds to specific expenditures. Temporary Regulations section 1.163-8T gives rules for tracing debt proceeds to expenditures.
• Prepaid interest, which generally can only be deducted over the period to which the prepayment applies. See section 461(g) for details.
• Limit the interest deduction if the corporation is a policyholder or beneficiary with respect to a life insurance, endowment, or annuity contract issued after June 8, 1997. For details, see section 264(f). Attach a statement showing the computation of the deduction.

Line 14. Depreciation

Enter on line 14a only the depreciation claimed on assets used in a trade or business activity. See the Instructions for Form 4562 or **Pub. 946,** How To Depreciate Property, to figure the amount of depreciation to enter on this line.

Complete and attach Form 4562 only if the corporation placed property in service during the tax year or claims depreciation on any car or other listed property.

Do not include any section 179 expense deduction on this line. This amount is not deductible by the corporation. Instead, it is passed through

to the shareholders on line 8 of Schedule K-1.

Line 15. Depletion

If the corporation claims a deduction for timber depletion, complete and attach **Form T,** Forest Activities Schedule.

 Do not deduct depletion for oil and gas properties. Each shareholder figures depletion on these properties under section 613A(c)(11). See the instructions on page 26 for Schedule K-1, line 23, item 2, for information on oil and gas depletion that must be supplied to the shareholders by the corporation.

Line 17. Pension, Profit-Sharing, etc., Plans

Enter the deductible contributions not claimed elsewhere on the return made by the corporation for its employees under a qualified pension, profit-sharing, annuity, or simplified employee pension (SEP) or SIMPLE plan, and under any other deferred compensation plan.

If the corporation contributes to an individual retirement arrangement (IRA) for employees, include the contribution in salaries and wages on page 1, line 8, or Schedule A, line 3, and not on line 17.

Employers who maintain a pension, profit-sharing, or other funded deferred compensation plan, whether or not qualified under the Internal Revenue Code and whether or not a deduction is claimed for the current tax year, generally must file the applicable form listed below.
• **Form 5500,** Annual Return/Report of Employee Benefit Plan. File this form for a plan that is not a one-participant plan (see below).
• **Form 5500-EZ,** Annual Return of One-Participant (Owners and Their Spouses) Retirement Plan. File this form for a plan that only covers the owner (or the owner and his or her spouse) but only if the owner (or the owner and his or her spouse) owns the entire business.

There are penalties for failure to file these forms on time and for overstating the pension plan deduction.

Line 18. Employee Benefit Programs

Enter amounts for fringe benefits paid or incurred on behalf of employees owning 2% or less of the corporation's stock. These fringe benefits include **(a)** employer contributions to certain accident and health plans, **(b)** the cost of up to $50,000 of group-term life insurance on an employee's life, and **(c)** meals and lodging furnished for the employer's convenience.

Do not deduct amounts that are an incidental part of a pension, profit-sharing, etc., plan included on line 17 or amounts reported elsewhere on the return.

Report amounts paid on behalf of more than 2% shareholders on line 7 or 8, whichever applies. A shareholder is considered to own more than 2% of the corporation's stock if that person owns on any day during the tax year more than 2% of the outstanding stock of the corporation

-15-

FIGURE A.15 *(Continued)*

or stock possessing more than 2% of the combined voting power of all stock of the corporation. See section 318 for attribution rules.

Line 19. Other Deductions

Enter the total of all allowable trade or business deductions that are **not** deductible elsewhere on page 1 of Form 1120S. Attach a schedule listing by type and amount each deduction included on this line.

Examples of other deductions include:
• Amortization (except as noted below)— see the Instructions for Form 4562 for more information. Complete and attach Form 4562 if the corporation is claiming amortization of costs that began during the tax year.
• Insurance premiums.
• Legal and professional fees.
• Supplies used and consumed in the business.
• Utilities.

Also, see **Special Rules** below for limits on certain other deductions.

Do not deduct on line 19:
• Items that must be reported separately on Schedules K and K-1.
• Qualified expenditures to which an election under section 59(e) may apply. See the instructions on page 26 for lines 16a and 16b of Schedule K-1 for details on treatment of these items.
• Amortization of reforestation expenditures under section 194. The corporation can elect to amortize up to $10,000 of qualified reforestation expenditures paid or incurred during the tax year. However, the amortization is not deducted by the corporation but the amortizable basis is instead separately allocated among the shareholders. See the instructions on page 28 for Schedule K-1, line 23, item 22 and Pub. 535 for more details.
• Fines or penalties paid to a government for violating any law. Report these expenses on Schedule K, line 19.
• Expenses allocable to tax-exempt income. Report these expenses on Schedule K, line 19.
• Net operating losses as provided by section 172 or the special deductions in sections 241 through 249 (except the

election to amortize organizational expenditures under section 248). These deductions cannot be claimed by an S corporation.

Note: *Shareholders are allowed, subject to limitations, to deduct from gross income the corporation's net operating loss. See section 1366.*

Special Rules

Commercial revitalization deduction. If the corporation constructs, purchases, or substantially rehabilitates a qualified building in a renewal community, it may qualify for a deduction of either **(a)** 50% of qualified capital expenditures in the year the building is placed in service or **(b)** amortization of 100% of the qualified capital expenditures over a 120-month period beginning with the month the building is placed in service. If the corporation elects to amortize these expenditures, complete and attach Form 4562. To qualify, the building must be nonresidential (as defined in section 168(e)(2)) and placed in service by the corporation. The corporation must be the original user of the building unless it is substantially rehabilitated. The amount of the qualified expenditures cannot exceed the lesser of $10 million or the amount allocated to the building by the commercial revitalization agency of the state in which the building is located. Any remaining expenditures are depreciated over the regular depreciation recovery period. See **Pub. 954,** Tax Incentives for Distressed Communities, and section 1400I for details.

Rental real estate. The corporation cannot deduct commercial revitalization expenditures for a building placed in service as rental real estate. Instead, the commercial revitalization deduction for rental real estate is reported separately to shareholders; see line 23, item 25, of Schedule K-1.

Travel, meals, and entertainment. Subject to limitations and restrictions discussed below, a corporation can deduct ordinary and necessary travel, meals, and entertainment expenses paid or incurred in its trade or business. Also, special rules apply to deductions for gifts, skybox rentals, luxury water travel,

convention expenses, and entertainment tickets. See section 274 and Pub. 463 for more details.

Travel. The corporation cannot deduct travel expenses of any individual accompanying a corporate officer or employee, including a spouse or dependent of the officer or employee, unless:
• That individual is an employee of the corporation and
• His or her travel is for a bona fide business purpose and would otherwise be deductible by that individual.

Meals and entertainment. Generally, the corporation can deduct only 50% of the amount otherwise allowable for meals and entertainment expenses paid or incurred in its trade or business. In addition (subject to exceptions under section 274(k)(2)):
• Meals must not be lavish or extravagant;
• A bona fide business discussion must occur during, immediately before, or immediately after the meal; and
• An employee of the corporation must be present at the meal.

See section 274(n)(3) for a special rule that applies to expenses for meals consumed by individuals subject to the hours of service limits of the Department of Transportation.

Membership dues. The corporation may deduct amounts paid or incurred for membership dues in civic or public service organizations, professional organizations (such as bar and medical associations), business leagues, trade associations, chambers of commerce, boards of trade, and real estate boards. However, no deduction is allowed if a principal purpose of the organization is to entertain, or provide entertainment facilities for, members or their guests. In addition, corporations may not deduct membership dues in any club organized for business, pleasure, recreation, or other social purpose. This includes country clubs, golf and athletic clubs, airline and hotel clubs, and clubs operated to provide meals under conditions favorable to business discussion.

Worksheet for Line 22a

1. Enter gross receipts for the tax year (see section 1362(d)(3)(B) for gross receipts from the sale of capital assets)* . . . . _____
2. Enter passive investment income as defined in section 1362(d)(3)(C)* . _____
3. Enter 25% of line 1 (If line 2 is less than line 3, stop here. You are not liable for this tax.) . . . . _____

4. Excess passive investment income— Subtract line 3 from line 2 . . _____
5. Enter deductions directly connected with the production of income on line 2 (see section 1375(b)(2))* . . _____
6. Net passive income—Subtract line 5 from line 2 . . . . _____
7. Divide amount on line 4 by amount on line 2 . . . . _____ %

8. Excess net passive income—Multiply line 6 by line 7 . . . . . . _____
9. Enter taxable income (see instructions for taxable income below) . . . _____
10. Enter smaller of line 8 or line 9 . _____
11. Excess net passive income tax—Enter 35% of line 10. Enter here and on line 22a, page 1, Form 1120S . . . _____

*Income and deductions on lines 1, 2, and 5 are from total operations for the tax year. This includes applicable income and expenses from page 1, Form 1120S, as well as those reported separately on Schedule K. See section 1375(b)(4) for an exception regarding lines 2 and 5.

Line 9 of Worksheet—Taxable income

Line 9 taxable income is defined in Regulations section 1.1374-1(d). Figure this income by completing lines 1 through 28 of **Form 1120,** U.S. Corporation Income Tax Return. Include the Form 1120 computation with the worksheet computation you attach to Form 1120S. You do not have to attach the schedules, etc., called for on Form 1120. However, you may want to complete certain Form 1120 schedules, such as Schedule D (Form 1120) if you have capital gains or losses.

FIGURE A.15 *(Continued)*

Entertainment facilities. The corporation cannot deduct an expense paid or incurred for a facility (such as a yacht or hunting lodge) used for an activity usually considered entertainment, amusement, or recreation.

Note: *The corporation may be able to deduct otherwise nondeductible meals, travel, and entertainment expenses if the amounts are treated as compensation and reported on Form W-2 for an employee or on Form 1099-MISC for an independent contractor.*

Lobbying expenses. Do not deduct amounts paid or incurred to participate or intervene in any political campaign on behalf of a candidate for public office, or to influence the general public regarding legislative matters, elections, or referendums. In addition, corporations generally cannot deduct expenses paid or incurred to influence Federal or state legislation, or to influence the actions or positions of certain Federal executive branch officials. However, certain in-house lobbying expenditures that do not exceed $2,000 are deductible. See section 162(e) for more details.

Clean-fuel vehicles and certain refueling property. A deduction is allowed for part of the cost of qualified clean-fuel vehicle property and qualified clean-fuel vehicle refueling property placed in service during the tax year. For more details, see section 179A and Pub. 535.

Certain corporations engaged in farming. Section 464(f) limits the deduction for certain expenditures of S corporations engaged in farming that use the cash method of accounting, and whose prepaid farm supplies are more than 50% of other deductible farming expenses. Prepaid farm supplies include expenses for feed, seed, fertilizer, and similar farm supplies not used or consumed during the year. They also include the cost of poultry that would be allowable as a deduction in a later tax year if the corporation were to **(a)** capitalize the cost of poultry bought for use in its farm business and deduct it ratably over the lesser of 12 months or the useful life of the poultry and **(b)** deduct the cost of poultry bought for resale in the year it sells or otherwise disposes of it. If the limit applies, the corporation can deduct prepaid farm supplies that do not exceed 50% of its other deductible farm expenses in the year of payment. The excess is deductible only in the year the corporation uses or consumes the supplies (other than poultry, which is deductible as explained above). For exceptions and more details on these rules, see **Pub. 225,** Farmer's Tax Guide.

Line 21. Ordinary Income (Loss)

Enter this income or loss on line 1 of Schedule K. Line 21 income is not used in figuring the tax on line 22a or 22b. See the instructions for line 22a for figuring taxable income for purposes of line 22a or 22b tax.

Tax and Payments

Line 22a. Excess Net Passive Income Tax

If the corporation has always been an S corporation, the excess net passive income tax does not apply.

If the corporation has accumulated earnings and profits (E&P) at the close of its tax year, has passive investment income for the tax year that is in excess of 25% of gross receipts, **and** has taxable income at year-end, the corporation must pay a tax on the excess net passive income. Complete lines 1 through 3 and line 9 of the worksheet on page 16 to make this determination. If line 2 is greater than line 3 and the corporation has taxable income (see instructions for line 9 of worksheet), it must pay the tax. Complete a separate schedule using the format of lines 1 through 11 of the worksheet on page 16 to figure the tax. Enter the tax on line 22a, page 1, Form 1120S, and attach the computation schedule to Form 1120S.

Reduce each item of passive income passed through to shareholders by its portion of tax on line 22a. See section 1366(f)(3).

Line 22b. Tax From Schedule D (Form 1120S)

Enter the built-in gains tax from line 22 of Part III of Schedule D. See the instructions for Part III of Schedule D to determine if the corporation is liable for the tax.

Line 22c

Include in the total for line 22c the following:

Investment credit recapture tax. The corporation is liable for investment credit recapture attributable to credits allowed for tax years for which the corporation was not an S corporation. Figure the corporation's investment credit recapture tax by completing **Form 4255,** Recapture of Investment Credit.

To the left of the line 22c total, enter the amount of recapture tax and "Tax From Form 4255." Attach Form 4255 to Form 1120S.

LIFO recapture tax. The corporation may be liable for the additional tax due to LIFO recapture under Regulations section 1.1363-2 if:
• The corporation used the LIFO inventory pricing method for its last tax year as a C corporation, or
• A C corporation transferred LIFO inventory to the corporation in a nonrecognition transaction in which those assets were transferred basis property.

The additional tax due to LIFO recapture is figured for the corporation's last tax year as a C corporation or for the tax year of the transfer, whichever applies. See the Instructions for Forms 1120 and 1120-A to figure the tax. The tax is paid in four equal installments. The C corporation must pay the first installment by the due date (not including extensions) of Form 1120 for the

corporation's last tax year as a C corporation or for the tax year of the transfer, whichever applies. The S corporation must pay each of the remaining installments by the due date (not including extensions) of Form 1120S for the 3 succeeding tax years. Include this year's installment in the total amount to be entered on line 22c. To the left of the total on line 22c, enter the installment amount and "LIFO tax."

Interest due under the look-back method for completed long-term contracts. If the corporation owes interest, attach **Form 8697,** Interest Computation Under the Look-Back Method for Completed Long-Term Contracts. To the left of the total on line 22c, enter the amount owed and "From Form 8697."

Interest due under the look-back method for property depreciated under the income forecast method. If the corporation owes interest, attach **Form 8866,** Interest Computation Under the Look-Back Method for Property Depreciated Under the Income Forecast Method. To the left of the total on line 22c, enter the amount owed and "From Form 8866."

Line 23d

If the S corporation is a beneficiary of a trust and the trust makes a section 643(g) election to credit its estimated tax payments to its beneficiaries, include the corporation's share of the payment (reported to the corporation on Schedule K-1 (Form 1041)) in the total amount entered on line 23d. Also, to the left of line 23d, enter "T" and the amount of the payment.

Line 24. Estimated Tax Penalty

A corporation that fails to make estimated tax payments when due may be subject to an underpayment penalty for the period of underpayment. Use **Form 2220,** Underpayment of Estimated Tax by Corporations, to see if the corporation owes a penalty and to figure the amount of the penalty. If you attach Form 2220 to Form 1120S, be sure to check the box on line 24 and enter the amount of any penalty on this line.

Line 27. Direct Deposit of Refund

If the corporation wants its refund directly deposited into its checking or savings account at any U.S. bank or other financial institution instead of having a check sent to the corporation, complete Form 8050 and attach it to the corporation's return. However, the corporation cannot have its refund from an amended return directly deposited.

Schedule A. Cost of Goods Sold

Generally, inventories are required at the beginning and end of each tax year if the production, purchase, or sale of merchandise is an income-producing factor. See Regulations section 1.471-1.

-17-

FIGURE A.15 *(Continued)*

However, if the corporation is a qualifying taxpayer or a qualifying small business taxpayer, it may adopt or change its accounting method to account for inventoriable items in the same manner as materials and supplies that are not incidental (unless its business is a tax shelter (as defined in section 448(d)(3))).

A **qualifying taxpayer** is a taxpayer that, for each prior tax year ending after December 16, 1998, has average annual gross receipts of $1 million or less for the 3-tax-year period ending with that prior tax year. See Rev. Proc. 2001-10, 2001-2 I.R.B. 272 for details.

A **qualifying small business taxpayer** is a taxpayer **(a)** that, for each prior tax year ending on or after December 31, 2000, has average annual gross receipts of $10 million or less for the 3-tax-year period ending with that prior tax year and **(b)** whose principal business activity is not an ineligible activity. See Rev. Proc. 2002-28, 2002-18 I.R.B. 815 for details.

Under this accounting method, inventory costs for raw materials purchased for use in producing finished goods and merchandise purchased for resale are deductible in the year the finished goods or merchandise are sold (but not before the year the corporation paid for the raw materials or merchandise if it is also using the cash method). For additional guidance on this method of accounting for inventoriable items, see Pub. 538.

Enter amounts paid for all raw materials and merchandise during the tax year on line 2. The amount the corporation can deduct for the tax year is figured on line 8.

Section 263A Uniform Capitalization Rules. The uniform capitalization rules of section 263A are discussed under **Limitations on Deductions** on page 13. See those instructions before completing Schedule A.

Line 1. Inventory at Beginning of Year

If the corporation is changing its method of accounting for the current tax year to no longer account for inventories, it must refigure last year's closing inventory using its new method of accounting and enter the result on line 1. If there is a difference between last year's closing inventory and the refigured amount, attach an explanation and take it into account when figuring the corporation's section 481(a) adjustment (explained on page 4).

Line 4. Additional Section 263A Costs

An entry is required on this line only for corporations that have elected a simplified method of accounting.

For corporations that have elected the **simplified production method,** additional section 263A costs are generally those costs, other than interest, that were not capitalized under the corporation's method of accounting immediately prior to the effective date of

section 263A that are required to be capitalized under section 263A. For new corporations, additional section 263A costs are the costs, other than interest, that must be capitalized under section 263A, but which the corporation would not have been required to capitalize if it had existed before the effective date of section 263A. For more details, see Regulations section 1.263A-2(b).

For corporations that have elected the **simplified resale method,** additional section 263A costs are generally those costs incurred with respect to the following categories.
- Off-site storage or warehousing.
- Purchasing.
- Handling, such as processing, assembly, repackaging, and transporting.
- General and administrative costs (mixed service costs).

For details, see Regulations section 1.263A-3(d).

Enter on line 4 the balance of section 263A costs paid or incurred during the tax year not includable on lines 2, 3, and 5.

Line 5. Other Costs

Enter on line 5 any other inventoriable costs paid or incurred during the tax year not entered on lines 2 through 4.

Line 7. Inventory at End of Year

See Regulations sections 1.263A-1 through 1.263A-3 for details on figuring the amount of additional section 263A costs to be included in ending inventory.

If the corporation accounts for inventoriable items in the same manner as materials and supplies that are not incidental, enter on line 7 the portion of its raw materials and merchandise purchased for resale that is included on line 6 and was not sold during the year.

Lines 9a Through 9e. Inventory Valuation Methods

Inventories can be valued at:
- Cost;
- Cost or market value (whichever is lower); or
- Any other method approved by the IRS that conforms to the requirements of the applicable regulations cited below.

However, if the corporation is using the cash method of accounting, it is required to use cost.

Corporations that account for inventoriable items in the same manner as materials and supplies that are not incidental may currently deduct expenditures for direct labor and all indirect costs that would otherwise be included in inventory costs.

The average cost (rolling average) method of valuing inventories generally does not conform to the requirements of the regulations. See Rev. Rul. 71-234, 1971-1 C.B. 148.

Corporations that use erroneous valuation methods must change to a method permitted for Federal income tax purposes. To make this change, use Form 3115.

On line 9a, check the method(s) used for valuing inventories. Under "lower of cost or market," *market* (for normal goods) means the current bid price prevailing on the inventory valuation date for the particular merchandise in the volume usually purchased by the taxpayer. For a manufacturer, market applies to the basic elements of cost— raw materials, labor, and burden. If section 263A applies to the taxpayer, the basic elements of cost must reflect the current bid price of all direct costs and all indirect costs properly allocable to goods on hand at the inventory date.

Inventory may be valued below cost when the merchandise is unsalable at normal prices or unusable in the normal way because the goods are subnormal due to damage, imperfections, shopwear, etc., within the meaning of Regulations section 1.471-2(c). These goods may be valued at a current bona fide selling price, minus direct cost of disposition (but not less than scrap value) if such a price can be established.

If this is the first year the Last-in, First-out (LIFO) inventory method was either adopted or extended to inventory goods not previously valued under the LIFO method provided in section 472, attach **Form 970,** Application To Use LIFO Inventory Method, or a statement with the information required by Form 970. Also check the LIFO box on line 9c. On line 9d, enter the amount or the percent of total closing inventories covered under section 472. Estimates are acceptable.

If the corporation changed or extended its inventory method to LIFO and had to write up its opening inventory to cost in the year of election, report the effect of this write-up as income (line 5, page 1) proportionately over a 3-year period that begins with the tax year of the LIFO election (section 472(d)).

See Pub. 538 for more information on inventory valuation methods.

Schedule B. Other Information

Be sure to answer the questions and provide other information in items 1 through 8.

Line 7

Complete line 7 if the corporation **(a)** was a C corporation before it elected to be an S corporation **or** the corporation acquired an asset with a basis determined by reference to its basis (or the basis of any other property) in the hands of a C corporation and **(b)** has net unrealized built-in gain (defined below) in excess of the net recognized built-in gain from prior years.

The corporation is liable for section 1374 tax if **(a)** and **(b)** above apply and it has a net recognized built-in gain (section 1374(d)(2)) for its tax year.

The corporation's net unrealized built-in gain is the amount, if any, by

FIGURE A.15 *(Continued)*

which the fair market value of the assets of the corporation at the beginning of its first S corporation year (or as of the date the assets were acquired, for any asset with a basis determined by reference to its basis (or the basis of any other property) in the hands of a C corporation) exceeds the aggregate adjusted basis of such assets at that time.

Enter on line 7 the corporation's net unrealized built-in gain reduced by the net recognized built-in gain for prior years. See sections 1374(c)(2) and (d)(1).

Line 8

Check the box on line 8 if the corporation was a C corporation in a prior year and has accumulated earnings and profits (E&P) at the close of its 2003 tax year. For details on figuring accumulated E&P, see section 312. If the corporation has accumulated E&P, it may be liable for tax imposed on excess net passive income. See the instructions for line 22a, page 1, of Form 1120S for details on this tax.

Line 9

Total receipts is the sum of the following amounts:
• Gross receipts or sales (page 1, line 1a).
• All other income (page 1, lines 4 and 5).
• Income reported on Schedule K, lines 3a, 4a, 4b(2), and 4c.
• Income or net gain reported on Schedule K, lines 4d(2), 4e(2), 4f, 5, and 6.
• Income or net gain reported on Form 8825, lines 2, 19, and 20a.

General Instructions for Schedules K and K-1. Shareholders' Shares of Income, Credits, Deductions, etc.

Purpose of Schedules

The corporation is liable for taxes on lines 22a, 22b, and 22c, page 1, Form 1120S. Shareholders are liable for income tax on their shares of the corporation's income (reduced by any taxes paid by the corporation on income) and must include their share of the income on their tax return whether or not it is distributed to them. Unlike most partnership income, S corporation income is **not** self-employment income and is not subject to self-employment tax.

Schedule K is a summary schedule of all shareholders' shares of the corporation's income, deductions, credits, etc. Schedule K-1 shows each shareholder's separate share. Attach a copy of each shareholder's Schedule K-1 to the Form 1120S filed with the IRS. Keep a copy as a part of the corporation's records, and give each shareholder a separate copy.

The total pro rata share items (column (b)) of all Schedules K-1 should equal the amount reported on the same line of

Schedule K. Lines 1 through 20 of Schedule K correspond to lines 1 through 20 of Schedule K. Other lines do not correspond, but instructions explain the differences.

Be sure to give each shareholder a copy of the Shareholder's Instructions for Schedule K-1 (Form 1120S). These instructions are available separately from Schedule K-1 at most IRS offices.

Note: *Instructions that apply only to line items reported on Schedule K-1 may be prepared and given to each shareholder instead of the instructions printed by the IRS.*

Substitute Forms

The corporation **does not** need IRS approval to use a substitute Schedule K-1 if it is an exact copy of the IRS schedule, **or** if it contains only those lines the taxpayer is required to use, and the lines have the same numbers and titles and are in the same order as on the IRS Schedule K-1. In either case, the substitute schedule must include the OMB number and either **(a)** the Shareholder's Instructions for Schedule K-1 (Form 1120S) or **(b)** instructions that apply to the items reported on Schedule K-1 (Form 1120S).

The corporation must request IRS approval to use other substitute Schedules K-1. To request approval, write to Internal Revenue Service, Attention: Substitute Forms Program Coordinator, SE:W:CAR:MP:T:T:SP, 1111 Constitution Avenue, NW, Washington, DC 20224.

The corporation may be subject to a penalty if it files a substitute Schedule K-1 that does not conform to the specifications of Rev. Proc. 2003-73, 2003-39 I.R.B. 647.

Shareholder's Pro Rata Share Items

General Rule

Items of income, loss, deductions, etc., are allocated to a shareholder on a daily basis, according to the number of shares of stock held by the shareholder on each day during the tax year of the corporation. See the instructions for item A.

A shareholder who disposes of stock is treated as the shareholder for the day of disposition. A shareholder who dies is treated as the shareholder for the day of the shareholder's death.

Special Rules

Termination of shareholder's interest. If a shareholder terminates his or her interest in a corporation during the tax year, the corporation, with the consent of all affected shareholders (including the one whose interest is terminated), may elect to allocate income and expenses, etc., as if the corporation's tax year consisted of 2 separate tax years, the first of which ends on the date of the shareholder's termination.

To make the election, the corporation must attach a statement to a timely filed original or amended Form 1120S for the

tax year for which the election is made. In the statement, the corporation must state that it is electing under section 1377(a)(2) and Regulations section 1.1377-1(b) to treat the tax year as if it consisted of 2 separate tax years. The statement must also explain how the shareholder's entire interest was terminated (e.g., sale or gift), and state that the corporation and each affected shareholder consent to the corporation making the election. A single statement may be filed for all terminating elections made for the tax year. If the election is made, write "Section 1377(a)(2) Election Made" at the top of each affected shareholder's Schedule K-1.

For more details on the election, see Temporary Regulations section 1.1377-1T(b).

Qualifying dispositions. If a qualifying disposition takes place during the tax year, the corporation may make an irrevocable election to allocate income and expenses, etc., as if the corporation's tax year consisted of 2 tax years, the first of which ends on the close of the day the qualifying disposition occurs.

A qualifying disposition is:

1. A disposition by a shareholder of at least 20% of the corporation's outstanding stock in one or more transactions in any 30-day period during the tax year,

2. A redemption treated as an exchange under section 302(a) or 303(a) of at least 20% of the corporation's outstanding stock in one or more transactions in any 30-day period during the tax year, or

3. An issuance of stock that equals at least 25% of the previously outstanding stock to one or more new shareholders in any 30-day period during the tax year.

To make the election, the corporation must attach a statement to a timely filed original or amended Form 1120S for the tax year for which the election is made. In the statement, the corporation must state that it is electing under Regulations section 1.1368-1(g)(2)(i) to treat the tax year as if it consisted of separate tax years, give the facts relating to the qualifying disposition (e.g., sale, gift, stock issuance, or redemption), and state that each shareholder who held stock in the corporation during the tax year consents to the election. A single election statement may be filed for all elections made under this special rule for the tax year.

For more details on the election, see Temporary Regulations section 1.1368-1T(g)(2).

Specific Instructions (Schedule K-1 Only)

General Information

On each Schedule K-1, complete the date spaces at the top; enter the names, addresses, and identifying numbers of the shareholder and corporation; complete items A through D; and enter the

FIGURE A.15 *(Continued)*

shareholder's pro rata share of each item. **Schedule K-1 must be prepared and given to each shareholder on or before the day on which Form 1120S is filed.**

Note: *Space has been provided on line 23 (Supplemental Information) of Schedule K-1 for the corporation to provide additional information to shareholders. This space, if sufficient, should be used in place of any attached schedules required for any lines on Schedule K-1, or other amounts not shown on lines 1 through 22 of Schedule K-1. Please be sure to identify the applicable line number next to the information entered below line 23.*

Special Reporting Requirements for Corporations With Multiple Activities

If items of income, loss, deduction, or credit from more than one activity (determined for purposes of the passive activity loss and credit limitations) are reported on lines 1, 2, or 3 of Schedule K-1, the corporation must provide information for each activity to its shareholders. See **Passive Activity Reporting Requirements** on page 11 for details on the reporting requirements.

Special Reporting Requirements for At-Risk Activities

If the corporation is involved in one or more at-risk activities for which a loss is reported on Schedule K-1, the corporation must report information separately for each at-risk activity. See section 465(c) for a definition of at-risk activities.

For each at-risk activity, the following information must be provided on an attachment to Schedule K-1:

1. A statement that the information is a breakdown of at-risk activity loss amounts.

2. The identity of the at-risk activity; the loss amount for the activity; other income and deductions; and other information that relates to the activity.

Specific Items

Item A

If there was no change in shareholders or in the relative interest in stock the shareholders owned during the tax year, enter the percentage of total stock owned by each shareholder during the tax year. For example, if shareholders X and Y each owned 50% for the entire tax year, enter 50% in item A for each shareholder. Each shareholder's pro rata share items (lines 1 through 20 of Schedule K-1) are figured by multiplying the Schedule K amount on the corresponding line of Schedule K by the percentage in item A.

If there was a change in shareholders or in the relative interest in stock the shareholders owned during the tax year, each shareholder's percentage of ownership is weighted for the number of days in the tax year that stock was owned. For example, A and B each held 50% for half the tax year and A, B, and C

held 40%, 40%, and 20%, respectively, for the remaining half of the tax year. The percentage of ownership for the year for A, B, and C is figured as follows and is then entered in item A.

	a	b	c (a × b)	
	% of total stock owned	% of tax year held	% of ownership for the year	
A	50	50	25	
	40	50	+20	45
B	50	50	25	
	40	50	+20	45
C	20	50	10	10
Total	. . . .			100%

If there was a change in shareholders or in the relative interest in stock the shareholders owned during the tax year, each shareholder's pro rata share items generally are figured by multiplying the Schedule K amount by the percentage in item A. However, if a shareholder terminated his or her entire interest in the corporation during the year or a qualifying disposition took place, the corporation may elect to allocate income and expenses, etc., as if the tax year consisted of 2 tax years, the first of which ends on the day of the termination or qualifying disposition. See **Special Rules** on page 19 for more details. Each shareholder's pro rata share items are figured separately for each period on a daily basis, based on the percentage of stock held by the shareholder on each day.

Item C

If the corporation is a registration-required tax shelter or has invested in a registration-required tax shelter, it must enter its tax shelter registration number in item C. Also, a corporation that has invested in a registration-required shelter must furnish a copy of its Form 8271 to its shareholders. See Form 8271 for more details.

Specific Instructions (Schedules K and K-1, Except as Noted)

Income (Loss)

Reminder: Before entering income items on Schedule K or K-1, be sure to reduce the items of income for the following:

1. Built-in gains tax (Schedule D, Part III, line 22). Each recognized built-in gain item (within the meaning of section 1374(d)(3)) is reduced by its proportionate share of the built-in gains tax.

2. Excess net passive income tax (line 22a, page 1, Form 1120S). Each item of passive investment income (within the meaning of section 1362(d)(3)(C)) is reduced by its proportionate share of the net passive income tax.

Line 1. Ordinary Income (Loss) From Trade or Business Activities

Enter the amount from line 21, page 1. Enter the income or loss without reference to **(a)** shareholders' basis in the stock of the corporation and in any indebtedness of the corporation to the shareholders (section 1366(d)), **(b)** shareholders' at-risk limitations, and **(c)** shareholders' passive activity limitations. These limitations, if applicable, are determined at the shareholder level.

If the corporation is involved in more than one trade or business activity, see **Passive Activity Reporting Requirements** on page 11 for details on the information to be reported for each activity. If an at-risk activity loss is reported on line 1, see **Special Reporting Requirements for At-Risk Activities** above.

Line 2. Net Income (Loss) From Rental Real Estate Activities

Enter the net income or loss from rental real estate activities of the corporation from **Form 8825,** Rental Real Estate Income and Expenses of a Partnership or an S Corporation. Each Form 8825 has space for reporting the income and expenses of up to eight properties.

If the corporation has income or loss from more than one rental real estate activity reported on line 2, see **Passive Activity Reporting Requirements** on page 11 for details on the information to be reported for each activity. If an at-risk activity loss is reported on line 2, see **Special Reporting Requirements for At-Risk Activities** above.

Line 3. Income and Expenses of Other Rental Activities

Enter on lines 3a and 3b of Schedule K (line 3 of Schedule K-1) the income and expenses of rental activities other than those reported on Form 8825. If the corporation has more than one rental activity reported on line 3, see **Passive Activity Reporting Requirements** on page 11 for details on the information to be reported for each activity. If an at-risk activity loss is reported on line 3, see **Special Reporting Requirements for At-Risk Activities** above. Also see **Rental Activities** on page 8 for a definition and other details on other rental activities.

Lines 4a Through 4f. Portfolio Income (Loss)

Enter portfolio income (loss) on lines 4a through 4f. See **Portfolio Income** on page 9 for the definition of portfolio income. Do not reduce portfolio income by deductions allocated to it. Report such deductions (other than interest expense) on line 9 of Schedules K and K-1. Interest expense allocable to portfolio income is generally investment interest expense and is reported on line 11a of Schedules K and K-1.

Line 4a. Enter only taxable interest on this line from portfolio income. Interest income derived in the ordinary course of the corporation's trade or business, such

-20-

as interest charged on receivable balances, is reported on line 5, page 1, Form 1120S. See Temporary Regulations section 1.469-2T(c)(3).

Lines 4b(1) and 4b(2). Enter only taxable ordinary dividends on these lines. Enter on line 4b(1) all qualified dividends from line 4b(2).

Qualified dividends. Except as provided below, qualified dividends are dividends received after December 31, 2002, from domestic corporations and qualified foreign corporations.

Exceptions. The following dividends are not qualified dividends:
• Dividends the corporation received on any share of stock held for less than 61 days during the 121-day period that began 60 days before the ex-dividend date. When determining the number of days the corporation held the stock, it cannot count certain days during which the corporation's risk of loss was diminished. See Pub. 550 for more details. The ex-dividend date is the first date following the declaration of a dividend on which the purchaser of a stock is not entitled to receive the next dividend payment. When counting the number of days the corporation held the stock, include the day the corporation disposed of the stock but not the day the corporation acquired it.
• Dividends attributable to periods totaling more than 366 days that the corporation received on any share of preferred stock held for less than 91 days during the 181-day period that began 90 days before the ex-dividend date. When determining the number of days the corporation held the stock, do not count certain days during which the corporation's risk of loss was diminished. See Pub. 550 for more details. Preferred dividends attributable to periods totaling less than 367 days are subject to the 61-day holding period rule above.
• Dividends that relate to payments that the corporation is obligated to make with respect to short sales or positions in substantially similar or related property.
• Dividends paid by a regulated investment company that are not treated as qualified dividend income under section 854.
• Dividends paid by a real estate investment trust that are not treated as qualified dividend income under section 857(c).

Qualified foreign corporation. A foreign corporation is a qualified foreign corporation if it is:
1. Incorporated in a possession of the United States or
2. Eligible for benefits of a comprehensive income tax treaty with the United States that the Secretary determines is satisfactory for this purpose and that includes an exchange of information program. See Notice 2003-69, 2003-42 I.R.B. 851 for details.

If the foreign corporation does not meet either 1 or 2 above, then it may be treated as a qualified foreign corporation for any dividend paid by the corporation if

the stock associated with the dividend paid is readily tradable on an established securities market in the United States.

However, qualified dividends do not include dividends paid by the following foreign entities in either the tax year of the distribution or the preceding tax year:
• A foreign investment company (section 1246(b)),
• A passive foreign investment company (section 1297), or
• A foreign personal holding company (section 552).

See Notice 2003-79 for more details.

Lines 4d(1) and 4d(2). Enter on line 4d(1) the Post-May 5, 2003, gain or loss from line 6a of Schedule D (Form 1120S). Enter on line 4d(2) the gain (loss) for the entire year from line 6b of Schedule D (Form 1120S).

Lines 4e(1) and 4e(2). Enter on line 4e(1) the Post-May 5, 2003, gain or loss that is portfolio income (loss) from Schedule D (Form 1120S), line 13. Enter on line 4e(2) the gain or loss for the entire year that is portfolio income (loss) from Schedule D (Form 1120S), line 14.

⚠ *If any gain or loss from lines 6, 13, and 14 of Schedule D is not portfolio income (e.g., gain or loss from the disposition of nondepreciable personal property used in a trade or business), do not report this income or loss on lines 4d(1) through 4e(2). Instead, report it on line 6.*

Line 4f. Enter any other portfolio income not reported on lines 4a through 4e.

If the corporation holds a residual interest in a REMIC, report on an attachment for line 4f each shareholder's share of taxable income (net loss) from the REMIC (line 1b of Schedule Q (Form 1066)); excess inclusion (line 2c of Schedule Q (Form 1066)); and section 212 expenses (line 3b of Schedule Q (Form 1066)). Because Schedule Q (Form 1066) is a quarterly statement, the corporation must follow the Schedule Q (Form 1066) Instructions for Residual Interest Holder to figure the amounts to report to shareholders for the corporation's tax year.

Line 5. Net Section 1231 Gain (Loss) (Except From Casualty or Theft)
Enter on line 5a the Post-May 5, 2003, net section 1231 gain (loss) from Form 4797, line 7, column (h). Enter on line 5b the net section 1231 gain (loss) for the entire year from Form 4797, line 7, column (g). If the corporation had a gain prior to May 6, 2003, from any section 1231 property held more than 5 years, show the total of all such gains on an attachment to Schedule K-1 (do not include any gain attributable to straight-line depreciation from section 1250 property). Indicate on the statement that this amount should be included in the shareholder's computation of qualified 5-year gain only if the amount on the shareholder's Form 4797, line 7, is more than zero.

Do not include gain or loss from involuntary conversions due to casualty or theft on lines 5a or 5b. Report net gain or loss from involuntary conversions due to casualty or theft on line 6.

If the corporation is involved in more than one trade or business or rental activity, see **Passive Activity Reporting Requirements** on page 11 for details on the information to be reported for each activity. If an at-risk activity loss is reported on line 5, see **Special Reporting Requirements for At-Risk Activities** on page 20.

Line 6. Other Income (Loss)
Enter any other item of income or loss not included on lines 1 through 5. Items to be reported on line 6 include:
• Recoveries of tax benefit items (section 111).
• Gambling gains and losses (section 165(d)).
• Gains from the disposition of an interest in oil, gas, geothermal, or other mineral properties (section 1254).
• Net gain (loss) from involuntary conversions due to casualty or theft. The amount for this item is shown on **Form 4684,** Casualties and Thefts, line 38a or 38b.
• Any net gain or loss from section 1256 contracts from **Form 6781,** Gains and Losses From Section 1256 Contracts and Straddles.
• Gain from the sale or exchange of qualified small business stock (as defined in the Instructions for Schedule D) that is eligible for the 50% section 1202 exclusion. To be eligible for the section 1202 exclusion, the stock must have been held by the corporation for more than 5 years. Corporate shareholders are not eligible for the section 1202 exclusion. Additional limitations apply at the shareholder level. Report each shareholder's share of section 1202 gain on Schedule K-1. Each shareholder will determine if he or she qualifies for the section 1202 exclusion. Report on an attachment to Schedule K-1 for each sale or exchange the name of the qualified small business that issued the stock, the shareholder's share of the corporation's adjusted basis and sales price of the stock, and the dates the stock was bought and sold.
• Gain eligible for section 1045 rollover (replacement stock purchased by the corporation). Include only gain from the sale or exchange of qualified small business stock (as defined in the Instructions for Schedule D) that was deferred by the corporation under section 1045 and reported on Schedule D. See the Instructions for Schedule D for more details. Corporate shareholders are not eligible for the section 1045 rollover. Additional limitations apply at the shareholder level. Report each shareholder's share of the gain eligible for section 1045 rollover on Schedule K-1. Each shareholder will determine if he or she qualifies for the rollover. Report on an attachment to Schedule K-1 for each sale or exchange the name of the qualified

-21-

FIGURE A.15 *(Continued)*

small business that issued the stock, the shareholder's share of the corporation's adjusted basis and sales price of the stock, and the dates the stock was bought and sold.

• Gain eligible for section 1045 rollover (replacement stock not purchased by the corporation). Include only gain from the sale or exchange of qualified small business stock (as defined in the Instructions for Schedule D) the corporation held for more than 6 months but that **was not** deferred by the corporation under section 1045. See the Instructions for Schedule D for more details. A shareholder (other than a corporation) may be eligible to defer his or her pro rata share of this gain under section 1045 if he or she purchases other qualified small business stock during the 60-day period that began on the date the stock was sold by the corporation. Additional limitations apply at the shareholder level. Report on an attachment to Schedule K-1 for each sale or exchange the name of the qualified small business that issued the stock, the shareholder's share of the corporation's adjusted basis and sales price of the stock, and the dates the stock was bought and sold.

• If the corporation had a gain before May 6, 2003, from the disposition of non-depreciable personal property used in a trade or business held more than 5 years, show the total of all such gains on an attachment to Schedule K-1. Indicate on the statement that the shareholder should include this amount on line 5 of the worksheet for line 35 of Schedule D (Form 1040). If the income or loss is attributable to more than one activity, report the income or loss amount separately for each activity on an attachment to Schedule K-1 and identify the activity to which the income or loss relates.

If the corporation is involved in more than one trade or business or rental activity, see **Passive Activity Reporting Requirements** on page 11 for details on the information to be reported for each activity. If an at-risk activity loss is reported on line 6, see **Special Reporting Requirements for At-Risk Activities** on page 20.

Deductions

Line 7. Charitable Contributions

Enter the amount of charitable contributions paid during the tax year. On an attachment to Schedules K and K-1, show separately the dollar amount of contributions subject to each of the 50%, 30%, and 20% of adjusted gross income limits. For additional information, see **Pub. 526,** Charitable Contributions.

 An accrual basis S corporation **may not** *elect to treat a contribution as having been paid in the tax year the board of directors authorizes the payment if the contribution is not actually paid until the next tax year.*

Generally, no deduction is allowed for any contribution of $250 or more unless the corporation obtains a written acknowledgment from the charitable organization that shows the amount of cash contributed, describes any property contributed, and gives an estimate of the value of any goods or services provided in return for the contribution. The acknowledgment must be obtained by the due date (including extensions) of the corporation's return, or if earlier, the date the corporation files its return. Do not attach the acknowledgment to the tax return, but keep it with the corporation's records. These rules apply in addition to the filing requirements for Form 8283 described below.

Certain contributions made to an organization conducting lobbying activities are not deductible. See section 170(f)(9) for more details.

If the deduction claimed for noncash contributions exceeds $500, complete **Form 8283,** Noncash Charitable Contributions, and attach it to Form 1120S. The corporation must give a copy of its Form 8283 to every shareholder if the deduction for any item or group of similar items of contributed property exceeds $5,000, even if the amount allocated to any shareholder is $5,000 or less.

If the deduction for an item or group of similar items of contributed property is $5,000 or less, the corporation must report each shareholder's pro rata share of the amount of noncash contributions to enable individual shareholders to complete their own Forms 8283. See the Instructions for Form 8283 for more information.

If the corporation made a qualified conservation contribution under section 170(h), also include the fair market value of the underlying property before and after the donation, as well as the type of legal interest contributed, and describe the conservation purpose furthered by the donation. Give a copy of this information to each shareholder.

Line 8. Section 179 Expense Deduction

An S corporation may elect to expense part of the cost of certain property that the corporation purchased during the tax year for use in its trade or business or certain rental activities. See the Instructions for Form 4562 for more information.

Complete Part I of Form 4562 to figure the corporation's section 179 expense deduction. The corporation does not claim the deduction itself, but instead passes it through to the shareholders. Attach Form 4562 to Form 1120S and show the total section 179 expense deduction on Schedule K, line 8. Report each individual shareholder's pro rata share on Schedule K-1, line 8. Do not complete line 8 of Schedule K-1 for any shareholder that is an estate or trust.

If the corporation is an enterprise zone business, also report on an attachment to Schedules K and K-1 the cost of section 179 property placed in service during the year that is qualified zone property.

See the instructions for line 23 of Schedule K-1, item 3, for sales or other dispositions of property for which a section 179 expense deduction has passed through to shareholders. See item 4 for recapture if the business use of the property dropped to 50% or less.

Line 9. Deductions Related to Portfolio Income (Loss)

Enter on line 9 the deductions clearly and directly allocable to portfolio income (other than interest expense). Interest expense related to portfolio income is investment interest expense and is reported on line 11a of Schedules K and K-1. Generally, the line 9 expenses are section 212 expenses and are subject to section 212 limitations at the shareholder level.

Note: *No deduction is allowed under section 212 for expenses allocable to a convention, seminar, or similar meeting. Because these expenses are not deductible by shareholders, the corporation does not report these expenses on line 9 or line 10. The expenses are nondeductible and are reported as such on line 19 of Schedules K and K-1.*

Line 10. Other Deductions

Enter any other deductions not included on lines 7, 8, 9, and 15g. On an attachment, identify the deduction and amount, and if the corporation has more than one activity, the activity to which the deduction relates.

Examples of items to be reported on an attachment to line 10 include:

• Amounts (other than investment interest required to be reported on line 11a of Schedules K and K-1) paid by the corporation that would be allowed as itemized deductions on a shareholder's income tax return if they were paid directly by a shareholder for the same purpose. These amounts include, but are not limited to, expenses under section 212 for the production of income other than from the corporation's trade or business.

• Any penalty on early withdrawal of savings not reported on line 9 because the corporation withdrew funds from its time savings deposit before its maturity.

• Soil and water conservation expenditures (section 175).

• Expenditures paid or incurred for the removal of architectural and transportation barriers to the elderly and disabled that the corporation has elected to treat as a current expense. See section 190.

• Contributions to a capital construction fund.

• Interest expense allocated to debt-financed distributions. See Notice 89-35, 1989-1 C.B. 675, for more information.

• If there was a gain (loss) from a casualty or theft to property not used in a trade or business or for income-producing purposes, provide each shareholder with the needed information to complete Form 4684.

-22-

FIGURE A.15   *(Continued)*

Investment Interest

Complete lines 11a and 11b for all shareholders.

Line 11a. Investment Interest Expense

Include on this line the interest properly allocable to debt on property held for investment purposes. Property held for investment includes property that produces income (unless derived in the ordinary course of a trade or business) from interest, dividends, annuities, or royalties; and gains from the disposition of property that produces those types of income or is held for investment.

Investment interest expense **does not** include interest expense allocable to a passive activity.

Report investment interest expense only on line 11a of Schedules K and K-1.

The amount on line 11a will be deducted by individual shareholders on Schedule A (Form 1040), line 13, after applying the investment interest expense limitations of section 163(d).

For more information, see **Form 4952,** Investment Interest Expense Deduction.

Lines 11b(1) and 11b(2). Investment Income and Expenses

Enter on line 11b(1) only the investment income included on lines 4a, b(2), c, and f of Schedule K-1. Do not include other portfolio gains or losses on this line.

Enter on line 11b(2) only the investment expense included on line 9 of Schedule K-1.

If there are other items of investment income or expense included in the amounts that are required to be passed through separately to the shareholders on Schedule K-1, such as net short-term capital gain or loss, net long-term capital gain or loss, and other portfolio gains or losses, give each shareholder a schedule identifying these amounts.

Investment income includes gross income from property held for investment, the excess of net gain attributable to the disposition of property held for investment over net capital gain from the disposition of property held for investment, and any net capital gain from the disposition of property held for investment that each shareholder elects to include in investment income under section 163(d)(4)(B)(iii). Generally, investment income and investment expenses do not include any income or expenses from a passive activity. See Regulations section 1.469-2(f)(10) for exceptions.

Property subject to a net lease is not treated as investment property because it is subject to the passive loss rules. Do not reduce investment income by losses from passive activities.

Investment expenses are deductible expenses (other than interest) directly connected with the production of investment income. See the Instructions for Form 4952 for more information on investment income and expenses.

Credits

Note: *If the corporation has credits from more than one trade or business activity on line 12a or 13, or from more than one rental activity on line 12b, 12c, 12d, or 12e, it must report separately on an attachment to Schedule K-1, the amount of each credit and provide any other applicable activity information listed in* **Passive Activity Reporting Requirements** *on page 11. However,* **do not** *attach* **Form 3800,** *General Business Credit, to Form 1120S.*

Line 12a. Credit for Alcohol Used as Fuel

Enter on line 12a of Schedule K the credit for alcohol used as fuel attributable to trade or business activities. Enter on line 12d or 12e the credit for alcohol used as fuel attributable to rental activities. Figure the credit on **Form 6478,** Credit for Alcohol Used as Fuel, and attach it to Form 1120S. The credit must be included in income on page 1, line 5, of Form 1120S. See section 40(f) for an election the corporation can make to have the credit not apply.

Enter each shareholder's share of the credit for alcohol used as fuel on line 12a, 12d, or 12e of Schedule K-1.

If this credit includes the small ethanol producer credit, identify on a statement attached to each Schedule K-1 **(a)** the amount of the small producer credit included in the total credit allocated to the shareholder, **(b)** the number of gallons of qualified ethanol fuel production allocated to the shareholder, and **(c)** the shareholder's pro rata share, in gallons, of the corporation's productive capacity for alcohol.

Line 12b. Low-Income Housing Credit

Section 42 provides for a credit that may be claimed by owners of low-income residential rental buildings. If shareholders are eligible to claim the low-income housing credit, complete the applicable parts of **Form 8586,** Low-Income Housing Credit, and attach it to Form 1120S. Enter the credit figured by the corporation on Form 8586, and any low-income housing credit received from other entities in which the corporation is allowed to invest, on the applicable line as explained below. The corporation must also complete and attach **Form 8609,** Low-Income Housing Credit Allocation Certification, and **Schedule A (Form 8609),** Annual Statement, to Form 1120S. See the Instructions for Form 8586 and Form 8609 for information on completing these forms.

Line 12b(1). If the corporation invested in a partnership to which the provisions of section 42(j)(5) apply, report on line 12b(1) the credit the partnership reported to the corporation on line 12a(1) of Schedule K-1 (Form 1065).

Line 12b(2). Report on line 12b(2) any low-income housing credit not reported on line 12b(1). This includes any credit from a partnership reported to the corporation on line 12a(2) of Schedule K-1 (Form 1065).

Note: *If part or all of the credit reported on line 12b(1) or 12b(2) is attributable to additions to qualified basis of property placed in service before 1990, report on an attachment to Schedules K and K-1 the amount of the credit on each line that is attributable to property placed in service (a) before 1990 and (b) after 1989.*

Line 12c. Qualified Rehabilitation Expenditures Related to Rental Real Estate Activities

Enter total qualified rehabilitation expenditures related to rental real estate activities of the corporation. For line 12c of Schedule K, complete the applicable lines of **Form 3468,** Investment Credit, that apply to qualified rehabilitation expenditures for property related to rental real estate activities of the corporation for which income or loss is reported on line 2 of Schedule K. See Form 3468 for details on qualified rehabilitation expenditures. Attach Form 3468 to Form 1120S.

For line 12c of Schedule K-1, enter each shareholder's pro rata share of the expenditures. On the dotted line to the left of the entry space for line 12c, enter the line number of Form 3468 on which the shareholder should report the expenditures. If there is more than one type of expenditure, or the expenditures are from more than one line 2 activity, report this information separately for each expenditure or activity on an attachment to Schedules K and K-1.

Note: *Qualified rehabilitation expenditures* **not** *related to rental real estate activities must be listed separately on line 23 of Schedule K-1.*

Line 12d. Credits (Other Than Credits Shown on Lines 12b and 12c) Related to Rental Real Estate Activities

Enter on line 12d any other credit (other than credits on lines 12b and 12c) related to rental real estate activities. On the dotted line to the left of the entry space for line 12d, identify the type of credit. If there is more than one type of credit or the credit is from more than one line 2 activity, report this information separately for each credit or activity on an attachment to Schedules K and K-1. These credits may include any type of credit listed in the instructions for line 13.

Line 12e. Credits Related to Other Rental Activities

Enter on line 12e any credit related to other rental activities for which income or loss is reported on line 3 of Schedules K and K-1. On the dotted line to the left of the entry space for line 12e, identify the type of credit. If there is more than one type of credit or the credit is from more than one line 3 activity, report this information separately for each credit or activity on an attachment to Schedules K and K-1. These credits may include any type of credit listed in the instructions for line 13.

-23-

FIGURE A.15   *(Continued)*

Line 13. Other Credits

Enter on line 13 any other credit, except credits or expenditures shown or listed for lines 12a through 12e of Schedules K and K-1 or the credit for Federal tax paid on fuels (which is reported on line 23c of page 1). On the dotted line to the left of the entry space for line 13, identify the type of credit. If there is more than one type of credit or the credit is from more than one activity, report this information separately for each credit or activity on an attachment to Schedules K and K-1.

The credits to be reported on line 13 and other required attachments follow.
• Credit for backup withholding on dividends, interest, or patronage dividends.
• Nonconventional source fuel credit. Figure this credit on a separate schedule and attach it to Form 1120S. See section 29 for rules on figuring the credit.
• Qualified electric vehicle credit (Form 8834).
• Unused investment credit from cooperatives. If the corporation is a member of a cooperative that passes an unused investment credit through to its members, the credit is in turn passed through to the corporation's shareholders.
• Work opportunity credit (Form 5884).
• Welfare-to-work credit (Form 8861).
• Credit for increasing research activities (Form 6765).
• Enhanced oil recovery credit (Form 8830).
• Disabled access credit (Form 8826).
• Renewable electricity production credit (Form 8835).
• Empowerment zone and renewal community employment credit (Form 8844).
• Indian employment credit (Form 8845).
• Credit for employer social security and Medicare taxes paid on certain employee tips (Form 8846).
• Orphan drug credit (Form 8820).
• New markets credit (Form 8874).
• Credit for contributions to selected community development corporations (Form 8847).
• Credit for small employer pension start-up costs (Form 8881).
• Credit for employer-provided child care facilities and services (Form 8882).
• New York Liberty Zone business employee credit (Form 8884).
• Qualified zone academy bond credit (Form 8860).
• General credits from an electing large partnership.

See the instructions for line 21 (Schedule K) and line 23 (Schedule K-1) to report expenditures qualifying for the **(a)** rehabilitation credit not related to rental real estate activities, **(b)** energy credit, or **(c)** reforestation credit.

Adjustments and Tax Preference Items

Lines 14a through 14e must be completed for all shareholders.

Enter items of income and deductions that are adjustments or tax preference items for the alternative minimum tax

(AMT). See **Form 6251,** Alternative Minimum Tax—Individuals, or Schedule I of **Form 1041,** U.S. Income Tax Return for Estates and Trusts, to determine the amounts to enter and for other information.

Do not include as a tax preference item any qualified expenditures to which an election under section 59(e) may apply. Because these expenditures are subject to an election by each shareholder, the corporation cannot figure the amount of any tax preference related to them. Instead, the corporation must pass through to each shareholder on lines 16a and 16b of Schedule K-1 the information needed to figure the deduction.

Line 14a. Depreciation Adjustment on Property Placed in Service After 1986

Figure the adjustment for line 14a based only on tangible property placed in service after 1986 (and tangible property placed in service after July 31, 1986, and before 1987 for which the corporation elected to use the general depreciation system). **Do not** make an adjustment for motion picture films, videotapes, sound recordings, certain public utility property (as defined in section 168(f)(2)), property depreciated under the unit-of-production method (or any other method not expressed in a term of years), qualified Indian reservation property, property eligible for a special depreciation allowance, qualified revitalization expenditures, or the section 179 expense deduction.

For property placed in service **before 1999,** refigure depreciation for the AMT as follows (using the same convention used for the regular tax):
• For section 1250 property (generally, residential rental and nonresidential real property), use the straight line method over 40 years.
• For tangible property (other than section 1250 property) depreciated using the straight line method for the regular tax, use the straight line method over the property's class life. Use 12 years if the property has no class life.
• For any other tangible property, use the 150% declining balance method, switching to the straight line method the first tax year it gives a larger deduction, over the property's AMT class life. Use 12 years if the property has no class life.

Note: *See Pub. 946 for a table of class lives.*

For property placed in service **after 1998,** refigure depreciation for the AMT **only** for property depreciated for the regular tax using the 200% declining balance method. For the AMT, use the 150% declining balance method, switching to the straight line method the first tax year it gives a larger deduction, and the same convention and recovery period used for the regular tax.

Figure the adjustment by subtracting the AMT deduction for depreciation from the regular tax deduction and enter the

result on line 14a. If the AMT deduction is more than the regular tax deduction, enter the difference as a negative amount. Depreciation capitalized to inventory must also be refigured using the AMT rules. Include on this line the current year adjustment to income, if any, resulting from the difference.

Line 14b. Adjusted Gain or Loss

If the corporation disposed of any tangible property placed in service after 1986 (or after July 31, 1986, if an election was made to use the General Depreciation System), or if it disposed of a certified pollution control facility placed in service after 1986, refigure the gain or loss from the disposition using the adjusted basis for the AMT. The property's adjusted basis for the AMT is its cost or other basis minus all depreciation or amortization deductions allowed or allowable for the AMT during the current tax year and previous tax years. Enter on this line the difference between the regular tax gain (loss) and the AMT gain (loss). If the AMT gain is less than the regular tax gain, **or** the AMT loss is more than the regular tax loss, **or** there is an AMT loss and a regular tax gain, enter the difference as a negative amount.

If any part of the adjustment is allocable to net short-term capital gain (loss), net long-term capital gain (loss), or net section 1231 gain (loss), attach a schedule that identifies the amount of the adjustment allocable to each type of gain or loss. For a net long-term capital gain (loss), also identify the amount of the adjustment that is 28% rate gain (loss). For a net section 1231 gain (loss), also identify the amount of adjustment that is unrecaptured section 1250 gain. Also indicate the amount of any qualified 5-year gain and the portion of each amount that is post-May 5, 2003, gain or loss.

Line 14c. Depletion (Other Than Oil and Gas)

Do not include any depletion on oil and gas wells. The shareholders must figure their depletion deductions and preference items separately under section 613A.

Refigure the depletion deduction under section 611 for mines, wells (other than oil and gas wells), and other natural deposits for the AMT. Percentage depletion is limited to 50% of the taxable income from the property as figured under section 613(a), using only income and deductions for the AMT. Also, the deduction is limited to the property's adjusted basis at the end of the year, as refigured for the AMT. Figure this limit separately for each property. When refiguring the property's adjusted basis, take into account any AMT adjustments made this year or in previous years that affect basis (other than the current year's depletion).

Enter the difference between the regular tax and AMT deduction. If the AMT deduction is greater, enter the difference as a negative amount.

-24-

FIGURE A.15   *(Continued)*

Lines 14d(1) and 14d(2)

Generally, the amounts to be entered on these lines are only the income and deductions for oil, gas, and geothermal properties that are used to figure the amount on line 21, page 1, Form 1120S.

If there are any items of income or deductions for oil, gas, or geothermal properties included in the amounts that are required to be passed through separately to the shareholders on Schedule K-1, give each shareholder a schedule that shows, for the line on which the income or deduction is included, the amount of income or deductions included in the total amount for that line. Do not include any of these direct pass-through amounts on line 14d(1) or 14d(2). The shareholder is told in the Shareholder's Instructions for Schedule K-1 (Form 1120S) to adjust the amounts on lines 14d(1) and 14d(2) for any other income or deductions from oil, gas, or geothermal properties included on lines 2 through 10 and 23 of Schedule K-1 in order to determine the total income and deductions from oil, gas, and geothermal properties for the corporation.

Figure the amounts for lines 14d(1) and 14d(2) separately for oil and gas properties that are not geothermal deposits and for all properties that are geothermal deposits.

Give the shareholders a schedule that shows the separate amounts included in the computation of the amounts on lines 14d(1) and 14d(2).

Line 14d(1). Gross income from oil, gas, and geothermal properties. Enter the total amount of gross income (within the meaning of section 613(a)) from all oil, gas, and geothermal properties received or accrued during the tax year and included on page 1, Form 1120S.

Line 14d(2). Deductions allocable to oil, gas, and geothermal properties. Enter the amount of any deductions allowed for the AMT that are allocable to oil, gas, and geothermal properties.

Line 14e. Other Adjustments and Tax Preference Items

Attach a schedule that shows each shareholder's share of other items not shown on lines 14a through 14d(2) that are adjustments or tax preference items or that the shareholder needs to complete Form 6251 or Schedule I of Form 1041. See these forms and their instructions to determine the amount to enter.

Other adjustments or tax preference items include the following:
• Accelerated depreciation of real property under pre-1987 rules.
• Accelerated depreciation of leased personal property under pre-1987 rules.
• Long-term contracts entered into after February 28, 1986. Except for certain home construction contracts, the taxable income from these contracts must be figured using the percentage of completion method of accounting for the AMT.

• Losses from tax shelter farm activities. No loss from any tax shelter farm activity is allowed for the AMT.

Foreign Taxes

Lines 15a through 15h must be completed if the corporation has foreign income, deductions, or losses, or has paid or accrued foreign taxes. See **Pub. 514,** Foreign Tax Credit for Individuals, for more information.

Line 15a. Name of Foreign Country or U.S. Possession

Enter the name of the foreign country or U.S. possession from which the corporation had income or to which the corporation paid or accrued taxes. If the corporation had income from, or paid or accrued taxes to, **more than one** foreign country or U.S. possession, enter "See attached" and attach a schedule for each country for lines 15a through 15h.

Line 15b. Gross Income From All Sources

Enter the corporation's gross income from all sources, (both U.S. and foreign).

Line 15c. Gross Income Sourced at Shareholder Level

Enter the total gross income of the corporation that is required to be sourced at the shareholder level. This includes income from the sale of most personal property other than inventory, depreciable property, and certain intangible property. See Pub. 514 and section 865 for details. Attach a schedule showing the following information:
• The amount of this gross income (without regard to its source) in each category identified in the instructions for line 15d, including each of the listed categories.
• Specifically identify gains on the sale of personal property other than inventory, depreciable property, and certain intangible property on which a foreign tax of 10% or more was paid or accrued. Also list losses on the sale of such property if the foreign country would have imposed a 10% or higher tax had the sale resulted in a gain. See **Sales or Exchanges of Certain Personal Property** in Pub. 514 and section 865.
• Specify foreign source capital gains or losses within each separate limitation category. Also separately identify foreign source gains or losses within each separate limitation category that are 28% rate gains and losses, unrecaptured section 1250 gains, and qualified 5-year gains and indicate the post-May 5, 2003, portion of each.

Line 15d. Foreign Gross Income Sourced at Corporate Level

Separately report gross income from sources outside the United States by category of income as follows. See Pub. 514 for information on the categories of income.

Line 15d(1). Passive foreign source income.

Line 15d(2). Attach a schedule showing the amount of foreign source income

included in each of the following listed categories of income:
• Financial services income;
• High withholding tax interest;
• Shipping income;
• Dividends from each noncontrolled section 902 corporation;
• Dividends from a domestic international sales corporation (DISC) or a former DISC;
• Distributions from a foreign sales corporation (FSC) or a former FSC;
• Section 901(j) income; and
• Certain income re-sourced by treaty.

Line 15d(3). General limitation foreign source income (all other foreign source income).

Line 15e. Deductions Allocated and Apportioned at Shareholder Level

Enter on line 15e(1) the corporation's total interest expense (including interest equivalents under Temporary Regulations section 1.861-9T(b)). Do not include interest directly allocable under Temporary Regulations section 1.861-10T to income from a specific property. This type of interest is allocated and apportioned at the corporate level and is included on lines 15f(1) through (3). On line 15e(2), enter the total of all other deductions or losses that are required to be allocated at the shareholder level. For example, include on line 15e(2) research and experimental expenditures (see Regulations section 1.861-17(f)).

Line 15f. Deductions Allocated and Apportioned at Corporate Level to Foreign Source Income

Separately report corporate deductions that are apportioned at the corporate level to **(1)** passive foreign source income, **(2)** each of the listed foreign categories of income, and **(3)** general limitation foreign source income (see the instructions for line 15d). See Pub. 514 for more information.

Line 15g. Total Foreign Taxes

Enter in U.S. dollars the total foreign taxes (described in section 901 or section 903) that were paid or accrued by the corporation (according to its method of accounting for such taxes). Translate these amounts into U.S. dollars by using the applicable exchange rate (see Pub. 514).

Attach a schedule reporting the following information:

1. The total amount of foreign taxes (including foreign taxes on income sourced at the shareholder level) relating to each category of income (see instructions for line 15d).

2. The dates on which the taxes were paid or accrued, the exchange rates used, and the amounts in both foreign currency and U.S. dollars, for:
• Taxes withheld at source on interest.
• Taxes withheld at source on dividends.

-25-

FIGURE A.15 *(Continued)*

- Taxes withheld at source on rents and royalties.
  - Other foreign taxes paid or accrued.

Line 15h. Reduction in Taxes Available for Credit

Enter the total reductions in taxes available for credit. Attach a schedule showing the reductions for:
- Taxes on foreign mineral income (section 901(e)).
- Taxes on foreign oil and gas extraction income (section 907(a)).
- Taxes attributable to boycott operations (section 908).
- Failure to timely file (or furnish all of the information required on) Forms 5471 and 8865.
- Any other items (specify).

Other

Lines 16a and 16b. Section 59(e)(2) Expenditures

Generally, section 59(e) allows each shareholder to make an election to deduct the shareholder's pro rata share of the corporation's otherwise deductible qualified expenditures ratably over 10 years (3 years for circulation expenditures), beginning with the tax year in which the expenditures were made (or for intangible drilling and development costs, over the 60-month period beginning with the month in which such costs were paid or incurred). The term "qualified expenditures" includes only the following types of expenditures paid or incurred during the tax year:
- Circulation expenditures.
- Research and experimental expenditures.
- Intangible drilling and development costs.
- Mining exploration and development costs.

If a shareholder makes the election, the above items are not treated as tax preference items.

Because the shareholders are generally allowed to make this election, the corporation cannot deduct these amounts or include them as adjustments or tax preference items on Schedule K-1. Instead, on lines 16a and 16b of Schedule K-1, the corporation passes through the information the shareholders need to figure their separate deductions.

On line 16a, enter the type of expenditures claimed on line 16b. Enter on line 16b the qualified expenditures paid or incurred during the tax year to which an election under section 59(e) may apply. Enter this amount for all shareholders whether or not any shareholder makes an election under section 59(e). If the expenditures are for intangible drilling and development costs, enter the month in which the expenditures were paid or incurred (after the type of expenditures on line 16a). If there is more than one type of expenditure included in the total shown on line 16b (or intangible drilling and development costs were paid or incurred for more than 1 month), report

this information separately for each type of expenditure (or month) on an attachment to Schedules K and K-1.

Line 17. Tax-Exempt Interest Income

Enter on line 17 tax-exempt interest income, including any exempt-interest dividends received from a mutual fund or other regulated investment company. This information must be reported by individuals on line 8b of Form 1040. Generally, the basis of the shareholder's stock is increased by the amount shown on this line under section 1367(a)(1)(A).

Line 18. Other Tax-Exempt Income

Enter on line 18 all income of the corporation exempt from tax other than tax-exempt interest (e.g., life insurance proceeds). Generally, the basis of the shareholder's stock is increased by the amount shown on this line under section 1367(a)(1)(A).

Line 19. Nondeductible Expenses

Enter on line 19 nondeductible expenses paid or incurred by the corporation. Do not include separately stated deductions shown elsewhere on Schedules K and K-1, capital expenditures, or items for which the deduction is deferred to a later tax year. Generally, the basis of the shareholder's stock is decreased by the amount shown on this line under section 1367(a)(2)(D).

Line 20

Enter total distributions made to each shareholder other than dividends reported on line 22 of Schedule K. Noncash distributions of appreciated property are valued at fair market value. See **Distributions** on page 29 for the ordering rules on distributions.

Line 21 (Schedule K Only)

Attach a statement to Schedule K to report the corporation's total income, expenditures, or other information for items 1 through 28 of the line 23 (Schedule K-1 Only) instruction below.

Line 22 (Schedule K Only)

Enter total dividends paid to shareholders from accumulated earnings and profits. Report these dividends to shareholders on Form 1099-DIV. Do not report them on Schedule K-1.

Lines 22a and 22b (Schedule K-1 Only). Recapture of Low-Income Housing Credit

If recapture of part or all of the low-income housing credit is required because **(a)** prior year qualified basis of a building decreased or **(b)** the corporation disposed of a building or part of its interest in a building, see **Form 8611**, Recapture of Low-Income Housing Credit. The instructions for Form 8611 indicate when Form 8611 is completed by the corporation and what information is provided to shareholders when recapture is required.

Note: *If a shareholder's ownership interest in a building decreased because of a transaction at the shareholder level,*

the corporation must provide the necessary information to the shareholder to enable the shareholder to figure the recapture.

If the corporation filed **Form 8693**, Low-Income Housing Credit Disposition Bond, to avoid recapture of the low-income housing credit, no entry should be made on line 22 of Schedule K-1.

See Form 8586, Form 8611, and section 42 for more information.

Supplemental Information

Line 23 (Schedule K-1 Only)

Enter in the line 23 Supplemental Information space of Schedule K-1, or on an attached schedule if more space is needed, each shareholder's share of any information asked for on lines 1 through 27 that is required to be reported in detail, and items 1 through 28 below. Please identify the applicable line number next to the information entered in the Supplemental Information space. Show income or gains as a positive number. Show losses in parentheses.

1. Taxes paid on undistributed capital gains by a regulated investment company or a real estate investment trust (REIT). As a shareholder of a regulated investment company or a REIT, the corporation will receive notice on **Form 2439,** Notice to Shareholder of Undistributed Long-Term Capital Gains, of the amount of tax paid on undistributed capital gains.

2. Gross income and other information relating to oil and gas well properties that are reported to shareholders to allow them to figure the depletion deduction for oil and gas well properties. See section 613A(c)(11) for details.

The corporation cannot deduct depletion on oil and gas wells. Each shareholder must determine the allowable amount to report on his or her return. See Pub. 535 for more information.

3. Gain or loss on the sale, exchange, or other disposition of property for which a section 179 expense deduction has been passed through to shareholders. The corporation must provide all the following information with respect to a disposition of property for which a section 179 expense deduction was passed through to shareholders (see the instructions for line 4 on page 13).

    a. Description of the property.

    b. Date the property was acquired.

    c. Date of the sale or other disposition of the property.

    d. The shareholder's pro rata share of the gross sales price.

    e. The shareholder's pro rata share of the cost or other basis plus expense of sale (reduced as explained in the instructions for Form 4797, line 21).

    f. The shareholder's pro rata share of the depreciation allowed or allowable, determined as described in the instructions for Form 4797, line 22, but

-26-

FIGURE A.15 *(Continued)*

excluding the section 179 expense deduction.

g. The shareholder's pro rata share of the section 179 expense deduction (if any) passed through for the property and the corporation's tax year(s) in which the amount was passed through.

h. An indication if the disposition is from a casualty or theft.

i. For an installment sale made during the corporation's tax year, any information needed to complete **Form 6252,** Installment Sale Income. The corporation also must separately report the shareholder's pro rata share of all payments received for the property in future tax years. (Installment payments received for installment sales made in prior tax years should be reported in the same manner used in prior tax years.)

4. Recapture of section 179 expense deduction if business use of the property dropped to 50% or less. If the business use of any property (placed in service after 1986) for which a section 179 expense deduction was passed through to shareholders dropped to 50% or less (for a reason other than disposition), the corporation must provide all the following information.

a. The shareholder's pro rata share of the original basis and depreciation allowed or allowable (not including the section 179 expense deduction).

b. The shareholder's pro rata share of the section 179 expense deduction (if any) passed through for the property and the corporation's tax year(s) in which the amount was passed through.

5. Recapture of certain mining exploration expenditures (section 617).

6. Any information or statements the corporation is required to furnish to shareholders to allow them to comply with requirements under section 6111 (registration of tax shelters) or section 6662(d)(2)(B)(ii) (regarding adequate disclosure of items that may cause an understatement of income tax).

7. If the corporation is involved in farming or fishing activities, report the gross income from these activities to shareholders.

8. Any information needed by a shareholder to compute the interest due under section 453(l)(3). If the corporation elected to report the dispositions of certain timeshares and residential lots on the installment method, each shareholder's tax liability must be increased by the shareholder's pro rata share of the interest on tax attributable to the installment payments received during the tax year.

9. Any information needed by a shareholder to compute the interest due under section 453A(c). If an obligation arising from the disposition of property to which section 453A applies is outstanding at the close of the year, each shareholder's tax liability must be increased by the tax due under section 453A(c) on the shareholder's pro rata share of the tax deferred under the installment method.

10. Any information needed by a shareholder to properly capitalize interest as required by section 263A(f). See **Section 263A uniform capitalization rules** on page 13 for more information.

11. If the corporation is a closely held S corporation (defined in section 460(b)) and it entered into any long-term contracts after February 28, 1986, that are accounted for under either the percentage of completion-capitalized cost method or the percentage of completion method, it must attach a schedule to Form 1120S showing the information required in items (a) and (b) of the instructions for lines 1 and 3 of Part II for **Form 8697,** Interest Computation Under the Look-Back Method for Completed Long-Term Contracts. It must also report the amounts for Part II, lines 1 and 3, to its shareholders. See the Instructions for Form 8697 for more information.

12. Expenditures qualifying for the **(a)** rehabilitation credit not related to rental real estate activities, **(b)** energy credit, or **(c)** reforestation credit. Complete and attach Form 3468 to Form 1120S. See Form 3468 and related instructions for information on eligible property and the lines on Form 3468 to complete. Do not include that part of the cost of the property the corporation has elected to expense under section 179. Attach to each Schedule K-1 a separate schedule in a format similar to that shown on Form 3468 detailing each shareholder's pro rata share of qualified expenditures. Also indicate the lines of Form 3468 on which the shareholders should report these amounts.

13. Recapture of investment credit. Complete and attach **Form 4255,** Recapture of Investment Credit, when investment credit property is disposed of, or it no longer qualifies for the credit, before the end of the recapture period or the useful life applicable to the property. State the type of property at the top of Form 4255, and complete lines 2, 4, and 5, whether or not any shareholder is subject to recapture of the credit. Attach to each Schedule K-1 a separate schedule providing the information the corporation is required to show on Form 4255, but list only the shareholder's pro rata share of the cost of the property subject to recapture. Also indicate the lines of Form 4255 on which the shareholders should report these amounts.

The corporation itself is liable for investment credit recapture in certain cases. See the instructions for line 22c, page 1, Form 1120S, for details.

14. Any information needed by a shareholder to compute the recapture of the qualified electric vehicle credit. See Pub. 535 for more information.

15. Recapture of new markets credit (Form 8874).

16. Any information a shareholder may need to figure recapture of the Indian employment credit. Generally, if the corporation terminates a qualified employee less than 1 year after the date of initial employment, any Indian

employment credit allowed for a prior tax year by reason of wages paid or incurred to that employee must be recaptured. For details, see section 45A(d).

17. Nonqualified withdrawals by the corporation from a capital construction fund.

18. Unrecaptured section 1250 gain. Figure this amount for each section 1250 property in Part III of Form 4797 (except property for which gain is reported using the installment method on Form 6252) for which you had an entry in Part I of Form 4797 by subtracting line 26g of Form 4797 from the **smaller** of line 22 or line 24 of Form 4797. Figure the total of these amounts for all section 1250 properties. Generally, the result is the corporation's unrecaptured section 1250 gain. However, if the corporation is reporting gain on the installment method for a section 1250 property held more than 1 year, see the next paragraph to figure the unrecaptured section 1250 gain on that property allocable to this tax year. Report each shareholder's pro rata share of the total amount as "Unrecaptured section 1250 gain."

The total unrecaptured section 1250 gain for an installment sale of section 1250 property held more than 1 year is figured in a manner similar to that used in the preceding paragraph. However, the total unrecaptured section 1250 gain must be allocated to the installment payments received from the sale. To do so, the corporation generally must treat the gain allocable to each installment payment as unrecaptured section 1250 gain until all such gain has been used in full. Figure the unrecaptured section 1250 gain for installment payments received during the tax year as the **smaller** of (a) the amount from line 26 or line 37 of Form 6252 (whichever applies) or (b) the total unrecaptured section 1250 gain for the sale reduced by all gain reported in prior years (excluding section 1250 ordinary income recapture). However, if the corporation chose not to treat all of the gain from payments received after May 6, 1997, and before August 24, 1999, as unrecaptured section 1250 gain, use only the amount the corporation chose to treat as unrecaptured section 1250 gain for those payments to reduce the total unrecaptured section 1250 gain remaining to be reported for the sale.

If the corporation received a Schedule K-1 or Form 1099-DIV from an estate, a trust, a REIT, or a mutual fund reporting "unrecaptured section 1250 gain," **do not** add it to the corporation's own unrecaptured section 1250 gain. Instead, report it as a separate amount. For example, if the corporation received a Form 1099-DIV from a REIT with unrecaptured section 1250 gain, report it as "Unrecaptured section 1250 gain from a REIT."

Also report as a separate amount any gain from the sale or exchange of an interest in a partnership attributable to unrecaptured section 1250 gain. See Regulations section 1.1(h)-1 and attach a

-27-

FIGURE A.15 *(Continued)*

statement required under Regulations section 1.1(h)-1(e).

19. 28% rate gain (loss). Figure this amount attributable to collectibles from the amount reported on Schedule D (Form 1120S) line 14. A **collectibles gain (loss)** is any long-term gain or deductible long-term loss from the sale or exchange of a collectible that is a capital asset.

Collectibles include works of art, rugs, antiques, metal (such as gold, silver, platinum bullion), gems, stamps, coin, alcoholic beverages, and certain other tangible property.

Also, include gain (but not loss) from the sale or exchange of an interest in a partnership or trust held for more than 1 year and attributable to unrealized appreciation of collectibles. For details, see Regulations section 1.1(h)-1. Also attach the statement required under Regulations section 1.1(h)-1(e).

20. Qualified 5-year gain. Attach a statement to each Schedule K-1 indicating the amount of net long-term gain (not losses) from the disposition of assets (excluding stock that could qualify for section 1202 gain) held more than 5 years that are portfolio income included on line 14 of Schedule D (Form 1120S). Also indicated the aggregate amount of all section 1231 gains from property held more than 5 years. Qualified 5-year gains should be reported only for the portion of the tax year before May 6, 2003. Do not include any section 1231 gain attributable to straight-line depreciation from section 1250 property. Indicate on the statement that this amount should be included in the shareholder's computation of qualified 5-year gain only if the amount on the shareholder's Form 4797, line 7, column (g), is more than zero, and that none of the gain is unrecaptured section 1250 gain.

21. If the corporation is a closely held S corporation (defined in section 460(b)(4)) and it depreciated certain property placed in service after September 13, 1995, under the income forecast method, it must attach to Form 1120S the information specified in the instructions for Form 8866, line 2, for the 3rd and 10th tax years beginning after the tax year the property was placed in service. It must also report the line 2 amounts to its shareholders. See the Instructions for Form 8866 for more details.

22. Amortization of reforestation expenditures. Report the amortizable basis and year in which the amortization began for the current year and the 7 preceding years. For limits that may apply, see section 194 and Pub. 535.

23. Any information needed by a shareholder to figure the interest due under section 1260(b). If any portion of a constructive ownership transaction was open in any prior year, each shareholder's tax liability must be increased by the shareholder's pro rata share of interest due on any deferral of gain recognition. See section 1260(b) for details, including how to figure the interest.

24. Any information needed by a shareholder to figure the extraterritorial income exclusion. See **Extraterritorial Income Exclusion** on page 11 for more information.

25. Commercial revitalization deduction from rental real estate activities. See **Line 19—Other Deductions** for the **Special Rules** that apply to the deduction.

26. If the corporation participates in a transaction that must be disclosed on Form 8886 (see page 7), both the corporation and its shareholders may be required to file Form 8886. The corporation must determine if any of its shareholders are required to disclose the transaction and provide those shareholders with information they will need to file Form 8886. This determination is based on the category(s) under which a transaction qualified for disclosures. See the instructions for Form 8886 for details.

27. Recapture of the credit for employer-provided child care facilities and services (Form 8882).

28. Any other information the shareholders need to prepare their tax returns.

Schedule L. Balance Sheets per Books

The balance sheets should agree with the corporation's books and records. Include certificates of deposit as cash on line 1 of Schedule L.

If the S election terminated during the tax year, the year-end balance sheet generally should agree with the books and records at the end of the C short year. However, if the corporation elected under section 1362(e)(3) to have items assigned to each short year under normal tax accounting rules, the year-end balance sheet should agree with the books and records at the end of the S short year.

Line 5. Tax-Exempt Securities

Include on this line:
- State and local government obligations, the interest on which is excludible from gross income under section 103(a), and
- Stock in a mutual fund or other regulated investment company that distributed exempt-interest dividends during the tax year of the corporation.

Line 24. Retained Earnings

If the corporation maintains separate accounts for appropriated and unappropriated retained earnings, it may want to continue such accounting for purposes of preparing its financial balance sheet. Also, if the corporation converts to C corporation status in a subsequent year, it will be required to report its appropriated and unappropriated retained earnings on separate lines of Schedule L of Form 1120.

Line 25. Adjustments to Shareholders' Equity

Some examples of adjustments to report on this line include:
- Unrealized gains and losses on securities held "available for sale."
- Foreign currency translation adjustments.
- The excess of additional pension liability over unrecognized prior service cost.
- Guarantees of employee stock (ESOP) debt.
- Compensation related to employee stock award plans.

If the total adjustment to be entered is a negative amount, enter the amount in parentheses.

Schedule M-1. Reconciliation of Income (Loss) per Books With Income (Loss) per Return

Line 3b. Travel and Entertainment

Include on this line:
- Meals and entertainment not allowed under section 274(n).
- Expenses for the use of an entertainment facility.
- The part of business gifts over $25.
- Expenses of an individual allocable to conventions on cruise ships over $2,000.
- Employee achievement awards over $400.
- The part of the cost of entertainment tickets that exceeds face value (also subject to 50% limit).
- The part of the cost of skyboxes that exceeds the face value of nonluxury box seat tickets.
- The part of the cost of luxury water travel not allowed under section 274(m).
- Expenses for travel as a form of education; nondeductible club dues.
- Other travel and entertainment expenses.

-28-

FIGURE A.15 *(Continued)*

194

		(a) Accumulated adjustments account	(b) Other adjustments account	(c) Shareholders' undistributed taxable income previously taxed
1	Balance at beginning of tax year . . .	-0-	-0-	
2	Ordinary income from page 1, line 21 .	10,000		
3	Other additions	20,000	5,000	
4	Loss from page 1, line 21	( )		
5	Other reductions	(36,000)	( )	
6	Combine lines 1 through 5	(6,000)	5,000	
7	Distributions other than dividend distributions	-0-	5,000	
8	Balance at end of tax year. Subtract line 7 from line 6	(6,000)	-0-	

Schedule M-2. Analysis of Accumulated Adjustments Account, Other Adjustments Account, and Shareholders' Undistributed Taxable Income Previously Taxed

Column (a). Accumulated Adjustments Account

The accumulated adjustments account (AAA) is an account of the S corporation that generally reflects the accumulated undistributed net income of the corporation for the corporation's post-1982 years. S corporations with accumulated E&P must maintain the AAA to determine the tax effect of distributions during S years and the post-termination transition period. An S corporation without accumulated E&P does not need to maintain the AAA in order to determine the tax effect of distributions. Nevertheless, if an S corporation without accumulated E&P engages in certain transactions to which section 381(a) applies, such as a merger into an S corporation with accumulated E&P, the S corporation must be able to calculate its AAA at the time of the merger for purposes of determining the tax effect of post-merger distributions. Therefore, it is recommended that the AAA be maintained by all S corporations.

On the first day of the corporation's first tax year as an S corporation, the balance of the AAA is zero. At the end of the tax year, adjust the AAA for the items for the tax year as explained below and in the order listed.

1. Increase the AAA by income (other than tax-exempt income) and the excess of the deduction for depletion over the basis of the property subject to depletion (unless the property is an oil and gas property the basis of which has been allocated to shareholders).
2. Generally, decrease the AAA by deductible losses and expenses, nondeductible expenses (other than expenses related to tax-exempt income and Federal taxes attributable to a C

corporation tax year), and the sum of the shareholders' deductions for depletion for any oil or gas property held by the corporation as described in section 1367(a)(2)(E). However, if the total decreases under 2 exceeds the total increases under 1 above, the excess is a "net negative adjustment." If the corporation has a net negative adjustment, **do not** take it into account under 2. Instead, take it into account only under 4 below.
3. Decrease AAA (but not below zero) by property distributions (other than dividend distributions from accumulated E&P), unless the corporation elects to reduce accumulated E&P first. See **Distributions** below for definitions and other details.
4. Decrease AAA by any net negative adjustment. For adjustments to the AAA for redemptions, reorganizations, and corporate separations, see Regulations section 1.1368-2(d).

Note: *The AAA may have a negative balance at year end. See section 1368(e).*

Column (b). Other Adjustments Account

The other adjustments account is adjusted for tax-exempt income (and related expenses) and Federal taxes attributable to a C corporation tax year. After these adjustments are made, the account is reduced for any distributions made during the year. See **Distributions** below.

Column (c). Shareholders' Undistributed Taxable Income Previously Taxed

The shareholders' undistributed taxable income previously taxed account, also called previously taxed income (PTI), is maintained only if the corporation had a balance in this account at the start of its 2003 tax year. If there is a beginning balance for the 2003 tax year, no adjustments are made to the account except to reduce the account for distributions made under section 1375(d) (as in effect before the enactment of the Subchapter S Revision Act of 1982). See **Distributions** below for the order of distributions from the account.

Each shareholder's right to nontaxable distributions from PTI is personal and

cannot be transferred to another person. The corporation is required to keep records of each shareholder's net share of PTI.

Distributions

General rule. Unless the corporation makes one of the elections described below, property distributions (including cash) are applied in the following order to reduce accounts of the S corporation that are used to figure the tax effect of distributions made by the corporation to its shareholders:

1. Reduce the AAA determined without regard to any net negative adjustment for the tax year (but not below zero). If distributions during the tax year exceed the AAA at the close of the tax year determined without regard to any net negative adjustment for the tax year, the AAA is allocated pro rata to each distribution made during the tax year. See section 1368(c).
2. Reduce shareholders' PTI account for any section 1375(d) (as in effect before 1983) distributions. A distribution from the PTI account is tax free to the extent of a shareholder's basis in his or her stock in the corporation.
3. Reduce accumulated E&P. Generally, the S corporation has accumulated E&P only if it has not distributed E&P accumulated in prior years when the S corporation was a C corporation (section 1361(a)(2)). See section 312 for information on E&P. The only adjustments that can be made to the accumulated E&P of an S corporation are (a) reductions for dividend distributions; (b) adjustments for redemptions, liquidations, reorganizations, etc.; and (c) reductions for investment credit recapture tax for which the corporation is liable. See sections 1371(c) and (d)(3).
4. Reduce the other adjustments account.
5. Reduce any remaining shareholders' equity accounts.

Elections relating to source of distributions. The corporation may modify the above ordering rules by making one or more of the following elections:

1. *Election to distribute accumulated E&P first.* If the corporation has accumulated E&P and

-29-

FIGURE A.15   *(Continued)*

wants to distribute this E&P before making distributions from the AAA, it may elect to do so with the consent of all its affected shareholders (section 1368(e)(3)(B)). This election is irrevocable and applies only for the tax year for which it is made. For details on making the election, see **Statement regarding elections** below.

2. *Election to make a deemed dividend.* If the corporation wants to distribute all or part of its accumulated E&P through a deemed dividend, it may elect to do so with the consent of all its affected shareholders (section 1368(e)(3)(B)). Under this election, the corporation will be treated as also having made the election to distribute accumulated E&P first. The amount of the deemed dividend cannot exceed the accumulated E&P at the end of the tax year, reduced by any actual distributions of accumulated E&P made during the tax year. A deemed dividend is treated as if it were a pro rata distribution of money to the shareholders, received by the shareholders, and immediately contributed back to the corporation, all on the last day of the tax year. This election is irrevocable and applies only for the tax year for which it is made. For details on making the election, see **Statement regarding elections** below.

3. *Election to forego PTI.* If the corporation wants to forego distributions of PTI, it may elect to do so with the consent of all its affected shareholders (section 1368(e)(3)(B)). Under this election, paragraph 2 under the **General rule** on page 29 does not apply to any distribution made during the tax year. This election is irrevocable and applies only for the tax year for which it is made. For details on making the election, see **Statement regarding elections** below.

Statement regarding elections. To make any of the above elections, the corporation must attach a statement to a timely filed original or amended Form 1120S for the tax year for which the election is made. In the statement, the corporation must identify the election it is making and must state that each shareholder consents to the election. The statement of election to make a deemed dividend must include the amount of the deemed dividend distributed to each shareholder. For more details on the election, see Temporary Regulations section 1.1368-1T(f)(5).

Example

The following example shows how the Schedule M-2 accounts are adjusted for items of income (loss), deductions, and distributions reported on Form 1120S. In this example, the corporation has no PTI or accumulated E&P.

Items per return are:

1. Page 1, line 21 income—$10,000
2. Schedule K, line 2 loss—($3,000)
3. Schedule K, line 4a income—$4,000
4. Schedule K, line 4b(2) income—$16,000
5. Schedule K, line 7 deduction—$24,000
6. Schedule K, line 10 deduction—$3,000
7. Schedule K, line 13 work opportunity credit—$6,000

8. Schedule K, line 17 tax-exempt interest—$5,000
9. Schedule K, line 19 nondeductible expenses—$6,000 (reduction in salaries and wages for work opportunity credit), and
10. Schedule K, line 20 distributions—$65,000.

Based on return items 1 through 10 and starting balances of zero, the columns for the AAA and the other adjustments account are completed as shown in the Schedule M-2 Worksheet on page 29.

For the AAA, the worksheet line 3—$20,000 amount is the total of the Schedule K, lines 4a and 4b(2) income of $4,000 and $16,000. The worksheet line 5—$36,000 amount is the total of the Schedule K, line 2 loss of ($3,000), line 7 deduction of $24,000, line 10 deduction of $3,000, and the line 19 nondeductible expenses of $6,000. The worksheet line 7 is zero. The AAA at the end of the tax year (figured without regard to distributions and the net negative adjustment of $6,000) is zero, and distributions cannot reduce the AAA below zero.

For the other adjustments account, the worksheet line 3 amount is the Schedule K, line 17, tax-exempt interest income of $5,000. The worksheet line 7 amount is $5,000, reducing the other adjustments account to zero. The remaining $60,000 of distributions are not entered on Schedule M-2.

Paperwork Reduction Act Notice. We ask for the information on this form to carry out the Internal Revenue laws of the United States. You are required to give us the information. We need it to ensure that you are complying with these laws and to allow us to figure and collect the right amount of tax.

You are not required to provide the information requested on a form that is subject to the Paperwork Reduction Act unless the form displays a valid OMB control number. Books or records relating to a form or its instructions must be retained as long as their contents may become material in the administration of any Internal Revenue law. Generally, tax returns and return information are confidential, as required by section 6103.

The time needed to complete and file this form and related schedules will vary depending on individual circumstances. The estimated average times are:

Form	Recordkeeping	Learning about the law or the form	Preparing the form	Copying, assembling, and sending the form to the IRS
1120S	65 hr., 45 min.	25 hr., 11 min.	47 hr., 44 min.	5 hr., 54 min.
Sch. D (1120S)	10 hr., 2 min.	4 hr., 31 min.	9 hr., 32 min.	1 hr., 20 min.
Sch. K-1 (1120S)	16 hr., 58 min.	10 hr., 36 min.	15 hr., 4 min.	1 hr., 4 min.

We Welcome Comments on Forms. If you have comments concerning the accuracy of these time estimates or suggestions for making these forms simpler, we would be happy to hear from you. You can write to the Tax Products Coordinating Committee, Western Area Distribution Center, Rancho Cordova, CA 95743-0001. **Do not** send the tax form to this address. Instead, see **Where To File** on page 3.

FIGURE A.15 *(Continued)*

Form 1065, U.S. Return of Partnership Income Filed by a Limited Liability Company (LLC)

This LLC has not elected to be taxed otherwise than as a partnership, so it reports income and expenses on this partnership return form. All of the income and deductions flow into one bucket of ordinary income on line 22 and each individual partner (LLC member) receives a Form K-1, on which is listed his or her share of the income, $56,000 in this case. The member pays income tax, as well as Social Security tax, on that $56,000 share of earnings.

As was the case with the S corporation, the LLC also made a $1,000 contribution to an eligible charity. This item is not deducted in computing the LLC income shared by the members, but one-third of that amount is listed separately on Form K-1 that each member receives. That member then lists that $333 contribution on his or her individual income tax return as an itemized deduction. (If the member does not itemize deductions, the tax benefit of the charitable contribution is lost forever.)

As for the S corporation tax return, Form K-1 for a member provides a laundry list of items that "flow through" to the members. (Only one Form K-1 is reproduced here, but as each of these three members own 33.3 percent of the LLC, each would receive an identical Form K-1.)

Department of the Treasury
Internal Revenue Service

U.S. Return of Partnership Income

For calendar year 2003, or tax year beginning .... , 2003, and ending .... , 20..... .
▶ **See separate instructions.**

OMB No. 1545-0099

2003

A Principal business activity	Use the IRS label. Other-wise, print or type.	Name of partnership	D Employer Identification number
SALES		CLEAN CAT PROCESSORS, LLC	55 : 5555555
B Principal product or service		Number, street, and room or suite no. If a P.O. box, see page 14 of the instructions.	E Date business started
PET SUPPLIES		111 MAIN ST., SUITE 1	1/1/03
C Business code number		City or town, state, and ZIP code	F Total assets (see page 14 of the instructions)
453910		EAST OVERSHOE, VA 55555	$ 217,000

G Check applicable boxes: **(1)** ☑ Initial return **(2)** ☐ Final return **(3)** ☐ Name change **(4)** ☐ Address change **(5)** ☐ Amended return
H Check accounting method: **(1)** ☐ Cash **(2)** ☐ Accrual **(3)** ☐ Other (specify) ▶ ....
I Number of Schedules K-1. Attach one for each person who was a partner at any time during the tax year ▶ ....

Caution: *Include **only** trade or business income and expenses on lines 1a through 22 below. See the instructions for more information.*

Income

1a	Gross receipts or sales	1a	1,000,000		
b	Less returns and allowances	1b		1c	1,000,000
2	Cost of goods sold (Schedule A, line 8)			2	600,000
3	Gross profit. Subtract line 2 from line 1c			3	400,000
4	Ordinary income (loss) from other partnerships, estates, and trusts *(attach schedule)*			4	
5	Net farm profit (loss) *(attach Schedule F (Form 1040))*			5	
6	Net gain (loss) from Form 4797, Part II, line 18			6	
7	Other income (loss) *(attach schedule)*			7	
8	**Total income (loss).** Combine lines 3 through 7			8	400,000

Deductions (see page 15 of the instructions for limitations)

9	Salaries and wages (other than to partners) (less employment credits)			9	42,500
10	Guaranteed payments to partners			10	
11	Repairs and maintenance			11	12,000
12	Bad debts			12	
13	Rent			13	
14	Taxes and licenses			14	1,000
15	Interest			15	2,000
16a	Depreciation (if required, attach Form 4562)	16a	2,000		
b	Less depreciation reported on Schedule A and elsewhere on return	16b		16c	2,000
17	Depletion **(Do not deduct oil and gas depletion.)**			17	
18	Retirement plans, etc.			18	
19	Employee benefit programs			19	
20	Other deductions *(attach schedule)*			20	172,500
21	**Total deductions.** Add the amounts shown in the far right column for lines 9 through 20			21	232,000
22	**Ordinary income (loss)** from trade or business activities. Subtract line 21 from line 8			22	168,000

Sign Here

Under penalties of perjury, I declare that I have examined this return, including accompanying schedules and statements, and to the best of my knowledge and belief, it is true, correct, and complete. Declaration of preparer (other than general partner or limited liability company member) is based on all information of which preparer has any knowledge.

▶ ....   ▶
Signature of general partner or limited liability company member   Date

May the IRS discuss this return with the preparer shown below (see instructions)? ☐ Yes ☐ No

Paid Preparer's Use Only

Preparer's signature		Date		Check if self-employed ▶ ☐	Preparer's SSN or PTIN
Firm's name (or yours if self-employed), address, and ZIP code ▶			EIN ▶		
			Phone no.	(	)

For Paperwork Reduction Act Notice, see separate instructions.   Cat. No. 11390Z   Form **1065** (2003)

FIGURE A.16   IRS Form 1065 (U.S. Return of Partnership Income)

Schedule A   Cost of Goods Sold (see page 18 of the instructions)

1	Inventory at beginning of year	**1**	0
2	Purchases less cost of items withdrawn for personal use	**2**	720,000
3	Cost of labor	**3**	
4	Additional section 263A costs *(attach schedule)*	**4**	
5	Other costs *(attach schedule)*	**5**	
6	**Total.** Add lines 1 through 5	**6**	720,000
7	Inventory at end of year	**7**	120,000
8	**Cost of goods sold.** Subtract line 7 from line 6. Enter here and on page 1, line 2	**8**	600,000

9a Check all methods used for valuing closing inventory:

  (i) ☑ Cost as described in Regulations section 1.471-3

  (ii) ☐ Lower of cost or market as described in Regulations section 1.471-4

  (iii) ☐ Other (specify method used and attach explanation) ▶ ....

  b Check this box if there was a writedown of "subnormal" goods as described in Regulations section 1.471-2(c) . . . . ▶ ☐

  c Check this box if the LIFO inventory method was adopted this tax year for any goods *(if checked, attach Form 970)* . . ▶ ☐

  d Do the rules of section 263A (for property produced or acquired for resale) apply to the partnership? . . ☐ **Yes** ☑ **No**

  e Was there any change in determining quantities, cost, or valuations between opening and closing inventory? . ☐ **Yes** ☑ **No**
   If "Yes," attach explanation.

Schedule B   Other Information

		Yes	No
1	What type of entity is filing this return? Check the applicable box:		
	a ☐ Domestic general partnership **b** ☐ Domestic limited partnership		
	c ☑ Domestic limited liability company **d** ☐ Domestic limited liability partnership		
	e ☐ Foreign partnership **f** ☐ Other ▶		
2	Are any partners in this partnership also partnerships?		✔
3	During the partnership's tax year, did the partnership own any interest in another partnership or in any foreign entity that was disregarded as an entity separate from its owner under Regulations sections 301.7701-2 and 301.7701-3? If yes, see instructions for required attachment		✔
4	Is this partnership subject to the consolidated audit procedures of sections 6221 through 6233? If "Yes," see **Designation of Tax Matters Partner** below		✔
5	Does this partnership meet **all three** of the following requirements?		
	a The partnership's total receipts for the tax year were less than $250,000;		
	b The partnership's total assets at the end of the tax year were less than $600,000; **and**		
	c Schedules K-1 are filed with the return and furnished to the partners on or before the due date (including extensions) for the partnership return.		
	If "Yes," the partnership is not required to complete Schedules L, M-1, and M-2; Item F on page 1 of Form 1065; or Item J on Schedule K-1		✔
6	Does this partnership have any foreign partners? If "Yes," the partnership may have to file Forms 8804, 8805 and 8813. See page 20 of the instructions		✔
7	Is this partnership a publicly traded partnership as defined in section 469(k)(2)?		✔
8	Has this partnership filed, or is it required to file, **Form 8264,** Application for Registration of a Tax Shelter? . .		✔
9	At any time during calendar year 2003, did the partnership have an interest in or a signature or other authority over a financial account in a foreign country (such as a bank account, securities account, or other financial account)? See page 20 of the instructions for exceptions and filing requirements for Form TD F 90-22.1. If "Yes," enter the name of the foreign country. ▶		✔
10	During the tax year, did the partnership receive a distribution from, or was it the grantor of, or transferor to, a foreign trust? If "Yes," the partnership may have to file Form 3520. See page 20 of the instructions		✔
11	Was there a distribution of property or a transfer (e.g., by sale or death) of a partnership interest during the tax year? If "Yes," you may elect to adjust the basis of the partnership's assets under section 754 by attaching the statement described under **Elections Made By the Partnership** on page 9 of the instructions		✔
12	Enter the number of **Forms 8865,** Return of U.S. Persons With Respect to Certain Foreign Partnerships, attached to this return . . . . ▶ 0		

Designation of Tax Matters Partner (see page 20 of the instructions)

Enter below the general partner designated as the tax matters partner (TMP) for the tax year of this return:

Name of designated TMP ▶		Identifying number of TMP ▶	
Address of designated TMP ▶			

Form **1065** (2003)

FIGURE A.16   *(Continued)*

Schedule K	Partners' Shares of Income, Credits, Deductions, etc.		
	(a) Distributive share items		**(b) Total amount**

1	Ordinary income (loss) from trade or business activities (page 1, line 22)	**1**	168,000
2	Net income (loss) from rental real estate activities *(attach Form 8825)*	**2**	
3a	Gross income from other rental activities **3a**		
b	Expenses from other rental activities *(attach schedule)* **3b**		
c	Net income (loss) from other rental activities. Subtract line 3b from line 3a	**3c**	
4	Portfolio income (loss) *(attach Schedule D (Form 1065) for lines 4d and 4e)*:		
a	Interest income	**4a**	
b	Dividends: **(1)** Qualified dividends ▶ .... **(2)** Total ordinary dividends ▶	**4b(2)**	
c	Royalty income	**4c**	
d	Net short-term capital gain (loss): **(1)** post-May 5, 2003 ▶ .... **(2)** Entire year ▶	**4d(2)**	
e	Net long-term capital gain (loss): **(1)** post-May 5, 2003 ▶ .... **(2)** Entire year ▶	**4e(2)**	
f	Other portfolio income (loss) *(attach schedule)*	**4f**	
5	Guaranteed payments to partners	**5**	
6a	Net section 1231 gain (loss) (post-May 5, 2003) *(attach Form 4797)*	**6a**	
b	Net section 1231 gain (loss) (entire year) *(attach Form 4797)* . .	**6b**	
7	Other income (loss) *(attach schedule)*	**7**	
8	Charitable contributions *(attach schedule)*	**8**	1,000
9	Section 179 expense deduction *(attach Form 4562)*.	**9**	
10	Deductions related to portfolio income (itemize)	**10**	
11	Other deductions *(attach schedule)*	**11**	
12a	Low-income housing credit: **(1)** From partnerships to which section 42(j)(5) applies	**12a(1)**	
	(2) Other than on line 12a(1)	**12a(2)**	
b	Qualified rehabilitation expenditures related to rental real estate activities *(attach Form 3468)*	**12b**	
c	Credits (other than credits shown on lines 12a and 12b) related to rental real estate activities	**12c**	
d	Credits related to other rental activities	**12d**	
13	Other credits	**13**	
14a	Interest expense on investment debts	**14a**	
b	**(1)** Investment income included on lines 4a, 4b(2), 4c, and 4f above	**14b(1)**	
	(2) Investment expenses included on line 10 above.	**14b(2)**	
15a	Net earnings (loss) from self-employment	**15a**	
b	Gross farming or fishing income	**15b**	
c	Gross nonfarm income	**15c**	
16a	Depreciation adjustment on property placed in service after 1986 . .	**16a**	
b	Adjusted gain or loss	**16b**	
c	Depletion (other than oil and gas)	**16c**	
d	**(1)** Gross income from oil, gas, and geothermal properties	**16d(1)**	
	(2) Deductions allocable to oil, gas, and geothermal properties . .	**16d(2)**	
e	Other adjustments and tax preference items *(attach schedule)* . .	**16e**	
17a	Name of foreign country or U.S. possession ▶ -------------------------------		
b	Gross income from all sources	**17b**	
c	Gross income sourced at partner level	**17c**	
d	Foreign gross income sourced at partnership level:		
	(1) Passive ▶ .... **(2)** Listed categories *(attach schedule)* ▶ .... **(3)** General limitation ▶	**17d(3)**	
e	Deductions allocated and apportioned at partner level:		
	(1) Interest expense ▶ .... **(2)** Other . . . . ▶	**17e(2)**	
f	Deductions allocated and apportioned at partnership level to foreign source income:		
	(1) Passive ▶ .... **(2)** Listed categories *(attach schedule)* ▶ .... **(3)** General limitation ▶	**17f(3)**	
g	Total foreign taxes (check one): ▶ Paid ☐ Accrued ☐	**17g**	
h	Reduction in taxes available for credit *(attach schedule)*	**17h**	
18	Section 59(e)(2) expenditures: **a** Type ▶ ------------------------------------ **b** Amount ▶	**18b**	
19	Tax-exempt interest income	**19**	
20	Other tax-exempt income	**20**	
21	Nondeductible expenses	**21**	
22	Distributions of money (cash and marketable securities)	**22**	
23	Distributions of property other than money	**23**	
24	Other items and amounts required to be reported separately to partners *(attach schedule)* .		

Row labels along left margin: Income (Loss); Deductions; Credits; Investment Interest; Self-Employment; Adjustments and Tax Preference Items; Foreign Taxes; Other.

Form **1065** (2003)

FIGURE A.16 *(Continued)*

Analysis of Net Income (Loss)

1 Net income (loss). Combine Schedule K, lines 1 through 7 in column (b). From the result, subtract the sum of Schedule K, lines 8 through 11, 14a, 17g, and 18b					**1**	167,000

2 Analysis by partner type:	**(i)** Corporate	**(ii)** Individual (active)	**(iii)** Individual (passive)	**(iv)** Partnership	**(v)** Exempt organization	**(vi)** Nominee/Other
a General partners		3				
b Limited partners						

Note: Schedules L, M-1 and M-2 are not required if Question 5 of Schedule B is answered "Yes."

Schedule L	**Balance Sheets per Books**	Beginning of tax year		End of tax year	
	Assets	**(a)**	**(b)**	**(c)**	**(d)**
1	Cash		FIRST YEAR		39,000
2a	Trade notes and accounts receivable			50,000	
b	Less allowance for bad debts				50,000
3	Inventories				120,000
4	U.S. government obligations				
5	Tax-exempt securities				
6	Other current assets (attach schedule)				
7	Mortgage and real estate loans				
8	Other investments (attach schedule)				
9a	Buildings and other depreciable assets . . .			10,000	
b	Less accumulated depreciation			2,000	8,000
10a	Depletable assets				
b	Less accumulated depletion				
11	Land (net of any amortization)				
12a	Intangible assets (amortizable only).				
b	Less accumulated amortization				
13	Other assets (attach schedule)				
14	**Total** assets				217,000
	Liabilities and Capital				
15	Accounts payable				55,000
16	Mortgages, notes, bonds payable in less than 1 year				
17	Other current liabilities (attach schedule) . . .				
18	All nonrecourse loans				
19	Mortgages, notes, bonds payable in 1 year or more				40,000
20	Other liabilities (attach schedule)				
21	Partners' capital accounts				122,000
22	**Total** liabilities and capital				217,000

Schedule M-1	**Reconciliation of Income (Loss) per Books With Income (Loss) per Return**		
1 Net income (loss) per books	35,000	**6** Income recorded on books this year not included on Schedule K, lines 1 through 7 (itemize):	
2 Income included on Schedule K, lines 1 through 4, 6b, and 7, not recorded on books this year (itemize):		**a** Tax-exempt interest $	
3 Guaranteed payments (other than health insurance)		**7** Deductions included on Schedule K, lines 1 through 11, 14a, 17g, and 18b, not charged against book income this year (itemize):	
4 Expenses recorded on books this year not included on Schedule K, lines 1 through 11, 14a, 17g, and 18b (itemize):		**a** Depreciation $	
a Depreciation $			
b Travel and entertainment $		**8** Add lines 6 and 7	
....		**9** Income (loss) (Analysis of Net Income (Loss), line 1). Subtract line 8 from line 5	35,000
5 Add lines 1 through 4	35,000		

Schedule M-2	**Analysis of Partners' Capital Accounts**		
1 Balance at beginning of year	0	**6** Distributions: **a** Cash	135,000
2 Capital contributed: **a** Cash	75,000	**b** Property	
b Property		**7** Other decreases (itemize):	
3 Net income (loss) per books	167,000	....	
4 Other increases (itemize):			
....		**8** Add lines 6 and 7	135,000
5 Add lines 1 through 4	242,000	**9** Balance at end of year. Subtract line 8 from line 5	107,000

FIGURE A.16 *(Continued)*

CLEAN CAT PROCESSORS, INC.

Employer Identification Number 55-5555555

Form 1065, year ended 12/31/2003

Line 26, Other deductions

Professional services	$ 3,250
Office expense	2,500
Supplies	1,000
Insurance	5,000
Telephone	5,000
Payroll tax, regular employees	4,250
Advertising	150,000
Utilities	1,500
	$172,500

SCHEDULE K-1
(Form 1065)
Department of the Treasury
Internal Revenue Service

Partner's Share of Income, Credits, Deductions, etc.
► See separate instructions.
For calendar year 2003 or tax year beginning _____ , 2003, and ending _____ , 20 ___

OMB No. 1545-0099

2003

Partner's identifying number ► 000-00-0000	Partnership's identifying number ► 55 : 5555555
Partner's name, address, and ZIP code **ANNE WHO** **234 CAT COURT** **EAST OVERSHOE, VA 55555**	Partnership's name, address, and ZIP code **CLEAN CAT PROCESSORS, LLC** **111 MAIN ST., SUITE 1** **EAST OVERSHOE, VA 55555**

A This partner is a ☑ general partner ☐ limited partner
☐ limited liability company member
B What type of entity is this partner? ► **INDIVIDUAL**
C Is this partner a ☑ domestic or a ☐ foreign partner?

F Partner's share of liabilities (see instructions):
Nonrecourse . . . . $ _____
Qualified nonrecourse financing . $ _____
Other . . . . $ _____**31,667**

	(i) Before change or termination	(ii) End of year
D Enter partner's percentage of:		
Profit sharing . . . . %	_____ %	**33.3** %
Loss sharing . . . . %	_____ %	**33.3** %
Ownership of capital . . . . %	_____ %	**33.3** %

G Tax shelter registration number . ► _____

H Check here if this partnership is a publicly traded partnership as defined in section 469(k)(2) . . . . . ☐

E IRS Center where partnership filed return: **CINCINATTI**

I Check applicable boxes: (1) ☐ Final K-1 (2) ☐ Amended K-1

J Analysis of partner's capital account:

(a) Capital account at beginning of year	(b) Capital contributed during year	(c) Partner's share of lines 3, 4, and 7, Form 1065, Schedule M-2	(d) Withdrawals and distributions	(e) Capital account at end of year (combine columns (a) through (d))
0	25,000	55,667	(40,000)	40,667

	(a) Distributive share item		(b) Amount	(c) 1040 filers enter the amount in column (b) on:
Income (Loss)	**1** Ordinary income (loss) from trade or business activities . . .	**1**	55,667	See page 6 of Partner's Instructions for Schedule K-1 (Form 1065).
	2 Net income (loss) from rental real estate activities	**2**		
	3 Net income (loss) from other rental activities	**3**		
	4 Portfolio income (loss):			
	a Interest income	**4a**		Form 1040, line 8a
	b (1) Qualified dividends	**4b(1)**		Form 1040, line 9b
	(2) Total ordinary dividends	**4b(2)**		Form 1040, line 9a
	c Royalty income	**4c**		Sch. E, Part I, line 4
	d (1) Net short-term capital gain (loss) (post-May 5, 2003) . . .	**4d(1)**		Sch. D, line 5, col. (g)
	(2) Net short-term capital gain (loss) (entire year)	**4d(2)**		Sch. D, line 5, col. (f)
	e (1) Net long-term capital gain (loss) (post-May 5, 2003) . . .	**4e(1)**		Sch. D, line 12, col. (g)
	(2) Net long-term capital gain (loss) (entire year)	**4e(2)**		Sch. D, line 12, col. (f)
	f Other portfolio income (loss) *(attach schedule)*	**4f**		
	5 Guaranteed payments to partner	**5**		See pages 6 and 7 of Partner's Instructions for Schedule K-1 (Form 1065).
	6a Net section 1231 gain (loss) (post-May 5, 2003).	**6a**		
	b Net section 1231 gain (loss) (entire year)	**6b**		
	7 Other income (loss) *(attach schedule)*	**7**		
Deduc-tions	**8** Charitable contributions (see instructions) *(attach schedule)* . .	**8**	333	Sch. A, line 15 or 16
	9 Section 179 expense deduction.	**9**		See page 8 of Partner's Instructions for Schedule K-1 (Form 1065).
	10 Deductions related to portfolio income *(attach schedule)* . . .	**10**		
	11 Other deductions *(attach schedule)*.	**11**		
Credits	**12a** Low-income housing credit: **(1)** From section 42(j)(5) partnerships	**12a(1)**		Form 8586, line 5
	(2) Other than on line 12a(1)	**12a(2)**		
	b Qualified rehabilitation expenditures related to rental real estate activities	**12b**		See page 9 of Partner's Instructions for Schedule K-1 (Form 1065).
	c Credits (other than credits shown on lines 12a and 12b) related to rental real estate activities.	**12c**		
	d Credits related to other rental activities	**12d**		
	13 Other credits	**13**		

For Paperwork Reduction Act Notice, see Instructions for Form 1065.   Cat. No. 11394R   Schedule K-1 (Form 1065) 2003

FIGURE A.17   Schedule K-1 (Partner's Share of Income, Credits, Deductions, etc.)

(a) Distributive share item	(b) Amount	(c) 1040 filers enter the amount in column (b) on:
Investment Interest		
14a Interest expense on investment debts	14a	Form 4952, line 1
b (1) Investment income included on lines 4a, 4b(2), 4c, and 4f	14b(1)	See page 9 of Partner's Instructions for Schedule K-1 (Form 1065).
(2) Investment expenses included on line 10	14b(2)	
Self-employment		
15a Net earnings (loss) from self-employment	15a	Sch. SE, Section A or B
b Gross farming or fishing income	15b	See page 9 of Partner's Instructions for Schedule K-1 (Form 1065).
c Gross nonfarm income	15c	
Adjustments and Tax Preference Items		
16a Depreciation adjustment on property placed in service after 1986	16a	
b Adjusted gain or loss	16b	See pages 9 and 10 of Partner's Instructions for Schedule K-1 (Form 1065) and Instructions for Form 6251.
c Depletion (other than oil and gas)	16c	
d (1) Gross income from oil, gas, and geothermal properties	16d(1)	
(2) Deductions allocable to oil, gas, and geothermal properties	16d(2)	
e Other adjustments and tax preference items (attach schedule)	16e	
Foreign Taxes		
17a Name of foreign country or U.S. possession ▶		
b Gross income from all sources	17b	
c Gross income sourced at partner level	17c	
d Foreign gross income sourced at partnership level:		
(1) Passive	17d(1)	
(2) Listed categories (attach schedule)	17d(2)	
(3) General limitation	17d(3)	
e Deductions allocated and apportioned at partner level:		
(1) Interest expense	17e(1)	Form 1116, Part I
(2) Other	17e(2)	
f Deductions allocated and apportioned at partnership level to foreign source income:		
(1) Passive	17f(1)	
(2) Listed categories (attach schedule)	17f(2)	
(3) General limitation	17f(3)	
g Total foreign taxes (check one): ▶ ☐ Paid ☐ Accrued	17g	Form 1116, Part II
h Reduction in taxes available for credit (attach schedule)	17h	Form 1116, line 12
Other		
18 Section 59(e)(2) expenditures: **a** Type ▶		See page 10 of Partner's Instructions for Schedule K-1 (Form 1065).
b Amount	18b	
19 Tax-exempt interest income	19	Form 1040, line 8b
20 Other tax-exempt income	20	See page 10 of Partner's Instructions for Schedule K-1 (Form 1065).
21 Nondeductible expenses	21	
22 Distributions of money (cash and marketable securities)	22	
23 Distributions of property other than money	23	
24 Recapture of low-income housing credit:		
a From section 42(j)(5) partnerships	24a	Form 8611, line 8
b Other than on line 24a	24b	

Supplemental Information

25 Supplemental information required to be reported separately to each partner (attach additional schedules if more space is needed):

....

....

....

....

....

....

FIGURE A.17 *(Continued)*

SCHEDULE K-1 (Form 1065) Department of the Treasury Internal Revenue Service	Partner's Share of Income, Credits, Deductions, etc. ▶ See separate instructions. For calendar year 2003 or tax year beginning _____ , 2003, and ending _____ , 20	OMB No. 1545-0099 2003

Partner's identifying number ▶ 111-11-1111	Partnership's identifying number ▶ 55 : 5555555
Partner's name, address, and ZIP code **BAXTER WHEN** **345 CAT AVENUE** **EAST OVERSHOE, VA 55555**	Partnership's name, address, and ZIP code **CLEAN CAT PROCESSORS, LLC** **111 MAIN ST., SUITE 1** **EAST OVERSHOE, VA 55555**

A This partner is a ☑ general partner ☐ limited partner ☐ limited liability company member

B What type of entity is this partner? ▶ **INDIVIDUAL**

C Is this partner a ☑ domestic or a ☐ foreign partner?

F Partner's share of liabilities (see instructions):
Nonrecourse . . . . $ ....
Qualified nonrecourse financing . $ ....
Other . . . . $ 31,667

G Tax shelter registration number . ▶ ....

	(i) Before change or termination	(ii) End of year
D Enter partner's percentage of:		
Profit sharing . . . . %	.... %	**33.3** %
Loss sharing . . . . %	.... %	**33.3** %
Ownership of capital . . . . %	.... %	**33.3** %

H Check here if this partnership is a publicly traded partnership as defined in section 469(k)(2) . . . . . ☐

E IRS Center where partnership filed return: **CINCINATTI**

I Check applicable boxes: **(1)** ☐ Final K-1 **(2)** ☐ Amended K-1

J Analysis of partner's capital account:

(a) Capital account at beginning of year	(b) Capital contributed during year	(c) Partner's share of lines 3, 4, and 7, Form 1065, Schedule M-2	(d) Withdrawals and distributions	(e) Capital account at end of year (combine columns (a) through (d))
0	25,000	55,667	(40,000)	40,667

	(a) Distributive share item		(b) Amount	(c) 1040 filers enter the amount in column (b) on:
Income (Loss)	1	Ordinary income (loss) from trade or business activities . . .	**1**	55,667	See page 6 of Partner's Instructions for Schedule K-1 (Form 1065).
	2	Net income (loss) from rental real estate activities	**2**		
	3	Net income (loss) from other rental activities	**3**		
	4	Portfolio income (loss):			
	a	Interest income	**4a**		Form 1040, line 8a
	b	(1) Qualified dividends	**4b(1)**		Form 1040, line 9b
		(2) Total ordinary dividends	**4b(2)**		Form 1040, line 9a
	c	Royalty income	**4c**		Sch. E, Part I, line 4
	d	(1) Net short-term capital gain (loss) (post-May 5, 2003) . .	**4d(1)**		Sch. D, line 5, col. (g)
		(2) Net short-term capital gain (loss) (entire year)	**4d(2)**		Sch. D, line 5, col. (f)
	e	(1) Net long-term capital gain (loss) (post-May 5, 2003) . .	**4e(1)**		Sch. D, line 12, col. (g)
		(2) Net long-term capital gain (loss) (entire year) . . .	**4e(2)**		Sch. D, line 12, col. (f)
	f	Other portfolio income (loss) (attach schedule)	**4f**		
	5	Guaranteed payments to partner	**5**		See pages 6 and 7 of Partner's Instructions for Schedule K-1 (Form 1065).
	6a	Net section 1231 gain (loss) (post-May 5, 2003).	**6a**		
	b	Net section 1231 gain (loss) (entire year)	**6b**		
	7	Other income (loss) (attach schedule)	**7**		
Deductions	8	Charitable contributions (see instructions) (attach schedule) . .	**8**	333	Sch. A, line 15 or 16
	9	Section 179 expense deduction.	**9**		See page 8 of Partner's Instructions for Schedule K-1 (Form 1065).
	10	Deductions related to portfolio income (attach schedule) . . .	**10**		
	11	Other deductions (attach schedule).	**11**		
Credits	12a	Low-income housing credit: **(1)** From section 42(j)(5) partnerships	**12a(1)**		Form 8586, line 5
		(2) Other than on line 12a(1)	**12a(2)**		
	b	Qualified rehabilitation expenditures related to rental real estate activities	**12b**		See page 9 of Partner's Instructions for Schedule K-1 (Form 1065).
	c	Credits (other than credits shown on lines 12a and 12b) related to rental real estate activities.	**12c**		
	d	Credits related to other rental activities	**12d**		
	13	Other credits	**13**		

For Paperwork Reduction Act Notice, see Instructions for Form 1065. Cat. No. 11394R **Schedule K-1 (Form 1065) 2003**

FIGURE A.17 *(Continued)*

SCHEDULE K-1
(Form 1065)
Department of the Treasury
Internal Revenue Service

Partner's Share of Income, Credits, Deductions, etc.

▶ See separate instructions.

For calendar year 2003 or tax year beginning _____ , 2003, and ending _____ , 20 ____

OMB No. 1545-0099

2003

Partner's identifying number ▶	222-22-2222	Partnership's identifying number ▶	55 : 5555555

Partner's name, address, and ZIP code	Partnership's name, address, and ZIP code
CAROL WHAT **678 FELINE FREEWAY** **EAST OVERSHOE, VA 55555**	**CLEAN CAT PROCESSORS, LLC** **111 MAIN ST., SUITE 1** **EAST OVERSHOE, VA 55555**

A This partner is a ☑ general partner ☐ limited partner
☐ limited liability company member

B What type of entity is this partner? ▶ **INDIVIDUAL**

C Is this partner a ☑ domestic or a ☐ foreign partner?

	(i) Before change or termination	(ii) End of year

D Enter partner's percentage of:
Profit sharing . . . . _____ % **33.3** %
Loss sharing . . . . _____ % **33.3** %
Ownership of capital . . . . . _____ % **33.3** %

E IRS Center where partnership filed return: **CINCINATTI**

F Partner's share of liabilities (see instructions):
Nonrecourse . . . . $ _____
Qualified nonrecourse financing . $ _____
Other . . . . $ _____**31,667**

G Tax shelter registration number . ▶ _____

H Check here if this partnership is a publicly traded partnership as defined in section 469(k)(2) . . . . . ☐

I Check applicable boxes: **(1)** ☐ Final K-1 **(2)** ☐ Amended K-1

J Analysis of partner's capital account:

(a) Capital account at beginning of year	(b) Capital contributed during year	(c) Partner's share of lines 3, 4, and 7, Form 1065, Schedule M-2	(d) Withdrawals and distributions	(e) Capital account at end of year (combine columns (a) through (d))
0	25,000	55,667	(40,000)	40,667

	(a) Distributive share item		(b) Amount	(c) 1040 filers enter the amount in column (b) on:
	1 Ordinary income (loss) from trade or business activities . . .	**1**	55,667	See page 6 of Partner's Instructions for Schedule K-1 (Form 1065).
	2 Net income (loss) from rental real estate activities	**2**		
	3 Net income (loss) from other rental activities	**3**		
	4 Portfolio income (loss):			
	a Interest income	**4a**		Form 1040, line 8a
	b (1) Qualified dividends	**4b(1)**		Form 1040, line 9b
	(2) Total ordinary dividends	**4b(2)**		Form 1040, line 9a
	c Royalty income	**4c**		Sch. E, Part I, line 4
	d (1) Net short-term capital gain (loss) (post-May 5, 2003) . . .	**4d(1)**		Sch. D, line 5, col. (g)
	(2) Net short-term capital gain (loss) (entire year)	**4d(2)**		Sch. D, line 5, col. (f)
	e (1) Net long-term capital gain (loss) (post-May 5, 2003) . . .	**4e(1)**		Sch. D, line 12, col. (g)
	(2) Net long-term capital gain (loss) (entire year)	**4e(2)**		Sch. D, line 12, col. (f)
	f Other portfolio income (loss) (attach schedule)	**4f**		
	5 Guaranteed payments to partner	**5**		See pages 6 and 7 of Partner's Instructions for Schedule K-1 (Form 1065).
	6a Net section 1231 gain (loss) (post-May 5, 2003)	**6a**		
	b Net section 1231 gain (loss) (entire year)	**6b**		
	7 Other income (loss) (attach schedule)	**7**		
	8 Charitable contributions (see instructions) (attach schedule) .	**8**	333	Sch. A, line 15 or 16
	9 Section 179 expense deduction	**9**		See page 8 of Partner's Instructions for Schedule K-1 (Form 1065).
	10 Deductions related to portfolio income (attach schedule) . . .	**10**		
	11 Other deductions (attach schedule)	**11**		
	12a Low-income housing credit: **(1)** From section 42(j)(5) partnerships	**12a(1)**		Form 8586, line 5
	(2) Other than on line 12a(1)	**12a(2)**		
	b Qualified rehabilitation expenditures related to rental real estate activities	**12b**		
	c Credits (other than credits shown on lines 12a and 12b) related to rental real estate activities.	**12c**		See page 9 of Partner's Instructions for Schedule K-1 (Form 1065).
	d Credits related to other rental activities	**12d**		
	13 Other credits	**13**		

Income (Loss) / Deductions / Credits

For Paperwork Reduction Act Notice, see Instructions for Form 1065.   Cat. No. 11394R   **Schedule K-1 (Form 1065) 2003**

FIGURE A.17 (Continued)

Form **SS-4**

(Rev. December 2001)

Department of the Treasury
Internal Revenue Service

Application for Employer Identification Number

(For use by employers, corporations, partnerships, trusts, estates, churches,
government agencies, Indian tribal entities, certain individuals, and others.)

See separate instructions for each line.   Keep a copy for your records.

EIN

OMB No. 1545-0003

Type or print clearly.

1	Legal name of entity (or individual) for whom the EIN is being requested

2	Trade name of business (if different from name on line 1)	3	Executor, trustee, "care of" name

4a	Mailing address (room, apt., suite no. and street, or P.O. box)	5a	Street address (if different) (Do not enter a P.O. box.)

4b	City, state, and ZIP code	5b	City, state, and ZIP code

6	County and state where principal business is located

7a	Name of principal officer, general partner, grantor, owner, or trustor	7b	SSN, ITIN, or EIN

8a Type of entity   (check only one box)

☐ Sole proprietor (SSN) _____
☐ Partnership
☐ Corporation (enter form number to be filed) ▶ _____
☐ Personal service corp.
☐ Church or church-controlled organization
☐ Other nonprofit organization (specify) ▶ _____
☐ Other (specify) ▶

☐ Estate (SSN of decedent) _____
☐ Plan administrator (SSN) _____
☐ Trust (SSN of grantor) _____
☐ National Guard   ☐ State/local government
☐ Farmers' cooperative   ☐ Federal government/military
☐ REMIC   ☐ Indian tribal governments/enterprises
Group Exemption Number (GEN) _____

8b If a corporation, name the state or foreign country
(if applicable) where incorporated

State	Foreign country

9 Reason for applying   (check only one box)

☐ Started new business (specify type) ▶ _____

☐ Hired employees (Check the box and see line 12.)
☐ Compliance with IRS withholding regulations
☐ Other (specify) ▶

☐ Banking purpose (specify purpose) ▶ _____
☐ Changed type of organization (specify new type) ▶ _____
☐ Purchased going business
☐ Created a trust (specify type) ▶ _____
☐ Created a pension plan (specify type) ▶ _____

10	Date business started or acquired (month, day, year)	11	Closing month of accounting year

12 First date wages or annuities were paid or will be paid (month, day, year). **Note:** *If applicant is a withholding agent, enter date income will
first be paid to nonresident alien. (month, day, year)* . . . . ▶

13 Highest number of employees expected in the next 12 months. **Note:** *If the applicant does not
expect to have any employees during the period, enter "-0-".* . . . . ▶

Agricultural	Household	Other

14 Check **one** box that best describes the principal activity of your business.

☐ Construction   ☐ Rental & leasing   ☐ Transportation & warehousing
☐ Real estate   ☐ Manufacturing   ☐ Finance & insurance

☐ Health care & social assistance   ☐ Wholesale–agent/broker
☐ Accommodation & food service   ☐ Wholesale–other   ☐ Retail
☐ Other (specify)

15 Indicate principal line of merchandise sold; specific construction work done; products produced; or services provided.

16a Has the applicant ever applied for an employer identification number for this or any other business? . . . . , ☐ Yes   ☐ No

Note: *If "Yes," please complete lines 16b and 16c.*

16b If you checked"Yes"online 16a, give applicant's legal name and trade name shown on prior application if different from line 1 or 2 above.

Legal name ▶ _____   Trade name ▶ _____

16c Approximate date when, and city and state where, the application was filed. Enter previous employer identification number if known.

Approximate date when filed (mo., day, year)	City and state where filed	Previous EIN

| **Third
Party
Designee**	Complete this section **only** if you want to authorize the named individual to receive the entityís EIN and answer questions about the completion of this form.	
	Designee's name	Designee's telephone number (include area code)
(   )
	Address and ZIP code	Designee's fax number (include area code)
(   )

Under penalties of perjury, I declare that I have examined this application, and to the best of my knowledge and belief, it is true, correct, and complete.

Applicant's telephone number (include area code)
(   )

Name and title (type or print clearly)

Applicant's fax number (include area code)
(   )

Signature ▶   Date ▶

For Privacy Act and Paperwork Reduction Act Notice, see separate instructions.   Cat. No. 16055N   Form **SS-4** (Rev. 12-2001)

FIGURE A.18

Form **4626**

Department of the Treasury
Internal Revenue Service

Alternative Minimum Tax–Corporations

See separate instructions.
Attach to the corporation's tax return.

OMB No. 1545-0175

2003

Name		Employer identification number

Note: *See page 1 of the instructions to find out if the corporation is a small corporation exempt from the AMT under section 55(e).*

1	Taxable income or (loss) before net operating loss deduction	1	
2	**Adjustments and preferences:**		
a	Depreciation of post-1986 property	2a	
b	Amortization of certified pollution control facilities	2b	
c	Amortization of mining exploration and development costs	2c	
d	Amortization of circulation expenditures (personal holding companies only)	2d	
e	Adjusted gain or loss	2e	
f	Long-term contracts	2f	
g	Merchant marine capital construction funds	2g	
h	Section 833(b) deduction (Blue Cross, Blue Shield, and similar type organizations only)	2h	
i	Tax shelter farm activities (personal service corporations only)	2i	
j	Passive activities (closely held corporations and personal service corporations only)	2j	
k	Loss limitations	2k	
l	Depletion	2l	
m	Tax-exempt interest income from specified private activity bonds	2m	
n	Intangible drilling costs	2n	
o	Other adjustments	2o	
3	Pre-adjustment alternative minimum taxable income (AMTI). Combine lines 1 through 2o	3	
4	**Adjusted current earnings (ACE) adjustment:**		
a	ACE from line 10 of the worksheet on page 11 of the instructions	4a	
b	Subtract line 3 from line 4a. If line 3 exceeds line 4a, enter the difference as a negative amount. See examples on page 6 of the instructions	4b	
c	Multiply line 4b by 75% (.75). Enter the result as a positive amount	4c	
d	Enter the excess, if any, of the corporation's total increases in AMTI from prior year ACE adjustments over its total reductions in AMTI from prior year ACE adjustments (see page 6 of the instructions). Note: *You must enter an amount on line 4d (even if line 4b is positive).*	4d	
e	ACE adjustment.
If line 4b is zero or more, enter the amount from line 4c
If line 4b is less than zero, enter the **smaller** of line 4c or line 4d as a negative amount	}	4e	
5	Combine lines 3 and 4e. If zero or less, stop here; the corporation does not owe any AMT	5	
6	Alternative tax net operating loss deduction (see page 7 of the instructions)	6	
7	**Alternative minimum taxable income.** Subtract line 6 from line 5. If the corporation held a residual interest in a REMIC, see page 7 of the instructions	7	
8	**Exemption phase-out** (if line 7 is $310,000 or more, skip lines 8a and 8b and enter -0- on line 8c):		
a	Subtract $150,000 from line 7 (if completing this line for a member of a controlled group, see page 7 of the instructions). If zero or less, enter -0-	8a	
b	Multiply line 8a by 25% (.25)	8b	
c	Exemption. Subtract line 8b from $40,000 (if completing this line for a member of a controlled group, see page 7 of the instructions). If zero or less, enter -0-	8c	
9	Subtract line 8c from line 7. If zero or less, enter -0-	9	
10	Multiply line 9 by 20% (.20)	10	
11	Alternative minimum tax foreign tax credit (see page 7 of the instructions)	11	
12	Tentative minimum tax. Subtract line 11 from line 10	12	
13	Regular tax liability before all credits except the foreign tax credit and possessions tax credit	13	
14	**Alternative minimum tax.** Subtract line 13 from line 12. If zero or less, enter -0-. Enter here and on Form 1120, Schedule J, line 4, or the appropriate line of the corporation's income tax return	14	

For Paperwork Reduction Act Notice, see page 10 of the instructions.   Cat. No. 12955I   Form **4626** (2003)

FIGURE A.19

Adjusted Current Earnings Worksheet

See ACE Worksheet Instructions (which begin on page 8).

1	Pre-adjustment AMTI. Enter the amount from line 3 of Form 4626			**1**	
2	ACE depreciation adjustment:				
a	AMT depreciation		**2a**		
b	ACE depreciation:				
	(1) Post-1993 property	**2b(1)**			
	(2) Post-1989, pre-1994 property . .	**2b(2)**			
	(3) Pre-1990 MACRS property . . .	**2b(3)**			
	(4) Pre-1990 original ACRS property .	**2b(4)**			
	(5) Property described in sections 168(f)(1) through (4)	**2b(5)**			
	(6) Other property	**2b(6)**			
	(7) Total ACE depreciation. Add lines 2b(1) through 2b(6) . . .		**2b(7)**		
c	ACE depreciation adjustment. Subtract line 2b(7) from line 2a			**2c**	
3	Inclusion in ACE of items included in earnings and profits (E&P):				
a	Tax-exempt interest income		**3a**		
b	Death benefits from life insurance contracts		**3b**		
c	All other distributions from life insurance contracts (including surrenders)		**3c**		
d	Inside buildup of undistributed income in life insurance contracts .		**3d**		
e	Other items (see Regulations sections 1.56(g)-1(c)(6)(iii) through (ix) for a partial list)		**3e**		
f	Total increase to ACE from inclusion in ACE of items included in E&P. Add lines 3a through 3e			**3f**	
4	Disallowance of items not deductible from E&P:				
a	Certain dividends received		**4a**		
b	Dividends paid on certain preferred stock of public utilities that are deductible under section 247 .		**4b**		
c	Dividends paid to an ESOP that are deductible under section 404(k)		**4c**		
d	Nonpatronage dividends that are paid and deductible under section 1382(c)		**4d**		
e	Other items (see Regulations sections 1.56(g)-1(d)(3)(i) and (ii) for a partial list)		**4e**		
f	Total increase to ACE because of disallowance of items not deductible from E&P. Add lines 4a through 4e			**4f**	
5	Other adjustments based on rules for figuring E&P:				
a	Intangible drilling costs		**5a**		
b	Circulation expenditures		**5b**		
c	Organizational expenditures		**5c**		
d	LIFO inventory adjustments		**5d**		
e	Installment sales		**5e**		
f	Total other E&P adjustments. Combine lines 5a through 5e			**5f**	
6	Disallowance of loss on exchange of debt pools			**6**	
7	Acquisition expenses of life insurance companies for qualified foreign contracts . . .			**7**	
8	Depletion			**8**	
9	Basis adjustments in determining gain or loss from sale or exchange of pre-1994 property .			**9**	
10	**Adjusted current earnings.** Combine lines 1, 2c, 3f, 4f, and 5f through 9. Enter the result here and on line 4a of Form 4626			**10**	

-11-

FIGURE A.19 *(Continued)*

Is an investment in a corporation a type of equity or is it debt?

This list of factors that courts have considered and on which they have based many decisions, was created by the staff of the Congressional Joint Committee on Taxation in 1989. Bear in mind that this document is not authoritative as an IRS regulation would be, but it is one of the few government documents, except for court transcripts, that provides some guidance. (See the discussion in Chapter 2.)

1. Is there a written unconditional promise to pay on demand or on a specific date a certain sum of money in return for an adequate consideration in money or money's worth, and to pay a fixed rate of interest?
2. Is there a preference over, or lack of subordination to, other interests in the corporation?
3. Is there a relatively low corporate debt/equity ratio?
4. Is there a lack of convertibility into the stock of the corporation?
5. Is there independence between the holdings of the stock of the corporation and the holdings of the interest in question?
6. Is there an intent of the parties to create a creditor-debtor relationship?
7. Are there principal and interest payments that are not subject to the risks of the corporation's business?
8. Is there the existence of security to ensure the payment of interest and principal, including sinking fund arrangements, if appropriate?
9. Is the existence of rights of enforcement and default remedies?
10. Is there an expectation of repayment?

11. Does the holder lack voting and management rights (except in the case of default or similar circumstances)?

12. Is there availability of other credit sources at similar terms?

13. Is there the ability to transfer the interest freely?

14. Are the interest payments not contingent on or subject to management or board of directors' discretion?

15. Is the labeling and financial statement classification of the instrument debt?

Useful Addresses

Securities and Exchange Commission (SEC) Contact Information

Small Business Ombudsman
U.S. Securities and Exchange Commission
450 Fifth Street, N.W.
Mail Stop 3-4
Washington, DC 20549
800-SEC-0330
www.sec.gov/smbus

Addresses of Secretaries of State Business Sections

Most states have Internet sites that provide forms and other information about business registration in that state. However, Internet addresses do change. If an Internet address following does not work, try the National Association of Secretaries of State at: http://www.nass.org/sos/sosflags.html. This site provides links to business registration offices of most states.

Secretary of State of Alabama
Corporation Section
Montgomery, AL 36103-5616
334-242-5324
http://www.sos.state.al.us/business/domestic.htm

State of Alaska
Department of Commerce and Economic Development
Division of Banking, Securities, and Corporations
P.O. Box 110807
Juneau, AK 99811-0807
907-465-2521
http://www.mycorporation.com/secretary-state/Alaska.htm

Arizona Corporation Commission
1300 West Washington
Phoenix, AZ 85007-2996
602-542-3135
http://www.cc.state.az.us/

Secretary of State
Corporation Division
Aegon Building
501 Woodlane, Suite 210
Little Rock, AR 72201
501-682-3409
http://www.sosweb.state.ar.us/

California Secretary of State
1500 11th Street
Sacramento, CA 95814
916-653-6814
http://www.ss.ca.gov/cgi-bin/contacts.cgi

Secretary of State of Colorado
Corporations Office
1560 Broadway, Suite 200
Denver, CO 80202
303-894-2200 or 303-894-2203
http://www.sos.state.co.us/

Office of Secretary of State
State of Connecticut
30 Trinity Street
Hartford, CT 06106
860-509-6001
http://www.sots.state.ct.us/

Office of Secretary of State
Department of State
Division of Corporations
P.O. Box 898
Dover, DE 19903
302-739-3073
http://www.state.de.us/corp/default.shtml

Florida Department of State
Secretary of State
Division of Corporations
P.O. Box 6327
Tallahassee, FL 32314
850-487-6866
http://www.dos.state.fl.us/doc/index.html

State of Georgia
Secretary of State
Corporations Division
Suite 315 West Tower
2 Martin Luther King, Jr. Drive
Atlanta, GA 30334
404-656-2817
http://www.sos.state.ga.us/corporations/

State of Hawaii
Department of Commerce and Consumer Affairs
Business Registration Division
1010 Richards Street
Honolulu, HI 96810
808-586-2727
http://www.ehawaiigov.org/initials/

Secretary of State of Idaho
700 W. Jefferson, Room 203
Boise, ID 83720-0080
208-334-2300
http://www.idsos.state.id.us/corp/corindex.htm

Secretary of State of Illinois
Department of Business Services
Room 328 Howlett Building
Springfield, IL 62756
217-782-2201 or 800-252-8980
http://www.sos.state.il.us/departments/business_services/

Secretary of State's Office, Corporations Division
302 West Washington Street, Room E-018
Indianapolis, IN 46204
317-232-6576
http://www.in.gov/sos/business/idnex.html

Secretary of State of Iowa
Hoover State Office Building, 2nd floor
Des Moines, IA 50319
515-281-5204
http://www.sos.state.ia.us/business/index.html

Kansas Secretary of State
Corporation Division
State Capitol, 2nd Floor
300 S.W. 10th Avenue
Topeka, KS 66612-1594
785-296-7456
http://www.kssos.org/business/business.html

Business Filings
Office of the Secretary of State
700 Capitol Avenue
Suite 152, State Capitol
Frankfort, KY 40601
502-564-3490
http://www.kysos.com/busser/corporations/corporations.asp

USEFUL ADDRESSES

Secretary of State of Louisiana
Commercial Division
P.O. Box 94125
Baton Rouge, LA 70804-9125
504-922-2675 or 800-259-0001
http://www.sec.state.la.us/comm/corp/corp-filings.htm

Secretary of State of Maine
Bureau of Corporations, Elections and Commissions
Division of Corporations
101 State House Station
Augusta, ME 04333-0101
207-287-4190
http://www.maine.gov/sos/cec/corp/

State of Maryland
State Department of Assessments and Taxation
301 W. Preston Street
Baltimore, MD 21201
410-767-1350
http://www.sos.state.md.us/

Massachusetts Secretary of the Commonwealth
Corporations Division
One Ashburton Place, Room 1717
Boston, MA 02108
617-727-9640
http://www.sec.state.ma.us/cor/coridx.htm

Michigan State Government
Department of Consumer & Industry Services
Corporation, Securities, and Land Development Bureau
Corporation Division
Corporations and Securities Bureau
P.O. Box 30054
Lansing, MI 48909-7554
517-334-6323
http://www.michigan.gov/businessstartup/ (Search for forms index)

Business Services Division
Office of the Secretary of State
180 State Office Building
100 Constitution Avenue
St. Paul, MN 55155-1299
612-296-2803
http://www.sos.state.mn.us/business/forms.html

Secretary of State of Mississippi
P.O. Box 136
Jackson, MS 39205-0136
601-359-1350
800-256-3494
http://www.sos.state.ms.us/

Secretary of State of Missouri
State Capitol, Room 209
P.O. Box 778
Jefferson City, MO 65102
573-751-4153
http://www.sos.mo.gov/section2.asp

USEFUL ADDRESSES

Business Services Bureau
Secretary of State of Montana
Montana State Capitol, Room 225
P.O. Box 202801
Helena, MT 59620-2801
406-444-3665
http://www.sos.state.mt.us/css/BSB/Filing_Forms.asp

Secretary of State of Nebraska
Corporate Division
State Capitol, Suite 1301
P.O. Box 94608
Lincoln, NE 68509-4608
402-471-4079
http://www.sos.state.ne.us/htm/corpmenu.htm

State of Nevada
Secretary of State
101 N. Carson Street, Suite 3
Carson City, NV 89701-4786
775-684-5708
http://sos.state.nv.us/../comm_rec/crforms/crforms.htm

Secretary of State of New Hampshire
Office of the Secretary of State
State House, Room 204
Concord, NH 03301-4989
603-225-4033
http://www.sos.nh.gov/corporate/index.html

State of New Jersey
Department of Treasury
Division of Revenue/Commercial Recording
P.O. Box 308
Trenton, NJ 08625-0308
609-530-6400
http://www.state.nj.us/Business/shtml

State of New Mexico
Public Regulation Commission
P.O. Drawer 1269
Santa Fe, NM 87504-1269
505-827-4500
http://www.state.nm.us/scc

New York State Department of State
Division of Corporations, State Records and Uniform Commercial
    Code
41 State Street
Albany, NY 12231-0001
518-473-2492
http://www.dos.state.ny.us/corp/corpspub.html

Secretary of State of North Carolina
The Corporations Division
300 N. Salisbury Street
Raleigh, NC 27603-5909
919-733-4201
http://www.secretary.state.nc.us/Corporations/

Secretary of State of North Dakota
Capitol Building
600 East Boulevard Avenue
Bismarck, ND 58505-0500
701-328-4284
http://www.state.nd.us/sec/businessserv/registrations/index

Ohio Secretary of State, Business Services Division
30 East Broad Street, 14th Floor
Columbus, OH 43266-0418
614-466-3910
http://www.sos.state.oh.us/sos//busiserv/index.html

Secretary of State of Oklahoma
Office of the Secretary of State
191 State Capitol
Oklahoma City, OK 73105
405-521-3911
http://www.sos.state.ok.us/business/business_filing.htm

Oregon Secretary of State
Corporation Division, Business Registry
Public Service Building
225 Capitol Street NE, Suite 151
Salem, OR 97310-1327
503-986-2222
http://www.filinginoregon.com/

Commonwealth of Pennsylvania
Department of State, Corporation Bureau
P.O. Box 8722
Harrisburg, PA 17105-8722
717-787-1057
http://www.dos.state.pa.us/corps/site/default.asp

Secretary of State of Rhode Island
First Stop Business Center
100 North Main Street
Providence, RI 02903
401-222-2185
http://www2.corps.state.ri.us/corporations/

Secretary of State of South Carolina
Office of the Secretary of State
Edgar Brown Building, Suite 525
P.O. Box 11350
Columbia, SC 29211
803-734-2170
http://www.scsos.com/

Secretary of State of South Dakota
State Capitol, Suite 204
500 East Capitol
Pierre, SD 57501-5070
605-773-4845
http://www.sdsos.gov/corporations/

USEFUL ADDRESSES

Secretary of State of Tennessee
Corporations Section
James K. Polk Building, Suite 1800
Nashville, TN 37243-0306
615-741-0537
http://www.state.tn.us/sos/service.htm

Secretary of State of Texas
Statutory Filings Division
Corporations Section
P.O. Box 13697
Austin, TX 78711-3697
512-463-5580
http://www.sos.state.tx.us/corp/forms/shtml

State of Utah
Department of Commerce
Division of Corporations
160 East 300 South
P.O. Box 146705
Salt Lake City, UT 84145-6705
801-530-4849
http://www.utah.gov/services/business.html

Secretary of State of Vermont
Office of the Secretary of State
Business Registry Division
109 State Street
Montpelier, VT 05609-1101
802-828-2386
http://www.sec.state.vt.us/corps/corpindex.htm

Commonwealth of Virginia
State Corporation Commission
Division of Information Resources
P.O. Box 1197
Richmond, VA 23218
804-371-9967 or 800-552-7945
http://www.state.va.us/scc/division/clk/brg.htm

Secretary of State of Washington
Office of the Secretary of State
Corporations Division
505 East Union, 2nd Floor
P.O. Box 40234
Olympia, WA 98504-0234
360-753-7115
http://www.secstate.wa.gov/corps/

Secretary of State of West Virginia
Building 1, Suite 157-K
1900 Kanawha Boulevard East
Charleston, WV 25305-0770
304-558-6000
http://www.wvsos.com/common/startbusiness.htm

Secretary of State of Wisconsin
Corporations Division
P.O. Box 7846
Madison, WI 53707-7848
608-266-3590
http://www.wdfi.org/corporations/

Secretary of State of Wyoming
Capitol Building
Cheyenne, WY 82002
307-777-6217
http://soswy.state.wy.us/corporat/corporat.htm

Office of the Secretary
District of Columbia
John A. Wilson Building
1350 Pennsylvania Avenue, NW
Washington, DC 20004
http://brc.dc.gov/whattodo/business/index.asp

Departamento de Estado
P.O. Box 9023271
San Juan, Puerto Rico 00902-3271
787-722-2121
http://www.estado.gobierno.pr/Corporaciones.htm

Office of Lieutenant Governor
Division of Corporation and Trademark
Kongens Gade #18
St. Thomas, USVI 00802
http://www.ltg.gov.vi/departments/corp.html#department

Short Course in Corporate Finance Terms

The most important number that most owners (stockholders) of corporations want to know is how much did the corporation earn during the last month, quarter, or year. To obtain a number, the corporation accounting staff keeps track of the numbers in such a way that they can be put together in what is generally called an income statement. (The numbers are for this example only and do not represent any real situation.)

The Blue Radish Corporation

Income Statement
For the Year 20XX

Total (gross) income, sales, or revenue. Although there is some technical distinction between these three terms, most people use them synonymously.	$1,000,000
From the total revenue, subtract the *cost of the goods (or services) sold.* Note that this is the cost of goods sold, and that is not necessarily the same as the cost of goods purchased at wholesale. (The corporation may have some of those purchases still on the shelf as inventory.)	600,000
The resulting difference is what is called *gross profit.*	400,000

Of course, the corporation does not operate in a vacuum. It has *operating expenses* such as rent, utilities, administrative salaries, office supplies, and so on. | 350,000

What is left is the *operating profit*. | 50,000

And there are *nonoperating expenses* that have to be deducted from the operating profit, the most famous of which is federal income tax. | 7,500

What is finally left is called *net income* or *net profit*. | $ 42,500

Now we can compute a favorite statistic, which is *net income per share of stock*. If 10,000 shares of stock were issued, we divide the net income by that 10,000 to arrive at a net income per share of $4.25. Obviously, this is not a significant statistic if one person owns all of the outstanding stock. However, if there are many stockholders with varying amounts of stock owned, it makes it easy for each stockholder to compute his or her share of the earnings in relation to their investment in the stock.

There is more to financial statements. Stockholders, as well as directors and management of the corporation, should want to know how much cash is left in the till (or the bank account), what other items the corporation owns, as well as what the corporation owes. To give us that information, the accounting staff creates a *balance sheet*.

The Blue Radish Corporation

Balance sheet
as of December 31, 20XX

The first class of items in this report is called *assets*. This term includes tangible items, such as currency in the cash register, merchandise held for sale to customers, machinery, vehicles, real estate, and so on. It also includes intangible items such as cash in the bank and accounts receivable from customers. The list for this corporation looks like this:

Cash in bank	$10,000
Accounts receivable	20,000
Inventory (radishes in the cooler, ready to ship to customers)	15,000
Machinery (scrubbing and packaging equipment)	50,000
Total assets	$95,000

It's nice to have lots of assets, but on the other hand, we have to account for what the corporation owes to other entities. In other words, we have to list the *liabilities*.

Account payable to Eccentric Farm (the radish grower)	$15,000
Loan from bank	30,000
Total liabilities	$45,000

We now have enough information to compute what the corporation is worth. It is worth the amount of its assets ($95,000) minus the amount of its liabilities ($45,000) which equals $50,000. This used to be called *net worth*, but the modern convention is to call it *equity*. It would be nice to know what created that equity, and the financial statements tell us as follows:

10,000 shares stock were originally issued for one dollar per share	$10,000
Net income of the corporation for this first year of operations	42,500
Subtotal	52,500
Before the end of the year, the corporation paid a dividend of $.25 per share to the stockholders. That, in effect, transfers $2,500 of equity from the corporation to the stockholders.	2,500
Equity at the end of the year	50,000
Total liabilities and equity	$95,000

You should be aware of some interrelationships between the income statement and the balance sheet. First, total assets should add to the same amount as the total of liabilities and equity. That's why it's called a balance sheet. Also, the net income of the corporation as computed on the income statement shows up on the balance sheet in the equity section. Why these interrelationships exist we will leave to the accounting theory courses, but it is important to know that they do exist and that if they do not exist in a set of financial statements, those statements should be viewed as unreliable.

Glossary

alternative minimum tax   A computation of income tax that must be made by most corporations with annual gross revenue of $5 million or more. The income tax computed by the regular tax rules is that compared to the income tax computed by the alternative minimum tax rules and the higher tax is what the corporation must pay to the IRS.

assets   Refer to the Short Course in Corporate Finance Terms in this Appendix.

balance sheet   Refer to the Short Course in Corporate Finance Terms in this Appendix.

bond   A formal document that indicates the holder thereof is owed a certain amount by the corporation and what interest rate will be paid. Generally, a bond is issued when the bondholder loans cash to the corporation by purchasing a bond. It should be noted that interest paid to bondholders by a corporation is usually tax deductible, whereas dividends paid to stockholders (both common and preferred) are not deductible by the corporation.

bondholder   An owner of a corporate bond; in essence, a creditor of the corporation.

C corporation   A term brought about by federal tax law and the IRS. This type of corporation pays its own tax on the income it earns. Its rate of tax and other tax factors have no relationship to the tax picture of the owners (stockholders) of the corporation. (See S corporation.)

chairman of the board   The chairperson of the board of directors. He or she is elected by the members of the board.

chief executive officer (CEO)   The individual responsible for the total operation of the company. Generally synonymous with the title of president and is appointed by majority vote of the directors.

chief financial officer (CFO)   The individual responsible for the financial records of the corporation and financial planning for the future of the business. May also hold title of treasurer.

chief operating officer (COO)   The individual responsible for the day to day operations of the whole corporation. He or she may also hold a formal title such as executive vice president.

class of stock   a means of separating stock in which some stockholders have certain rights and privileges that are denied to other stockholders.

close corporation   A means of streamlining corporate management hierarchy permitted by many states. It is designed for corporations with few stockholders, where most of the stockholders are also active as employees of the corporation (example: a family business). There is no board of directors, as stockholders operate as such, directly electing the corporate officers and participating in major management decisions. In other words, it recognizes the fact that a board of the directors interposed between stockholders and officers is often merely a formality and allows the elimination of such.

common stock   The most common class of stock. The owners of common stock share, pro rata to their percentage of ownership, with other common stockholders in dividends and other manifestations of the success of the corporation. Usually, but not always, owners of common stock have voting rights in the election of directors. (See voting rights and directors.)

convertible bond   Like convertible preferred stock, this type of bond can be converted to common stock under certain circumstances. Because of the fact that this bond (a corporate debt) may become stock (corporate ownership), there is always a question of whether the income paid to bondholders is deductible as interest or is really a disguised dividend and therefore not deductible.

convertible preferred stock   Under certain circumstances, and at the option of the preferred stockholder, this class of stock may be converted into common stock. The conversion rate (how many shares of common stock equal how many shares of preferred stock) should be set forth in the preferred stock certificates when they are issued.

corporate charter   A document that is issued by the state, when it creates a corporation, that specifies the name of the corporation, the initial incorporators, and what ownership securities (stocks) the corporation may issue. Historically, the charter specified the nature of the activity in which the corporation would engage, but modern procedure generally is to include no such specification or a specification which is so broad as to permit any type of activity.

corporation   An entity that is created by the state that can contract in its own name, sue in court and be sued, and, in general, conduct business in its own right. If the corporation is formed to conduct a profit-making business, it is initially owned by those who petitioned the state to form the corporation, but such ownership may be transferred to others after formation of the corporation. If a corporation is formed for a nonprofit activity, it may have members, but they are not owners. Unlike a live individual, a corporation may have infinite life, unless it is initially formed for a specific period of years.

cost of goods sold   Refer to the Short Course in Corporate Finance Terms in Appendix C.

cumulative preferred stock   Preferred stock on which, if the specified dividends have not been paid over one or more previous years, the cumulative feature requires that those prior dividends be paid before the dividends can be paid to common stockholders.

depreciation   An accounting process that spreads to cost of a long-lived asset over the useful life of the asset. (In the simplest method, the cost of a machine that was purchased for $50,000, with a five-year useful life would appear on the financial statements as an annual expense of $10,000 in each of those five years.)

directors   Individuals who are a elected by stockholders who have voting rights. It is the duty of each director to meet as a board to elect the corporate officers. Directors should also meet frequently to oversee the management of the company.

distribution   Cash, or other property, that is paid to owners of a business as a share of earnings of that business. While dividends to stockholders of a C corporation are a form of distribution, the term is usually reserved to describe payments to owners that are not dividends. Specifically, that includes payments to owners made by S corporations, limited liability companies, and partnerships.

dividend   An amount, paid out of present or prior corporate earnings, to stockholders. The amount and date of payment is determined by the board of directors.

equity   Refer to the Short Course in Corporate Finance Terms in Appendix C.

gross income   Refer to the Short Course in Corporate Finance Terms in Appendix C.

income   Refer to the Short Course in Corporate Finance Terms in Appendix C.

income statement   Refer to the Short Course in Corporate Finance Terms in Appendix C.

liabilities   Refer to the Short Course in Corporate Finance Terms in this Appendix C.

limited liability company   Form of doing business that is, in essence, a partnership with limited liability. Like a corporation, it must be created by the state before it can operate. The owners are known as members rather than partners.

liquidating dividend   A payment made to stockholders of a C corporation when the corporation is in the process of going out of business and liquidating its assets. These dividends may or may not be taxable to the stockholders, depending on various factors.

officers of a corporation   Most states require that a corporation, at a minimum, have a president, secretary, and treasurer. These officers are elected by the board of directors and serve at the pleasure of that board. Many states allow alternate names for these positions, such as chief executive officer. (See president, secretary, and treasurer.)

partnership   Form of doing business in which two or more individuals or other entities join together to operate a profitmaking business. The individual partners pay taxes on his or her share of the income, so the partnership pays no income tax. This form provides no limited liability to the owners and is therefore avoided except for the smallest of enterprises where the partners may have little or no assets. (See limited liability company for a viable alternative.)

preferred stock   A class of stock the owners of which have preference as to dividends before owners of common stock. Generally, the dividends are specified as a dollar amount when the stock is issued by the corporation, and once that dollar amount has been paid to the preferred stockholders, the common stockholders may be paid up to any amount, limited only by the decision of the board of directors and the amount of earnings available from which to pay the dividends.

registered agent   An individual who registers with the state as the person who will accept legal process to be served on the corporation. If a corporation does business in many states, it would have a registered agent for each state.

revenue   Refer to the Short Course in Corporate Finance Terms in Appendix C.

S corporation   A corporation that passes its income and other tax attributes through to its stockholders, and the stockholders pay the income tax on their share of the corporation's taxable income, regardless of whether or not they received cash from the corporation.

secretary   This position is also appointed by majority vote of the board of directors, and the individual is responsible for maintaining minutes of the meetings of the board of directors and attesting to various legal documents signed by the corporation, such as annual reporting to the state.

stock certificate   A document, often in a fancy form, that specifies how many shares of ownership (stock) in the corporation an individual or other entity owns.

stockholder   An owner of stock (common or preferred) in the corporation.

treasurer   The individual responsible for corporate cash and other corporate assets. He or she is appointed by the board of directors, and the position is generally required by state statute. It often is held by the same individual who is the chief financial officer.

voting rights   In C or S corporations, the right of stockholders to vote for members of the board of directors. Certain classes of stock, if so provided in the stock certificate, may be denied voting rights. This is often the case for preferred stock.